TENURE FOR SOCRATES

TENURE FOR SOCRATES

A Study in the Betrayal of the American Professor

JON HUER

Bergin & Garvey
New York • Westport, Connecticut • London

Library of Congress Cataloging-in-Publication Data

Huer, Jon.
    Tenure for Socrates : a study in the betrayal of the American
professor / Jon Huer.
        p.   cm.
    Includes bibliographical references and index.
    ISBN 0-89789-244-5
    1. College teachers—Tenure—United States.   2. Academic freedom—
United   States.   I.   Title.
    LB2335.7.H8   1991
    378.1'22—dc20   90–38827

British Library Cataloguing-in-Publication Data is available.

Library of Congress Catalog Card Number: 90–38827
ISBN: 0–89789–244–5

First published in 1991

Bergin & Garvey, One Madison Avenue, New York, NY 10010
An imprint of Greenwood Publishing Group, Inc.

Printed in the United States of America

∞

The paper used in this book complies with the
Permanent Paper Standard issued by the National
Information Standards Organization (Z39.48–1984).

10 9 8 7 6 5 4 3 2 1

To
Anyone who might find my thesis in this book agreeable,
and of course
to
Jonathan Blake Huer,
who always finds me agreeable,
with love

Institutions of higher education are conducted for the common good and not to further the interest of either the individual teacher or the institution as a whole. The common good depends upon the free search for *truth* and its free exposition. Academic freedom is essential to these purposes and applies to both teaching and research. Freedom in research is fundamental to the advancement of *truth*.

Statement from the American
Association of University
Professors, 1940

The University and each constituent institution shall protect faculty and students in their responsible exercise of the freedom to teach, to learn and otherwise to seek and speak the *truth*.

The *Code*. The University of
North Carolina System, 1988

Noble, gracious, the friend of *truth*, justice, courage, temperance, who are his kindred?

Socrates, in *The Republic*

Contents

Prologue: Why I Have Written This Book

Let us suppose that a professor who has just been granted tenure at the University of Ivory Tower is asked by the institution to take, in an appropriate ceremony, the following hypothetical Oath of Tenure:

The Oath of Tenure

Upon this occasion of the granting of tenure by my academic institution, I solemnly pledge the following Oath of Tenure before the University Community and the larger society for whose benefit I have been granted this privilege:

1. I shall always conduct myself as a scholar in pursuit of the truth and the truth only. I shall serve no other interests. Nor shall I be influenced by my peers, my profession, my own institution, or my self-interest. I shall always pursue the truth honestly, independently, and critically.

2. I shall to the best of my ability avoid partisan issues, personal political views, and sectarian interests that serve only limited segments of society. My scholarly activities will always serve all humanity. None shall be excluded or favored.

3. I shall seek no pecuniary rewards from commercial or contractual agreements in addition to my duties as a scholar or in lieu of my scholarship. Nor will such nonscholarly activities be presented as my scholarship. I shall be content with the intrinsic value of my reward as a scholar and with the security of tenure and the

protection of academic freedom that my scholarship has been accorded.

4. I shall in judging my fellow scholars consider only the quality of their scholarship. Neither the approval of established orthodoxy nor the quantity of standardized output shall be considered evidence of scholarly accomplishment. Only originality of conception, benefit to mankind, and intellectual integrity shall be considered primary criteria.

5. I shall express and publish only those ideas that are worthy of a wide audience. I shall neither write nor present works only for the sake of routine professional productivity. The ideas I express in classrooms and in writings shall be only those that I truly believe will benefit community, society, and humanity as a whole.

6. I shall neither seek nor desire administrative posts unrelated to scholarship. If chosen for an administrative role, I shall do my best to support and protect faculty scholarship, however unpopular or unorthodox. I shall always recognize the supremacy of scholarship above all administrative imperatives.

7. I shall avoid involvement in activities, both on and off campus, that may be inimical to the scholarly community. I shall consider my life and thought bound by a special contract with the institution and the larger society to be employed wisely, frugally, and fruitfully on their behalf.

To most contemporary professors the requirements in the Oath of Tenure would surely seem too demanding and the tone too alien. They would comment that it is more fitting for a monk in a monastery than for a professor in modern society. They would be inclined to dismiss it as irrelevant nonsense. However, if each paragraph is patiently—not summarily—considered, an average professor may have to admit that it is, on second thought, all very reasonable. There is nothing inherently objectionable in defining himself as a scholar in pursuit of the honest, independent, and critical truth. Nor is it unsupportable that the tenured professor should pursue only those activities that would contribute to the welfare of all mankind. Nor is it unreasonable to insist on originality, benefit, and integrity of thought as criteria in judging fellow scholars. Nor is it too much to ask the scholar to avoid administrative assignments, since his job is in scholarship, not management.

Tenure, and its attendant academic freedom, *does* demand these and other conditions in exchange for a comfortably secure life for the professor. If confronted with this fact insistently, no scholar could deny such conditions as inherently entailed in tenure and academic freedom. But why, at first blush, would such "conditions" for tenure seem so outlandish, so out of touch with reality, and cause great discomfort for today's professors?

To drive the point to its logical conclusion, add one final paragraph to the oath.

8. I shall always recognize and uphold the identity of tenure and pursuit of the truth, which is absolute, unconditional, and inviolate. I shall, in the event that pursuit of the truth is no longer the purpose of my academic life, voluntarily revoke my tenure privilege and resign from my post as a tenured scholar at this institution.

Of course this is an outrage. Under this oath, few professors could keep their job. But we must persist. Why? Obviously this question cannot be answered without pointing out the gulf between what professors take and what they give in return. They routinely expect the comfort and security entailed in tenure, and their expectation is absolutely and unconditionally expressed. But why would they consider anything required in exchange so outrageous?

The significance of all this cannot be overstated. The most wickedly money-conscious society is also the only society in existence that pays professors to do whatever they want as long as they seek and speak the truth. The most advanced market society in the world is also the only society that practices a wholly nonmarket idea with its professors. What is more remarkable, however, is that this point seems to entirely escape its most direct beneficiary himself, namely, the university professor.[1]

It is my considered opinion, accumulated after two decades of academic life, that tenure is given to the wrong people for the wrong reason. Those who *have* it do not *need* it, and those who *need* it do not *have* it. Those who have it do not need it because they do not use it, and those who need it cannot use it because they do not have it. The implications, I believe, are worth pondering.

For anyone who wishes to look at the American professoriate critically, now is perhaps the best time to do it. After the crisis of confidence in the 1970s and early 1980s, professors are just now riding the crest of economic prosperity and social esteem (relatively speaking). The typical professor is a member of the middle class. The harshness of earlier criticism and countercriticism involving professors is largely absent. Prosperity and contentment, at least for those who have made it and for those who expect to make it in the academic world, tend to lower the traditional aversion to self-criticism. Let us hope that this is the correct professorial mood of the moment and that they feel magnanimous toward critics from their own ranks.

Beneath the surface of peace and prosperity, however, not all is well with the professor at a tranquil university. For the seeming peace and prosperity mask serious trouble beneath. The self-satisfied professor is ignoring a vulnerable undercurrent—troublesome, ominous, and quite possibly destructive. The trouble is both in what he is *doing* and in what he is *not doing*. The professor has never been more secure economically or freer intellectually. Yet his voice in society is amplified only in its silence. With his livelihood secured by tenure and his thought protected by academic freedom, he refuses to partake in the affairs of society. In the main, the typical professor is neither seen nor heard in any meaningful way. The substance of his scholarship is thin; the narrowness of his vision makes him a public caricature; his work habits are slothful and his knowledge irrelevant. His relevance to the larger society, which underwrites his livelihood, is so tenuous that his existence or nonexistence makes little difference outside his Ivory Tower. Insulated in this protective shell, he scratches out another meaningless research paper for his colleagues in their narrow specialty. Professors as a whole do not speak to the public; they do not speak even among themselves. The typical professor has become the Little Man (or Woman) no one notices or cares. There is little to notice in what he does, and little to care in what he says.

Of course it is difficult to generalize the academic mood correctly. It varies from campus to campus, from subject to subject, and according to the tenure status of the professor. For the reasons that I will elaborate shortly, the "professor" we are now describing is one who is tenured and who deals with *academic ideas* as his main subject. Chemists and accountants may have their own woes, but they are rarely bothered by inner troubles that are inherent within their fields of study. Theirs are "problems" that must be resolved within the given range of possible solutions. Normally, it is the "academic" professors—typically philosophers, "social scientists," writers, historians, theologians, and other men and women of letters—who agonize over their own proper place in academia and the larger society. When I speak of professors, therefore, I mean these academic professors, especially those with tenure.

Under the sensibilities born of education and reflection, the academic professor frequently finds himself unhappy. His academic routines produce little that seems to be of any lasting significance. His social esteem is more image than substance. Aspiring to something more than job security, he finds that his economic reward often seems hollow and unsatisfying. The perks of tenure do not excite him or make him grateful any more; while lip service is paid to "academic freedom," he enjoys no real sense of freedom in his thought. Much to his surprise, the American professor often dreads that he is only half a step ahead of doom. It is no wonder that a recent Carnegie Foundation survey finds almost one-third of professors feeling "trapped" by their lives and careers.[2]

Unlike other occupations and careers, a professor's life is easily subjected to the question of meaning. Only a special habit of mind can find happiness in dealing with ideas as a vocation. No life becomes so easily devoid of meaning as does the academic life, for empty ideas, especially for the holders of an idea-occupation, are deadlier than the worst boredom that saps the worker's morale. The sought-after blessings of tenure are no panacea against self-doubt and remorse generated by empty ideas. Professors are both blessed and cursed with a "meaning-less" life. For professors must live and die with ideas, and practically all professorial troubles are essentially those of unexamined ideas. As such their troubles are remedied only by critical examination.

I am proposing that it is time for that self-examination. To begin now cannot hurt, but not to do so helps no one. That is my reason for writing this book.[3]

NOTES

1. For reasons of practical convenience and of the simple fact that the tenured seniority consists predominantly of male professors (five to one), I have decided to adopt the convention of using the "he" form to refer to both male and female seniors in this book.

2. Quoted in Christine M. Licata, *Post-Tenure Faculty Evaluation* (Washington, D.C.: Association for the Study of Higher Education, 1986), 3.

3. I suppose that the content and tone of this prologue should make it clear what kind of intellectual orientation is brought to bear upon the writing of this book. Whatever is not clear should be resolved as this book unfolds its argument. Therefore, it is unnecessary to elaborate my own biographical-intellectual-methodological background; this volume speaks for itself. As a general practice in this sort of criticism, furthermore, the author's intention ought to be clearly visible from page one. I believe this is largely the case in this book.

Professors especially, by virtue of their knowledge of human nature, are prone to cynicism. Many highly knowledgeable professors are actively cynical; the less-endowed are only passively so. Many professors are proud to be cynics-in-residence on campus. But cynicism, whatever its virtue in scholarship, deprives one of passion for doing what is right. Criticism is *not* cynicism although they may share certain elements, notably intellectual detachment. In fact, cynicism makes criticism ineffective to the extent it is tainted with cynicism. Both the critic and the cynic recognize evil in humanity, but only the critic wants something done about it. The cynic merely confirms his belief. I hope, perhaps against hope, that it would be obvious to the reader that this distinction has been preserved in this book.

Because this book is about tenure, I should clarify my own status. Yes, I hold a tenured position as an associate professor in the Department of Sociology at the University of North Carolina, Wilmington, North Carolina 28403. Obviously, this book could not have been written (unless I were insane) without this protection in tenure. It has taken me fifteen post–Ph.D. years, six different campuses, and five none-too-memorable books to attain the status. And the very publication of this book demonstrates what a wonderful thing tenure is. My special thanks goes to UNC–Wilmington for making this near-miracle possible.

Part I

Academic Tenure

Chapter 1

The Irrelevance of Tenure

Academic tenure for American professors is an extraordinarily self-contradictory phenomenon. A society whose view of things economic borders on cosmic significance grants a lifetime of job security to a segment of its population least demonstrative of economic value. With it, professors may freely do virtually whatever they wish. The job security is called tenure, and the guarantee academic freedom. In a society where "economic consideration" borders almost on religion, what it gets in return from professors, especially from the "academic" professors, is not worth the money it spends on them. Why would American society insist on such a potentially wasteful system for its professors? What do professors actually do with such a free guarantee for life? The issue is fraught with possibilities and perils.

For a typical professor, the pinnacle of academic life is the achievement of tenure. His success or failure is no more singularly expressed than through his tenure status. Through tenure he defines his career milestone and secures his elementary economic comfort. It is no overstatement to say that he lives for tenure and dies without it.

For his society, tenure is a special privilege granted for a specific service that presumably only the professor can render. The service is nothing special. It is, in fact, the only thing a professor can do for a living: devote his life to scholarship to benefit his community, society, and humanity for the sole purpose of improving happiness. By providing him with a carefree economic and intellectual environment, society demands in exchange an honest day's thought from him.

Reflection and experience easily compel the view that this is an unprofitable exchange for society. It gives the professor his special tenure privilege but gets in return only a subpar service. Tenure may serve the professor well, but it is not doing much for the society that grants it. The special provisions entailed in tenure and academic freedom, though occasional lip service may be paid to them, have been all but forgotten by the professor.

Few professors are conscious of the binding obligation that tenure imposes on them when they pursue it, for tenure is normally thought to liberate them. But it is entirely the wrong kind of liberation celebrated entirely for the wrong reason. Taken predominantly as a means of economic security among those who enjoy it, tenure has been made largely irrelevant by becoming meaningless. The tenured professor now enjoys an unprecedented freedom without fulfilling its elementary obligation. In doing so, he scores a few easy points for himself. Yet in the long run, he serves neither himself nor his society in a way that is mutually beneficial.

Tenure is a privilege, and all privileges eventually corrupt. Only periodic and pitiless self-criticism can retard the onset of routine corruption.

All social privileges are gained either by merit or by heredity. For merit, one must prove one's worth in physical combat, popularity contests in politics and economics, or open competition. For heredity, one must be of appropriate birth, which is much easier than proving merit. Thus claimed, one can enjoy the perks of privilege in legitimate comfort and security.

The tenure privilege in American universities is an aberration. With rare exceptions—so rare as to be meaningless—this privilege is gained neither by merit nor by heredity. It is acquired chiefly by luck (being in the right place at the right time), by connivance (expanding one's vita, not one's scholarship), or by demonstrating an infinite capacity for humility (sometimes called collegiality). These qualities may be necessary and valuable for survival in a highly competitive economic society. But professors do not live or compete in the economic society. Their existence is confined almost wholly to the university. In it survive and even prosper many individuals who may not do as well in a more openly competitive economic setting. It is a world of its own brotherhood, its own rituals, and its own determination of merits and demerits. What complicates this insulated world is the small inconvenient fact that its livelihood derives directly from the larger society, for a specific purpose for which the society is willing to pay the expense.

Undeserved privileges tend to cause occasional discomfort in the undeserving. Nervousness and insecurity inevitably follow. Professors are fierce in pursuit of tenure privilege and are often overly demonstrative of its significance. An undeserved privilege, perhaps a contradiction in terms, seldom brings joy to its possessor but causes much grief in its pursuit. For each privilege awarded to the undeserving is deprived from the truly deserving. Each undeserved privilege is a privilege deprived and wasted. It is almost universally felt among those who are conscious of it that those who have tenure do not need it or are unlikely to need it and that those who need it do not have it or are unlikely to get it.

This paradox did not escape John C. Livingston, professor of government and political science and acting dean at Sacramento State College at the time and a longtime observer of the academic scene. He was moved to comment that "Indeed I am persuaded that those who have been denied tenure would compose a better faculty than those on whose brows the garland of guaranteed lifetime employment has been laid. . . . (The) rejects would be more intense, more committed, more exciting, more innovative." Instead of merit, Livingston argues, mediocrity generally wins the privilege of tenure.[1]

It is indeed the supreme irony of academic life that tenure—a special privilege designed to free professors—has quietly enslaved them. Once enslaved, they no longer pretend to pursue the lofty ideas that give the professoriate as a whole its public image. Nor are they likely to be aware enough of the new reality to burden their conscience with the daily grind of trivia and insignificance. Through it all, they often imagine themselves to be free intellectuals and molders of minds in the grand pedagogical tradition. This delusion easily borders on both low comedy and high tragedy. The only saving grace for them may be that whatever is of monumental importance to them, whatever it is that moves them to great passion, is of no serious public consequence. More likely than not, it is the importance of a monumentally trivial quest, and it is the passion for a predictably insignificant purpose.

Tenure has always been two things at once. It has been hailed as the ultimate means to liberation of the mind from doctrinal orthodoxy. But it has also been prized as a simple escape from the humbling requisites of economic life. The former meaning has largely been lost, especially in the preceding decade, while the latter has claimed a virtual monopoly in the daily reality of working professors. It is tenure they dream about; it is how to get it that occupies most of their waking thoughts; and it is the exaltation of finally getting it, or the bemoaning of not getting it, that is the high or low point of an otherwise humdrum academic life. Tenure, established to liberate professors from their mundane economic needs, chains them to the very economic burden from which they dream of being liberated. Once a means to an end, tenure has become an end in itself. But as a fixed end, it gives its possessors no special joy for possessing it.

Professors may imagine their hero to be Socrates, but their private working model is Adam Smith. To them, tenure is first and last an economic factor. And that imperative of modern life has them groveling while they pursue it and gloating when they have gotten it through luck, connivance, and collegiality.

What is tenure? One of the unwritten rules of American universities is that the professor must be free from the pressures of economic necessity so that he can pursue his goals as scholar and teacher as honestly and independently as possible. To that end, the university grants him a special privilege known as tenure. Of all occupations in America, this tenure privilege is unique to the professor. Tenure is a lifetime guarantee of a job assuming continuous "good behavior" as a scholar and teacher. Tenure status is undoubtedly the most common yardstick available in academia to measure a professor's progress in his career. Currently over 60 percent of all professors have tenure at various institutions on different levels.[2] Understandably, a tenure decision generates much tension, both for the granting institution and for those who are being judged.

Normally a professor becomes eligible for tenure after an average probationary period of four years (about three for private institutions and about six for public universities and colleges). It is one of the quirks of university life that the professor, if denied tenure, must leave the job, as tenure is an up-or-out decision. Hence the drama and tension at tenure time. The drama and tension are all the more commonplace at tenure time because no one really knows what makes a "good" scholar and teacher. Elaborate procedures are established at most campuses for making fair tenure decisions. But such procedures have little or nothing to do with substantive fairness or accuracy in the evaluation process. Elaborately or otherwise, the wrong man can be hanged just as easily. But such procedures give apparent comfort to the inherent ambiguity. Because of such ambiguity, countless stories of unfair tenure decisions are told on college campuses.[3]

This is a very superficial description of the meaning of tenure. Beyond the immediate concern of granting and denying tenure lie the more complicated issues of academic freedom that tenure guarantees and of the goals of academic freedom whose pursuit tenure enables. But for the typical professor, pursuing tenure is enough. The rest will presumably take care of itself in the course of his life as a tenured senior professor at a university. The typical professor need not trouble himself, and normally does not, with the purpose of tenure and the meaning of academic freedom. Indeed, it would surprise him a great deal if asked *what* he was going to do with his tenure now that he has it. He would be speechless. It is like asking a new millionaire on Wall Street what he is going to do with his money. Making it was all he wanted.

Not all professors get tenure, of course, but the idea of tenure itself is taken for granted. A corporate employee puts in his day's work dreaming of becoming a vice president some day. A university professor pursues tenure in essentially the same way, although perhaps with a more realistic expectation of his goal. In both cases, the goal itself is perceived as real and attainable.

While the professor may share similar behavior traits with the corporate employee in the determined pursuit of their respective goals, the purpose of their goals *is* quite different. No serious corporate man troubles himself with the purpose of this goal or that. The vice presidency *is* the goal. No one will ask an economic man about the purpose of his economic goal. Pursuit of wealth precludes philosophy. But the professor is burdened, in private and public expectations, by the question of purpose. Pursuing wealth is not like pursuing scholarship, for scholarship *is* philosophy. That he is simply doing what is economically most self-serving does not dissolve the question of purpose when he finally gets tenure. There is more to it than simple job security. As the professor himself claims, there is the small matter of the *purpose* of tenure that pricks his conscience and continually bothers him. After all, the professor by his own claim is not an economic agent. He is a professor. This troublesome question is not quieted by economic security in tenure. In fact, it is only goaded by it.

Most professors have only a dim notion of how tenure, at least in its contemporary form, all began. A brief excursion into the origin of tenure as it is understood today illuminates the issue by giving it a historical perspective.

Although the origin of the twin concepts of tenure and academic freedom goes back to the beginning of the medieval university itself, its present form in America is the distinct product of an effort made by the American Association of University Professors (AAUP). It was with the emergence of the AAUP as spokesman for the American professoriate that the ancient practice of tenure was transformed into a form that is commonly recognizable today. Called into existence in 1913 by eighteen professors at Johns Hopkins University, the AAUP confronted and cajoled the university hierarchy of powerful trustees and presidents for professorial autonomy. It formulated principles of academic freedom tied to tenure and eventually prevailed on the reluctant and often hostile hierarchy to accept the principles.

At the turn of the century, academic tenure on most campuses in America operated on a gentlemen's agreement between individual faculty members and their institution. But without contractual obligations in force, the agreement often worked against the professor, the weaker of the two parties. Trustees and presidents were not always proper gentlemen. Mostly small and locally financed, typical American universities at the time were a fair playground for the overreaching trustees and presidents. Gentlemen-scholars did not insist on specific terms of employment and hence were extremely vulnerable to the whims of the hierarchy. Professors could be and were subject to dismissal without a hearing or recourse to due process.

Professor Edward A. Ross represents one such case. An economist at Stanford, he was forced to resign in 1900 when his opinion apparently displeased one Mrs. Stanford, the sole trustee of the university. In a classic case of academic freedom clashing with economic authority, the professor had denounced certain economic policies that were dear to Mrs. Stanford. Displeased to the imperious degree to which she had been accustomed by virtue of her wealth, she pressured the president to force the professor to resign. The dismissal became a well publicized cause célèbre, involving the national organization of economists. The Ross incident left a deep impression on a young professor at Stanford by the name of Arthur Lovejoy. He resigned from Stanford and moved to Johns Hopkins, where he began a decade of work organizing professors. Lovejoy's perseverance eventually culminated in the formation of the AAUP.

In 1915 the AAUP issued the first articulated statement of principle concerning academic freedom, titled "The General Report on Academic Freedom and Academic Tenure." Now growing in stature, the AAUP in 1925 produced jointly with the Association of American Colleges (AAC), an organizational arm of presidents, a "Conference Statement" as a significant step toward securing cooperation from administrators. By then, institutions of higher learning had grown in size and diversity. Presidents could no longer actively participate in the day-to-day management of their universities. Reliance on specialized administrators and academic departments became increasingly imperative. This development also favored the increasing autonomy of professors.

However, the contemporary model of tenure and academic freedom, mandating a formal agreement and an adversary procedure in cases of dismissal, was not created until 1940. In this year the AAUP and the AAC once again jointly produced a document that was to become the prototype for all later policy statements. The document specified seven years as the maximum probationary period and confirmed the principle of dismissal only under bona fide proof. The burden of proof for unfitness thus moved from the shoulders of professors to those of administrators. The AAUP and the AAC, not always on friendly terms during the years of struggle to define their respective roles in the academy, gradually came to accept the autonomy of the professoriate in the booming postwar years of land-grant higher education.

Those who take tenure security for granted might do well to remember the AAUP's struggle in its early years to represent the professoriate's interests. The odds were heavily against them. With few exceptions, colleges and universities were controlled by businessmen-trustees who did not always look upon "liberal" academics with tolerance. Many presidents, with concentrated power that came with the smallness of their institutions, were often accused of being autocratic and less than gentlemanly in their dealings with the faculty. The public sentiment, especially during World War I, frequently called on trustees and legislators to punish the "pacifist" traitors among college teachers. And within its own ranks, the AAUP was spurned by many gentleman-scholars as smacking of unionism.

Under these adverse circumstances and despite limited resources, the organization persevered. It investigated the many cases that called for its intervention and settled disputes as well as it could, sometimes with conciliatory gestures and sometimes with threats of censure. It articulated the principle of academic freedom now assumed by most professors and accepted by almost all public and private institutions in America. Many potential incidents were avoided by the mere possibility that the AAUP might investigate.

During the 1960s higher education burgeoned in America, resulting in an acute shortage of professors. This shortage profoundly affected the nature of tenure and academic freedom. It was in the 1960s that the new principle of academic freedom and permanent tenure became the standard, primarily to attract qualified teachers. Professors routinely expected to be tenured as part of established benefits. For the purpose of attracting enough teachers to fill the posts, not only did the offer of tenure become a permanent fixture on campus, but also many underqualified professors were easily tenured. This practice naturally lowered the quality of faculty in general and created a bottleneck in career mobility for many years to come.

During the political turmoil of the 1970s, and with the threat of declining enrollment, tenure and academic freedom came under attack, not always unjustifiably. Activist professors took to the streets and the public forum with their political beliefs. Protests and counterprotests were commonplace on campus. In academic freedom professors claimed their right of protest and immunity of penalty. A few legislators, urged on by self-styled patriots and moralists, called for the abolishment of tenure-based academic freedom altogether. Fortunately, no such draconian initiative ever passed a state house. However, the public outcry demonstrated once again, as it had done during World War I and the McCarthy era, the fragility of the professor's protective cocoon.[4]

In the 1980s, a tenured professor has seldom been dismissed. On the one hand, this demonstrates the universally accepted notion of tenure security. The professoriate is happy with this state of affairs. On the other hand, and perhaps ominously, this state of groggy peace for the professor indicates that something may be amiss at the academy. This thought makes some people uneasy. The feeling is that something important in the meaning of academic freedom, which the founders of the AAUP fought so hard to achieve, has been lost. To the extent that something is taken for granted, the original purpose is obviously lost. To the extent that the original purpose is lost, the legitimacy of its present existence becomes untenable.

In any society or era, the founding generation is always the most dynamic, the most dedicated, and the purest at heart. The revolutionary generation that destroys the old and ushers in the new always displays the very best of human virtues. Since not every generation can be its own destroyer and rebuilder, continuously renewing itself, the subsequent generations tend to absorb *less* of the virtuousness of the preceding generation. With the passage of time, every subsequent generation corrupts a little more than the preceding one, removing itself a little further from the original purpose. This is the inevitable conservative inertia in any generation in any society. To avoid this atrophy or degeneration, each generation may keep its remembrance alive by trying to revive the memory of the founders on their anniversary, reenacting the original dramas and reciting the earlier pledges. With each generation, however, the memory fades, the reenactment loses its significance, and the reciting becomes perfunctory and empty of meaning.

So it is with the professor. He rarely troubles himself with the question: Why was tenure fought for so hard?

In a strange way, tenure itself changes nothing in the professor. It has the least direct impact. Raises and promotions matter directly. They affect one's pocketbook. But tenure does nothing. It affects nothing at all in the day-to-day routines of academic life. But why is the professor so eager to get it? If academic freedom subsequent to tenure is so eagerly pursued, why is academic freedom so important to professors?

Strictly speaking, tenure is not a reward for a job well done or a down payment on the predicted excellence of future performance. Rather, tenure is a means to an end. What is the end? It is academic freedom. But academic freedom for what? The classic statement of purpose (for academic freedom) was expressed by the AAUP in 1940: "Institutions of higher education are conducted for the common good and not to further the interest of either the individual teacher or the institution as a whole. The common good depends upon the free search for the truth and its free expression." It simply says professors need freedom to express their ideas. This principle is so rhetorical and commonplace that, like "all men are created equal," it is enough to merely assume, not assert, its validity today. The statement continues: "Academic freedom is essential to these purposes and applies to both teaching and research." All later statements on the purpose of tenure and academic freedom simply restate this declaration.

Every writer on tenure and academic freedom agrees on the principle. Robert MacIver calls it "the endless search for the truth."[5] According to Clark Byse and Louis Joughin, tenure "enables a faculty member to teach, study, and act free from a large number of restraints and pressures which otherwise would inhibit independent thought and action."[6] The professor must "follow out any bold, vigorous, independent train of thought" to produce "honest judgment and independent criticism" and to pursue "the truth wherever it may lead."[7]

The standard purpose of tenure and academic freedom is simple enough: it frees the professor from the concerns of economic life, which ordinary workmen must endure, so that he may speak the truth in his honest and independent commitment to scholarship. Not a reward for a job well done, it is specifically designed to *protect* professors from the consequences of speaking the truth. Academic freedom, then, is justified only in pursuit of the truth. Tenure as a reward for a job well done and as a protective device for the freedom to pursue the truth may *end up* being the same thing. But they should not be presumed to be the same thing. However, the idea of truth as the precondition for tenure is so taken for granted that to hear it mentioned would surprise the professor.

Things that are taken for granted, however, tend to be things forgotten. It is more so for things that are made up of abstract ideas. At present, it takes a special effort for the professor to remind himself of the original, and still imperative, purpose of tenure. For him, pursuing tenure has been so consuming and overwhelming a task that pursuing the truth subsequent to it has been all but forgotten.

Thus, the professor feels his work is essentially done when he gets his tenure. Still in his (or her) thirties, suddenly he finds himself with little else to do. Teaching sooner or later loses its lustre and becomes tedious and repetitious. So does "research," one project being like another. It is a struggle just to stay afloat, semester after semester, year after year. For the truth-seeker, tenure *is* the truth. And it has been *achieved*. Now all that remains is the grinding out of a routine campus life maintaining the minimum requirements of his academic sinecure. It is both easy and difficult; it is both rewarding and demeaning; it is both pleasurable and painful. Hence, in his lucid moments of reflection, he feels trapped in his career, unfulfilled in his life. He has pursued tenure all his academic career, not truth. Now, in getting tenure, he has lost the very purpose of life.

The undercurrent of unease in a professor's life, however, is not disquieting enough to compel him to alter his commitment to a seemingly comfortable existence. Superficially he is well fixed for life. He has his public status to enjoy; he has his specialized colleagues for mutual support; he has the untenured faculty to lord over; he has his students to impress with his knowledge. One should not assume that the professor is easily moved by logic and reason only because he is a learned man. In most cases, established academic routines easily resolve what little need for reflection there is in the professor.

That he is doing well in public esteem and economic terms[8] spells instant trouble. For, by making it primarily a sign of career success, the professor has made his tenure *irrelevant* in the real sense. As tenure is taken wholly as a career and economic measure in a professor's life, the academic freedom it is supposed to produce has become meaningless. As academic freedom has become meaningless, the truth that the academic freedom is supposed to protect has been sacrificed. The professor has succeeded in a small measure, namely, in securing his immediate economic well-being, by failing in a large measure: he has made himself as a professor an irrelevant figure. He lives well off tenure and takes it easy in academic freedom. But his parasitic days may be numbered.

Tenure unused is tenure irrelevant. The easiest way to measure the relevance of anything is by *removing* it from the scene. An irrelevant post under the bridge, when removed, will not reduce the structural soundness of the bridge. Irrelevance, present or removed, causes no effect on the status quo. Now let us remove tenure from the professor. What would happen to the routine of academic life? Nothing. No stirring truth would be sacrificed since no stirring truth is being pursued *with* tenure. No academic freedom would be suppressed since no academic freedom is being exercised with tenure. No visible change would affect the professor since tenure is not a visible thing to wear, use, or exhaust. Tenure or no tenure would make little or no difference. Hence, tenure itself—and all that it implies—has become irrelevant. Herein, then, lies, the ultimate threat to tenure, academic freedom, and truth itself. For nothing destroys a special privilege faster than a special privilege that is no longer special. The professor relentlessly pursues his freedom, yet very little of it is ever used for the purpose for which it is pursued and granted. In this, he is a model citizen of his larger society.

Whatever may be professors' self-image, however solid their tenured security may appear, however safe and sound their academic routines may feel, this irrelevance makes them the most *expendable* of social groups. The wholesale disappearance of philosophy or sociology, as opposed to chemistry or accounting, will cause virtually no inconvenience to anyone but philosophers or sociologists themselves. But paradoxically, it is this very expendability that makes the academic professoriate potentially the most *valuable* group in society as well. For in this very expendability lies the essence of academic freedom. Academic freedom is a special, and less noticed, case of general freedom in society. But freedom, especially academic freedom, has been the most historically expendable of all commodities in society. It is this very expendability that makes it so precious. Yet, the professor who so eagerly seeks freedom is usually the one who so easily surrenders it.

It indeed is an extremely delicate task to transform expendability into something of extreme social value. But the professor who remains expendable without being valuable is an irrelevant entity. He cannot ask for a special privilege for an end that is not special. He can claim neither merit nor heredity. But he has in his sole possession the greatest weapon mankind has ever invented: he has tenure, and with it, academic freedom and truth on his side. And they are no mean complement to battle irrelevance and expendability. But *he* has to do the battle.

NOTES

1. John Livingston, "Tenure Everyone?" in *The Tenure Debate*, ed. Bardwell Smith (San Francisco: Jossey-Bass 1973), 69–70.

2. "The Annual Report on the Economic Status of the Profession 1987–1988," *Academe*. AAUP (March-April 1988): 14. Faculty's tenure and salary status are annually updated in this publication.

3. An excellent collection of case studies is found in Arthur S. Wilke, ed., *The Hidden Professoriate*. (Westport, Conn: Greenwood Press, 1979).

4. For the most authoritative account of tenure and academic freedom in the United States, see Richard Hofstadter and Walter P. Metzger, *The Development of Academic Freedom in the United States* (New York: Columbia University Press, 1965). Metzger's shorter version contained in Commission on Academic Tenure in Higher Education, *Faculty Tenure* (San Francisco: Jossey-Bass, 1973), 93–159 covers the medieval origin of tenure and academic freedom as well.

5. Robert MacIver, *Academic Freedom in Our Time* (New York: Columbia University Press, 1955), 6.

6. Clark Byse and Louis Joughin, *Tenure in American Higher Education* (Ithaca, · N.Y.: Cornell University Press, 1959), 2.

7. Fritz Machlup quoted in Byse and Joughin, *Tenure*, 3.

8. See AAUP, *Academe*. Quoted above.

Chapter 2

Academic Tenure and Market Tenure

Presently, not only is tenure sought for the wrong reason, but it is routinely awarded to a large group of faculty who have no pertinent use for it. The first case applies to "academic" professors who, in their pursuit of economic security, remember nothing about why tenure was originally established. The second applies to subject matters that, by virtue of their special functions, stand outside the original meaning of tenure and purpose of academic freedom. As much as tenure is wasted on some faculty members both in practice and as principle, it is also wasted on some *fields* as well. Certain subject areas in the university curriculum (e.g., chemistry and accounting) should involve no tenure application at all. As tenure is irrelevant to some academic professors in practice, as we have seen, it is also irrelevant to certain subject fields as a matter of misapplied principle. Simply stated, chemistry and accounting, among other such fields, do *not* need tenure or academic freedom.

This contention is surely to be disputed by both parties. But the immediate reaction has more to do with the habits of academics, which are among the least amenable to change, than with principle. I do not mean to "grade" different subject fields, since I do not see tenure as a badge of honor or superiority in comparing subject matters. However, in this and the next several chapters, if not the whole book, I hope to have the dispute laid to rest. In the process, the academic professor, as differentiated from the functional colleague, may be reminded of something about himself that he has largely forgotten.

It is obviously untrue that the undercurrent of moodiness described in the preceding chapter pervades *all* academic fields. The mathematics professor is hardly bothered by the question of his place in academia or the specter of obsolescence in society, as his sociology colleague might be. In the School of Business, the mood is much more upbeat than it is in the Department of Philosophy. Nursing instructors are much more sanguine about life in general than and untenured juniors in history. A Ph.D. candidate in physics tends to have an outlook on his future rather different from that of a doctoral candidate in political science. A student who prepares himself to be an accountant may not have the same foreboding of grimness in job prospects as one who wants to be a serious writer.

There are many layers of academic careers and many shades of economic prospect for those who pursue them. When a university holds a faculty meeting, members of many different schools, departments, and programs come to a single collective forum, commonly known as the "faculty." A faculty member from chemistry may converse with an art historian from the creative arts department about this or that subject. But their conversations will rarely stray into the profound or substantive; they will basically be limited to the latest sports scores, complaints about students or about cafeteria food, speculation on salary increases and administrative moves, and other campus gossip. The fact that these diverse members on campus are gathered in one place gives rise to the impression of one single body with many backgrounds united by a singular purpose and task. But this impression is largely false and serves no useful purpose.

Analysis demands, however, that we discern a definite pattern of association among the different layers and shades. A faculty member who teaches real-estate law has virtually nothing in common with a faculty member who teaches moral philosophy, and he obviously does not share the many grounds for foreboding and gloom (not necessarily intellectual ones) by which the philosopher may be afflicted. Aside from the traditional divisions of university curriculum among natural science, humanities, social science, and professional schools, we confront the factor of tenure in this conventional organizational chart. Which fields need tenure and which fields do not? Convention has it that all university professors in all different fields want and need tenure. For my critical analysis this will not do.

Forced by this analytic and practical necessity, I propose that we divide what is taught in the university into two simple categories: "academic" fields and "functional" fields. Whatever inadequacies and ambiguities this classification scheme may present, I will try to overcome them along the way. For the time being these two categories should serve the present purpose. After all, the best classification is neither most exhaustive nor most accurate; it is most serviceable for the purpose in hand. And the academic-functional dichotomy should do just that. The former needs tenure; the latter does not. New thinking requires new perspective; new perspective requires a new organization of thought. However comforting to our intellectual inertia, it would not help us to insist upon the conventional wisdom regarding the university professoriate just when we are trying to look at it critically.

As their most telling characteristic, "academic" fields are *useless* in themselves (as properly explained below) in the ongoing realities of society. The term "academic" itself normally means in popular usage something irrelevant, inconsequential, or impractical. "Useless" is a more direct term, which I find is representative of these various connotations. As we shall discover shortly, being useless is not as hopeless a cause as it may first appear. But it is a notion that nevertheless sets academic fields apart from the other, the "useful" fields, as a way of understanding our present issue.

To put it in a nutshell, society can do nicely without moral philosophers or social theorists. Propaganda (sometimes called communications or commercials) is useful; philosophy is not. Economics is useful; political economy is not. Social work is useful; sociology is not. Literacy is useful; literature is not. The simplest way to tell the two apart is to determine whether the holder of a particular field's knowledge can earn a living outside the university community, relying exclusively on his knowledge or skill. No modern society has a job that calls for an independent-minded philosopher or a social theorist. Academic professors have nothing to offer to the market that it would find useful. Participants in these fields of endeavor are acutely aware of this market problem and are quite self-conscious about it. Business majors routinely refer to social science as the "unemployment field."

That some philosophers, social scientists, writers, or historians find it necessary to learn new skills in order to change their careers in midlife—such as learning computers to make themselves marketable to a corporation—only proves the point. *As* philosophers, social scientists, writers, and historians, they are as useless outside academia as computer experts are in an Amish community. On the other hand, modern society would instantly become paralyzed without the full complements of its market fields that comprise its scientists, managers, producers, communicators, facilitators, and practitioners of all such technical specialties.

When the subject is tenure, it is normally those in useless academic fields who show intense interest. The degree of interest is more routine among the practitioners of useful fields. Tenure conflict is normally the province of academic fields. It is those in social science, history, philosophy, English literature, theology, and sometimes political economy (as an oddball member of the economics department) who get in tenure trouble or lock horns with administration over one issue or another. The desperation with which academic members fight for tenure and the frequency in which they get in trouble with administration are in odd contrast to the relative paucity of such trouble in functional fields.

The discerning reader is already in agreement that the professorial concerns expressed in the preceding chapter apply almost exclusively to academic, not functional, fields. In other words, the trouble over tenure, the specter of expendability, the foreboding over the meaning of this or that, visit those whose knowledge is practically useless outside the university. A philosopher cannot earn a living simply by philosophizing. Academic fields produce no results intrinsic to the fields that are in demand in ordinary society.

It is not surprising, then, that an absolute majority of those with a Ph.D. in one academic department or another enter universities as their primary occupational stations. Although in some fields, such as sociology, over 80 percent of doctorates become professors, overall more than twice as many academic degree holders enter university employment as "functional" degree holders. In other words, the marketable degree holders do not define their occupational choice overwhelmingly in institutions of higher learning. They can find it in the open marketplace other than the university setting.[1]

Students who choose academic fields as opposed to market fields as their career choice tend to make their choice essentially as a commitment. It is uncommon that a sociology graduate student or an aspiring writer would think urgently about the marketability of the field he, and increasingly she, has chosen. Even after the warnings of an impending bottleneck in the job market in recent years, students still chose these fields oblivious to the warnings. The market fields, on the other hand, tend to have smaller supply-demand gaps overall because the students tend to respond much more critically to the job market fluctuations.

As academics, professors in these useless fields deal primarily with *ideas*. Professors in market fields deal with *things*, or with ideas that can be easily converted to things. A business management teacher may talk about "identification" between employees and company as a crucial idea in modern management. But the idea must result in higher earnings and greater quarterly dividends. Media people refer to a new sitcom idea as a "concept," but the concept is directly related to concrete ratings. Ideas for ideas' sake could not be entertained seriously by a business teacher or by a media specialist. On the other hand, a philosopher could not talk about what is good for the company or its stockholders without compromising his freedom as a philosopher. To remain a true philosopher, he must remain essentially a dealer in useless ideas.

What makes anything useful in society? All useful things in society either give comfort to the existing social system or contribute to the convenience of life in a practical way. They are—or can be reduced to—normally measurable, definite quantities. Propaganda is useful to society as toilet paper is useful to life. To be useful and in demand in an ordinary social system, these are the simplest criteria to define and to satisfy. In America's market society the marketplace is where one useful item is exchanged for another useful item. The measure of usefulness is embodied in the item's "marketability." The totality of society, then, is presumed to exist in the totality of these exchanges. And the total worth of a society is also presumed to be represented in its total quantity of market exchanges.

Marketability is attained by its appeal to the largest number of people in any given time and place. Under no compulsion except the inner compulsion for agreeability, things are deemed marketable simply because they satisfy the self-interests of certain members of society. Sick people find medical help useful; Madison Avenue finds clever minds useful; corporations find consumers useful; hungry people find food useful.

Academic fields offer no such useful goods or services that are marketable. Even in the Golden Ages of humanity, moral advice was never deemed a marketable or even useful commodity. A buyer will not part with his money unless he expects satisfaction from its expenditure. Things that money can buy normally do not satisfy his moral yearnings. "True" philosophers, prophets, revolutionaries, and artists—the more radical versions of today's academic professors—have always been among the poorest of humanity. People will not spend money in large quantities on philosophy, prophecy, revolution, or the arts. Academic professors' daily nightmare consists of trying to find *some* cause of usefulness and marketability for their majors. Their daily agony is renewed in the impossibility of this task. Academic fields produce little or nothing that would appeal to a large number of people in a market society with an abundance of more pleasing goods. Their product (to use the marketing term for something entirely different) satisfies neither the needs of society nor the conveniences of life. It is never sufficiently appealing for people to pay for it. Many among the trustees and the public are, as Arthur DeBardeleben relates, "especially impressed by the argument that the academic social scientist or humanist is 'impractical' or 'unreliable.' "[2]   No one likes to buy impractical or unreliable products.

Understandably, feeling especially miniaturized among the more opulent and useful brother departments, schools, and programs, academic fields are rather defensive about their uselessness, often in the extreme. They try to overcome this obvious inferiority complex either by imitating the useful fields or by offering services to the useful fields in some technical capacities. A common example occurs when social scientists try to act like natural scientists or offer their services to be research technicians for "useful" projects. Even philosophers offer their services to business schools for joint projects on business ethics or other such feasible topics. Psychology presents an altogether different story. Although begun as a field dealing with an academic subject, it has aspired in its aim and method to imitate hard science. In an extremely confusing state of existence and self-image, it is at present neither an academic nor a functional field.

Either way, their aspirations and imitations tend to fall short, and it is a bitterly disappointing experience for the academically useless but practically ambitious academics. This tendency is more pronounced in some fields such as sociology, whose subject matter comes closer to the borderline case of usefulness than other academic fields. The useful fields, immensely supported by their marketability, treat academic fields by turns with sympathy, superiority, smugness, or abject neglect. For academic professors, it is an unrelenting struggle for respectability and, in many cases, for parity in salaries, facilities, student enrollments, and other campus differentials. There is no denying that a considerable difference exists in practical terms between academic fields and functional-market fields. Administrators generally adopt the marketability yardstick in setting faculty salaries. Most professors in academic fields are resigned to this unfairness as a simple and unavoidable fact of life.

But all is not lost for academic fields. For their *real value* lies precisely in the fact that they are entirely useless. Their knowledge is not for sale, therefore they need not appeal to or be dictated by the market. Since their continuing employment exists by virtue of their scholarship, not marketability, they need not concern themselves with practicality at all. Their uselessness, as well as their independence from the market and from practical consideration, makes them absolutely *free* and *autono-*

mous. In a perverse way, it is their uselessness in everyday life that makes them useful in higher life. Since usefulness is defined solely by the marketplace, on the other hand, by trying to become useful in some ways these academic fields would only end up making themselves useful neither as academic fields nor as market fields. Trying to be useful, they only harm their precious freedom and autonomy. By remaining useless, they become potentially the most important segment of society. Thus freed from the market, the university that houses academic fields is potentially the most vital place for pure, untainted human knowledge. I say *potentially* because this is a premise, not necessarily a reality. But here we are getting ahead of ourselves.

Why does the academic institution—or more generally, the larger society—expend its enormous resources on subject matters that bear no useful relation to society or life? Why does it support academic professors who could not possibly earn a living outside academia by marketing their knowledge or skill? These and other questions urgently require immediate response. Although their full answers would run the whole length of our argument in this book, we can say for now that society apparently has decided that these academic fields have, after all, some *vital services* to perform. Whatever form this benefit may take, it would be wholly different from the kind of benefit that is made available at the marketplace. A man who is examining the quality of toilet paper is liable to examine the quality of his social life. He may find that the good quality of toilet paper does not satisfy his yearnings for the quality of his *social* life. What his soul yearns for, if this is the case, cannot be satisfied by what is offered on the market. They are two different issues of life and society. It is essentially this *difference* in the subject matters of academic fields and functional fields, not in their imitated similarity, that salvages the former's hurt pride and sense of self-worth.

The mechanism through which these useless academic fields are made useful on campus is tenure. The end that is sought through tenure is academic freedom. The benefit embodied in the end, when it is properly understood, is the improvement of happiness in community, society, and humanity. Only with this benefit in mind does society expend its enormous resource on the otherwise useless academic professors. Without the university, they have no place else to go; without tenure, they cannot survive; without the protection of academic tenure, they are nonexistent. To say that their total survival depends on tenure privilege is to understate the case. If any segment of society depends on a special provision made exclusively for them, it is the academic faculty and its academic tenure. One without the other is meaningless.

The market fields, needless to say, do not depend on tenure for their survival. An accountant can work for a corporation just as easily as for a university's business department. So can a chemist. So can a nurse. So can an engineer. Obviously, some adjustments will be necessary to switch from one working environment to another. But the essence remains the same. It is this relatively easy transferability that gives market fields their general air of comfort and security. Their survival is not necessarily tied to academic life, and in fact industry and academia frequently exchange personnel for teaching positions. A purely academic mathematician may look down on a colleague previously associated with a corporation. But this is a minor snobbery that bears no significance on their transferability. Unlike a philosopher, a mathematician has his mathematics either at the marketplace or in a classroom.

Naturally, the keen attention paid to the issues of tenure normally comes from the academic faculty in one subject area or another. Except for rare occasions, it is the academic faculty that bears the brunt of tenure struggle. The burden of tenure conflict is almost always borne in inverse proportion to the marketability (or usefulness) of the field. The less useful, the more conflict. Whereas a moral philosopher looks upon tenure with the dread of a death sentence, an accountant in the business department looks upon it with a fair amount of nonchalance.

Job security—which is embodied in tenure—thus has two entirely different meanings. While it is wholly tied to tenure for academic professors, it is inconsequentially related to tenure for market professors. For the former, it is tenure. For the latter, it is the marketplace. For the former, getting tenure is the pinnacle of life. For the latter, getting tenure is fairly pro forma, depending on the strength of marketability. The university is the only place where academic professors find their judgment of fitness. The market professors can and do find their marketability at the marketplace. And the university makes allowance for their marketability when their faculty evaluation is conducted. Implicitly they are judged by different criteria from those applied to academic professors, on the grounds that they are market professors. This casts the matter of tenure in a slightly different light.

The most obvious argument for tenure is that it is necessary, both for the grantor and for the grantee. For the grantor, it is necessary to protect professors from their mundane concerns in exchange for their devotion to truth. For the grantee, it is necessary because he cannot survive or pursue the truth effectively without tenure. Both society and professors benefit from this arrangement. But this simple rule of tenure exchange does not apply, or applies only marginally, to functional fields. There are two basic reasons for saying so. One is that, as we have seen, their tenure security is made irrelevant by virtue of their inherent marketability.

The other reason, crucially important (as shall be developed more fully in later chapters), is that the market professors *have nothing to do with the truth*. They pursue facts. Truth is not a marketable commodity; facts are. Truth is what society wants from scholarship in exchange for the scholar's job security. Society simply pays for facts with research funds and investments. Truth is produced under the guarantee of freedom. Facts are produced under the terms of practicality. Truth irritates and often *threatens* the status quo. Facts *serve* the status quo. Thus, truth is utterly the product of tenure security and academic freedom. Facts are tied to the fluctuating fortunes of the marketplace.

Although convention dictates that we speak of academic tenure for both academic and market professors, we have seen that they are two entirely different notions. The former need tenure. The latter do not, at least not for the reasons for which tenure was established. In view of the critical urgency and significance we attach to academic tenure, it should not apply at all to nonacademic professors. Neither society nor market professors benefit from tenure. Simply, there is no need for it. Peace of mind achieved with academic tenure is essentially the same peace of mind derived from the market. The urgency that an academic professor feels about his tenure is only marginally relevant to a market professor.

Only academic professors, by virtue of their uselessness and pursuit of the truth, need the protection that tenure accords. By applying the principle of tenure to everyone on campus not only do we confuse the concept of tenure, we also dilute the purpose of tenure. The first implies the principle of need; the second, pursuit of the truth. One of the simplest measures of the scholarly integrity of a professor is how much of the given orthodoxy in the field is accepted by him. Orthodoxy in chemistry is accepted by necessity. Orthodoxy in sociology is accepted by choice. Doubting orthodoxy is an admirable and imperative quality in the latter. But the same trait could not be praised equally in the former, because they are two fundamentally different subjects. By doing his job right, a functional professor retains his job. But by doing his job right, in pursuit of truth, the academic professor instantly jeopardizes his job. Hence the critical importance of tenure for the academic professor. The unwritten tradition of confusing the two may serve our convenience, but not our reality. Only with this elemental realization may we begin to comprehend the true significance of tenure and freedom for the academic professor.

But then, what is the true significance of tenure and academic freedom?

NOTES

1. See Arthur S. Wilke, ed., *The Hidden Professoriate* (Westport, Conn.: Greenwood, 1979), especially 59–88.

2. Arthur DeBardeleben, "The University's External Constituency," in *Dimensions of Academic Freedom*, eds. Walter P. Metzger, Sanford H. Kadish, Arthur DeBardeleben, Eward J. Bloustein (Urbana: University of Illinois Press, 1969), 76.

Chapter 3

The Special Contract

In the ancient Orient the king would appoint a most respected scholar to a post whose job consisted solely of criticizing the king's conduct. With the job went the guarantee that no matter what he said about the king's conduct, he would not be punished for his honest opinion. It is an amazing feat of creativity that a modern market society appoints its most educated yet practically useless segment to a protected position just to tell the truth about the society itself. To guarantee absolute honesty, the society grants the scholar a special protective shield known as tenure. This "vision to subsidize free criticism and inquiry," observed Professor Walter Metzger, "is one of the remarkable achievements of man."[1]

The extraordinary nature of tenure and academic freedom can be summarized clearly in the simple fact that a society makes a special concession *against its own interest*. To guarantee someone else's freedom to truth is to risk a threat to one's own truth. Only a society that is recklessly self-confident or one that is foolish would recognize such a grand vision of truth. The tenure system enjoyed by the American professoriate is unique to contemporary American society and to professors. No other society and no other occupational group allow such a carte blanche to their members. "Freedom from accountability," an extreme version of tenure immunity, according to Robert M. O'Neal, "would be unacceptable for any other profession."[2] Yet, being neither self-confident nor foolish, American society's guarantee of academic freedom—and demand for honest truth in return—almost verges on heroic proportions.

Truth in general is never popular. For it to prosper, it requires special protection from and against society for the latter's own good. Tenure is the mechanism designed to promote truth, to protect the professor, and to help society along the way. No other historical arrangement similar to the present tenure system in American society, aside from the Oriental king's scholar–critic, has ever existed. Given the extraordinary nature of tenure and academic freedom, squandering this remarkable arrangement for truth through either abuse or sloth would amount to an act of equally extraordinary stupidity.

There are many ways to squander this special opportunity. One of the most relentlessly common ways is to use it as an "economic" incentive for higher productivity. But what is entailed in tenure is truth, not productivity. Truth cannot be multiplied in production as useful commodities can. Truth requires protection, not incentive, for truth is its own incentive. Used as incentive, tenure tends to attract the wrong kind of academics to produce the wrong kind of "truths." No good truth can come out of a situation prompted primarily by an economic incentive.

Another way of squandering it, equally common on campus, is in confusing academic freedom entailed in tenure with "neutrality." Respectable scholars have argued over the issue of university neutrality.[3] Sometimes the term "dispassionate" or "disinterested" substitutes for "neutrality." The idea has been perniciously attractive that professors must remain neutral on social issues in the best tradition of science and intellectual impartiality. But truth is not and cannot be approached neutrally; nor dispassionately, nor disinterestedly. Commitment, not neutrality; passion, not dispassion; and interest, not disinterest, are the basic ingredients of all truth. If one were to approach his subject with neutrality, dispassion, and disinterest, why would he *need* academic freedom to protect him at all?

Still another way of squandering, also equally common, is in forgetting the *original* and still the *only* principle of tenure. Tenure exists to protect those whose ideas, in their pursuit of the truth, *need* protection. Tenure protects truth by protecting the truth-seeker. Like all things in society that repeat, tenure becomes ritualized and tends to be taken for granted. Worse, it tends to reward those whose ideas, by their harmlessness or absence, least require tenure protection.

Harmless mediocrity may become routinized and standardized. At most campuses hardly anyone would get tenure if he attained something similar to the accomplishment of some of the most admired heroes in his field. It is unlikely that Socrates, had he lived now, would be given tenure by his professional colleagues in the department of philosophy. His truth would be too relentless, his autonomy too fierce, his moral precepts too disquieting, his uncorruptability too irritating. It is equally unlikely that Thorstein Veblen in economics, Beethoven in music, Marx in philosophy, or many others like them, would fare better now that there is tenure protection. With few exceptions, virtually all academic departments have become "conservative" by inaction and inertia. And it is not difficult to imagine what discomfort these heores would cause in their respective departments. That they fared poorly with the authorities in their real lives does not mean that they would fare any better today with their hypothetical academic colleagues who should know something about academic freedom. With absolute protection from tenure and academic freedom now in place, there is still no evidence of advancement either in truth or in the truth-seeker. As opposed to seeking the truth, academic corruption enjoys many variations in its expression.

Tenure makes what is useless useful and puts in demand what is without demand. This is an entirely unnatural process wholly alien to a market society where, in principle, supply and demand rule. (It is true that government regulations, support, or subsidies in many areas of industry and agriculture affect the market principle of supply and demand. But none are so permanently and unconditionally fixed as tenure and academic freedom.) Where there is no practical usefulness, society artificially creates it. Where there is no demand for academic fields, society artificially creates it. University jobs are maintained with the sole purpose of supporting academic professors, who are useless outside academia, so that they may do nothing but pursue the truth. For an avowed market society this is no mean accomplishment and no small puzzle.

Tenure is actually the only nonmarket concession that a market society allows. Normally, one sells what one can and buys what one must. In this simple scheme of things there is no room for buying and selling something for which there is no demand. Academic professors speak freely of "economic rewards," "job security," "promotion," "raises," and so on as concepts intrinsic to tenure. But these are economic terms applied to an essentially noneconomic phenomenon. If such purely economic concepts applied, few academic fields and fewer academic professors would be on campus. The academic professor finds himself having no leg to stand on if he insists on tenure as an economic concept. For tenure is a deliberately antieconomic system in theory (permanent employment) and in practice (monopolized employment).

Why does America's market society allow something that is manifestly antimarket in conception? Obviously, tenure has been developed through many seemingly small and insignificant events into the present form. No one person or organization (Arthur Lovejoy or the AAUP) is individually responsible for having created tenure singlehandedly. There is no way we can discern one Grand Design responsible for its present form. The forces that have created the system have been many—psychological, economic, social, religious, political, cultural. And we can only speculate after the fact what its function, hence its putative origin, may be in our contemporary society.

I believe it is the very nature of market society itself that *necessitates* tenure and academic freedom. The market society that grants this extraordinary freedom to professors cannot do very well without it. As much as the professor needs this special gesture from his society, his society also needs the professor. Both are desperately in *need* of each other. We know that the professor stands largely useless and undemanded at the marketplace. That explains why he must depend on the largesse of society for his livelihood. But his society needs him just as much, if not more. It has to do with the nature of America's market society.

America's liberal market society, in its relentlessly rational form, has increasingly become myopic, pedestrian, philistine, epicurean, hedonistic, selfish, brutish, nasty, anti-intellectual, and anticultural, and as a result self-destructive. The system as a whole is rotten to the core, and its corruption is so widespread and deep that anyone who wants a modicum of change ends up crying, "Where do you start?" Moral virtues and high-mindedness cannot compete with such ingredients for success that naturally prevail in an advanced market society. Truth is not an acceptable collateral to borrow a dime at the bank. Truth has no market value. If this market system were pushed to its logical limit, which it threatens to do in its rational progression, there would hardly be philosophers, artists, humanists or sociologists left in America. Nor would there be any truth at all. All would be liars, if all are not already.

Many, especially on Wall Street, may not grieve over the passing of such useless fields into oblivion, for their world begins with production and ends with consumption. But America as a society and civilization would surely be one shade more barbaric without some of these useless academics and their truth. In a modest way, and at least in basic assumptions, these useless academics are the guardians of a liberal market-democracy going full steam toward whatever destination it is logically approaching. That these academics are not doing a good job as guardians, or are actively participating in the process of cultural decay, is a different issue, an issue we shall take up presently. But the idea is nevertheless persuasive.

Tenure is a thorn in the side of liberal market-democracy in America. The pain it causes may not be great; the discomfort it creates may be ignored; the reminder it represents may be easily forgotten. But viewed from the academic side, it is the only significant antidote currently available to the relentlessly self-destructive market mechanism. Not counting the brother professors in the market fields for the reasons we noted, it is on the fragile shoulders of philosophers, writers, artists, sociologists, humanists, and what have you—those useless and pitifully undemanded academics—that what little civilization existing in American society rests. American society does not obviously want all its sons and daughters to be marketeers. It does not obviously believe that every issue of value must be decided at the auction.

Nothing in the Constitution of the United States guarantees academic freedom.[4] The guarantee of freedom of speech is a general principle that applies to all citizens. The guarantee of academic freedom is a specific principle that applies only to the professoriate. (But *not* to all professors. As noted, it is applicable only to "academic professors" in "academic fields." Again, this point obviously requires stupendous argument. The argument will be supported, I hope, throughout the rest of this book. For the time being, we shall consider it a yet-unsupported proposition.) The ultimate justification for the tenure protection of useless academic fields is that such a system is already in place. It exists as a *specific agreement* between society and professoriate. But what is this specific agreement?

Academic freedom in many ways is a misnomer. It would be more appropriate to call it "academic contract." For it is a specific contractual obligation for the specific purpose of extracting the wholly honest, independent, and critical truth from the professor. In exchange, society has granted the professor a special privilege given to no other segment of its population. The professor, on his part, must oblige by pursuing the truth as honestly, independently, and critically as possible. (Tenure granted to federal judges has nothing to do with academic truth. It is for "legal truth," which has everything to do with existing laws and nothing with truth. Even the United States Supreme Court justices must go by the law. None could presume to feel that truth is in his or her own conscience. The arbitrariness resulting from such "truths" would make legal administration virtually impossible.)

The view that the professoriate is the repository of highest truth beneficial to society is entirely an historical, not absolute or logical, decision. And this historical decision, hence its contract, applies as long as both parties uphold their sides of the agreement: society will protect the professor, the professor will pursue the truth. Society has every right to withdraw from the contract when the professor fails to live up to his obligation. The privilege remains in effect as long as the professor performs his contractual obligation. The right to freedom of speech is innate and absolute. But there is no such thing as an innate, absolute right to academic freedom. Unless the professor continues to fulfill his obligation to the contract—that is, pursuing the truth beneficial to society—his right merely returns to the constitutional right to free speech, which is not special. (We should not be too bothered by "truth beneficial to society" as yet. We will take up the issue in subsequent chapters.)

It cannot be stressed too strongly how special a contract is this tenure-protected academic freedom. It is given to a specific group for a specific purpose: namely, professors for truth. Society has apparently decided that the (academic) professor is the best and perhaps only seeker of truth in society. In a liberal market society this is perhaps a reasonable assumption. Money makers and employees of money makers are hardly in a position to pursue the truth. But because of this very special purpose, it is equally reasonable to insist on granting tenure only to (1) those who would make *most* of the opportunity (namely, academic professors), and (2) those, even among academic professors, who would do their society most *good* with the truth.

To confer this special function upon a market professor (say, an accounting teacher) who would do neither is certain to waste the privilege. The market professor in accounting, while being an excellent accountant, has nothing to do with pursuing the truth. His business is in counting money according to the rules of money counting, rules with which he has nothing to do. Even an honest accountant is, after all, an employee of market society. He does what market society tells him to do. This is, of course, no reflection on the man's private virtue or lack of it. It is just not his function to pursue the truth. Accounting, like other market fields in academia, requires accuracy and factualness, not truth. (I would extend this principle, although for different reasons, to athletic coaches and librarians. Strictly speaking, they are not "academics" and their jobs have nothing to do with pursuing the truth.) This does not mean that academic fields (such as philosophy) are inherently superior to market fields. It merely means that academic fields, by virtue of their otherwise useless existence in society, are in a *position* to pursue the truth, whereas those in functional fields are not.

To confer this special privilege upon someone, even an academic professor, who is slothful with it is also certain to waste the privilege. In other words, it must be granted to those who are most active with their time and effort and more obligatory with their truth-seeking role. By "active" I do not mean the usual measure of productivity: how many journal articles, books, presentations at professional meetings, committee assignments, and so forth. For most of these routine comings and goings of academia have little or nothing to do with the truth and much with the untruth. With rare exceptions, people who pursue the truth honestly, independently, and critically do not necessarily produce much that is acceptable to the established organs of publication. I do mean one's dynamic consciousness in pursuit of the truth. Nor do I mean by "obligatory" one's conformity to orthodoxy. Rather, I mean one's awareness of the serious meaning entailed in the terms of tenure and academic freedom. By this account, it is the *active* member *in pursuit of the truth*, not necessarily a "productive" one (for one can be falsely and dishonestly productive), who would need tenure and academic freedom. Seasoned academics in their more candid moments would admit that such a member is likely to be denied tenure.

Academic freedom thus wasted, or tenure made irrelevant by nonuse, is always the best argument for abolishing tenure altogether. Nothing argues more strongly against tenure privilege than tenure wasted on those who do not use it in active pursuit of the truth. A man who occupies a large space wasted with unused furniture is in a most vulnerable position to insist on his special privilege to hold onto the space in a crowded quarters. Nothing grieves the academy more than seeing tenure and academic freedom denied to a member who would have made most of it. As it stands, the academic landscape is littered with wasted tenure and academic freedom, and the unemployment office is full of those who would certainly make better use of the privilege.

Professor Rolf Sartorius defines academic freedom as the freedom "to engage in research, teaching, publication, and other such pursuits without fear of reprisals for the expression of unpopular opinion."[5] This is a fairly standard definition of academic freedom widely used by various scholars who have written on the subject.

However, professors discussing the issue, like Sartorius, are so intent on insisting upon that freedom that few, if any, worry about what to do with the academic freedom we already have that is unused. Like all other human declarations, the definition given by Sartorius evokes only formal significance and hence only a perfunctory response. Such declarations are useful mostly when the cause is in its infancy. As rhetorical rallying points and as catchy slogans, they tend to be highly exaggerated with their intended purposes. The professors who declared academic freedom as imperative, in the concrete form of tenure guarantee in the formative years of the AAUP, would have considered their work actually done when tenure acquired the status of a legal contract. Once tenure guarantee is secured, no one thinks about academic freedom unless it is a threat to tenure itself. With or without tenure, the typical academic professor knows he will not trouble his cause by pursuing unpopular opinion. With this happy decision, truth falls by the wayside. In almost no case is a professor's truth ever liberated in any visible way by the granting of tenure and the acquisition of academic freedom.

The trouble is that professors get their tenure by *suppressing* the expression of unpopular opinion, not *in order to* express unpopular opinion. Obviously this is a self-defeating usage or nonusage of tenure privilege. It is granted only to be wasted. One of the cardinal rules of the probationary years is that one should keep one's mouth shut and keep one's mind in neutral. Tenure thereby acquired rarely opens the shut mouth or engages the neutral mind. Academic freedom, according to the definition given above, is granted to those whose activity in research, teaching, and writing would be *truthful* enough to benefit society. Since truth is likely to irritate many, while being actually beneficial to them, tenure and academic freedom guarantee that there will be no harm done to the professor. Through its contract, society has guaranteed the professor this principle. The professor, in his present commitment, has no other choice but to pursue unpopular activities under this protection.

The irony of the whole thing is not only that the tenured professor does virtually nothing with his academic freedom. He also makes sure that anyone who is likely to do something with it will not get tenure. It is the case of bad money driving out good money. Tenure is justified as a principle only if the professor pursues the truth in his honest, critical, and autonomous way *and* as a result courts popular wrath for his truth. At present, tenure is neither given to those professors who need it nor held by those who put it to good use. During the 1980s, almost no tenured academic professor has been threatened with dismissal for his truth-pursuing activity. Virtually every case that comes to the AAUP for investigation or makes rounds at university campuses nowadays involves a junior member whose academic freedom has been violated by senior faculty. Those senior members not only waste their own tenure and academic freedom, they mostly prevent juniors from gaining that privilege.

The modern university, by its conservative inertia, has become the most hostile place for those interested in pursuing the truth. And tenure, once deemed precious, has become the most wasted, irrelevant principle. Neither anchored in the consciousness of the academy nor protected by tenure and academic freedom, truth has been virtually forgotten and abandoned by American professors. They fight for tenure when they do not have it. They declare truth as inviolate if it serves their tenure-pursuit. They endorse academic freedom in order to justify tenure. But once they get tenure, neither academic freedom nor truth is remembered.

Where no academic freedom is exercised in pursuit of the truth, however, it is easy to conclude that no justification exists for tenure itself. This less-than-complimentary view of current academic fields is a judgment that demands some hard evidence. It therefore requires that we take a closer and pitiless look at their current state of existence.

NOTES

1. Richard Hofstadter and Walter P. Metzger, *The Development of Academic Freedom in the United States* (New York: Columbia University Press, 1965), 506.

2. Robert M. O'Neal, "Tenure under Attack," in *The Tenure Debate*, ed. Bardwell Smith (San Francisco: Jossey-Bass, 1973), 181.

3. See Smith, *Tenure Debate*, especially 214–22.

4. See the various arguments in Edmund L. Pincoffs, ed., *The Concept of Academic Freedom* (Austin, TX: University of Texas Press, 1972) 64–70, 77–81.

5. Rolf Sartorius, "Tenure and Academic Freedom," in Pineoffs, *Concept of Academic Freedom*, 135.

Chapter 4

Nowhere Near the Truth

There is a certain quaint charm traditionally associated with the uselessness of an academic scholar. A scholar is supposed to be useless in the practical run of daily life with which his ordinary fellow citizens occupy themselves. After all, he is a scholar, insulated from the practical world, devoted wholly to issues significant only to him. Because of this very uselessness he is respected, admired, and often held in awe. But this picture postcard image of the scholar today as a university faculty member is as outdated in present reality as yesteryear's lab equipment in a high-tech era.

With the rare exceptions of the few liberal arts campuses here and there, and the even rarer exceptions of the few "professors" one finds on such campuses, the typical scholar today is closer to a common hustler, albeit a small-time hustler. Like all real-life hustlers, his main job is to sell. But unlike real-life hustlers, he has nothing tangible to sell. Hence arise the odd desperation and neurosis that are commonly observed in academic fields and among their practitioners. In the agonizing process of trying to make something useless useful, four byproducts become obvious. They are corruption in purpose, apology for the status quo, sycophancy as an attitude, and mediocrity in performance. The last three will be examined in subsequent chapters. In this chapter we shall examine the first byproduct.

In their attempt to present themselves as useful and functional, the academic fields have turned inward to *themselves* as the very purpose of their scholarly existence. With varying degrees of success, they have become infatuated with their own fields, not with the object of their fields.

Sociologists are largely preoccupied with sociology, not with society. Philosophers talk about philosophical methods more than about philosophies. Political scientists think more about science than about politics. Psychologists are thrilled about this experimental result or that, not how it may illuminate the human mind. Their shoptalk is that of a more useful scientific field. "Methods," "theory," "model-building," "paradigm," "principle," "hypothesis-testing," "conceptualization," "operationalization," "operant conditioning," and the like excite the academics.

They have a great deal to say about their own fields, but little or nothing about their subject matter. Few sociologists venture to say anything about their society; few philosophers give their philosophies. They read "classics" in their respective fields, but learn little or nothing *from* them. The modern academics know a great deal about this "school," that "theory," or the other "trend," but they have virtually nothing to state as their own truth. When a sociologist thinks as a *scholar*, he is free, imaginative, and even relevant. When he thinks as a *sociologist*, he is a methodologist, a party-line disciplinarian, and a wholly irrelevant babbler of the incomprehensible. The sociologist no longer studies society; he studies sociology. He looks for what is fashionable in the field and burrows his head in it for a comfortable niche. The subject matter of society requires breadth and scope; the *field* of sociology forces narrow-minded ignorance. Only when one is freed *from one's own field* does one gain any intellectual perspective at all. This is true of practically all academic fields. By being so professionally tied to their fields or specialties, however, academic professors have become virtual slaves to their own orthodoxy. Their mind can no longer exercise the academic freedom it has craved for so long.

Next, let me indulge in a necessarily unsympathetic look at two fields, sociology and philosophy, as typical examples of this corruption. It is doubtful that even the most unsympathetic view, however, would dampen the blithe cheeriness with which academics go about their daily routines.

Of the different academic fields, the most insecure with its own status is, perhaps, sociology. It is blessed in its history neither with the usefulness of functional science nor with the historical heritage of cultural contribution in the humanities. Nor does its practitioner come into the field with any personally rich biographical experience to enliven his subject. Whatever is taught in the sociology curriculum as a whole amounts to very little in substance. Most sociologists are terribly ignorant of values in literature, the arts, history, philosophy, political and economic theory. What little smatterings of liberal arts they have had in their undergraduate education are woefully inadequate for the breadth and scope their subject requires. This lack of classic training tends to give most sociologists the relentlessly narrow and technical mindset that the public caricature of a "sociologist" brings readily to mind.

Hopelessly tied to the "scientific model" borrowed from natural science, sociologists insist that theirs is a "young" discipline, soon to grow to maturity. This notion of young science gives them the comfort and security to explain away their inadequacy. They forget that "social science" has existed as long as, or perhaps longer than, physical science. Hammurabi's Codes were written long before any treatise on heavenly bodies, and Plato's *Republic* long before Newton's physics. Neither "social science" has been surpassed by later, more "scientific," discoveries—to the improved happiness of mankind. To be sure, neither Hammurabi nor Plato held a Ph.D or a position in "social science." But that is just being technical. Social science viewed this way, far from being young, is the oldest of all sciences. The main tools of social science—namely, words and ideas—have existed as long as society has existed. The claim of youthfulness is thus not only historically false, but, even when true, is still no excuse for its current state of deficiency. In the meantime, the sociologist (like other social scientists) sticks his head in the sand doing his specialized task like a real scientist.

But sociology, unlike other academic fields, is not a specialized discipline. It is broadly about *society*, which is neither scientific nor specialized. By specializing in a narrowly defined "scientific" subject area, however, the sociologist positions himself as a scholar with least competence to handle his subject matter. (Specialization protects ignorance in all academic fields.) This young, technically alert but intellectually incompetent sociologist does not grow into a mature scholar over time; he, and now increasingly she, merely becomes more technically elaborate in method, more narrow-minded in outlook, and certainly more conservative in scholarly ideas and actions. Time and repetition simply do not fill his or her intellectual and cultural void.

In order to write anything interesting, one must have read something interesting first. Good scholars always read a lot. One's usually limited experience is broadened through the experiences (real or fictional) of others. Literature enriches, historical writings inform, and philosophical analyses sharpen one's own life perspective. Sociologists, not unlike other academic professors, are almost primitive in this regard. Their "emotional vocabulary," the range of ability to "feel," is near zero. And it shows. Although their subject is society, little in their writing would suggest that sociologists know anything about it or have something interesting to say about the subject. They may know some facts about a particular aspect of society. But such facts hardly seem to relate to the real society in which we all live and about which we all have some notions. They are society-experts, yet their writings invariably demonstrate that they know little or nothing about society. Nor would sociologists themselves feel in moments of honest reflection that their own intellectual expectations raised in an earlier, more optimistic era have been fulfilled. They strive for a methodology that can be shared by all enterprisers with predictably forgettable results. What they produce is neither science nor art. Straddling uselessness as an intellectual discipline and usefulness with its technical aspiration, sociology finds itself in an awkward position on campus. It is in this sense that sociologists perhaps more than any others feel the crunch of external fear and internal self-doubt.

A good sociologist—or anyone who studies society and people—is at once a competent historian of society and an insightful observer of people in their intimate daily lives. The best sociology is thus exemplified in Arthur Miller's *The Death of a Salesman*, as much as in C. Wright Mills's *White Collar* or in David Riesman's *The Lonely Crowd*. By and large, what we get from academic sociologists (generally called "research results") is elaborately detailed without the feel of intimate life, which claims scientific objectivity without the historically enlightening grasp of society as a whole. It is neither personally insightful nor morally uplifting. They claim their work is about society and people, yet none of the drama of life and the sweep of society is ever present in their typical research. Those who are not sociologists learn next to nothing about themselves or their society from the labors of society-experts. What is produced in their "science" is generally pitiful as analysis, and what is carried out as their "research" is almost laughable to most sane people.

Born of the classic tradition of the humanities, however, it is not easy for sociology to be accepted into the more affluent scientific community in spite of its aspiration. Its genesis may be in the humanities, but its current hopes are in the functional sciences. Having been vaguely positioned between science and art, the notion of scholarship in something called "sociology" (a peculiarly American phenomenon) has always been suspect. In its effort to make itself useful and respectable, however, it has increasingly adopted the functional rather than academic model for self-image and for its methods of daily operation. Substantial scholarship, fairly abundant in its earlier development, has now been replaced by "functional" research. Sociologists must appear "scientific," talk "research," and work with the "computer." Because of its ambivalence in status, sociology is perhaps the most appearance-conscious of all academic disciplines. Hence many sociologists are fascinated more by the fact of research than by its result. It is certainly easier to collect data than to justify how it is supposed to contribute to knowledge. Its excessive fear of moralist passion has deprived sociology of its vitality and relevance. In consequence, it is driven to find its purpose in "scientific research" and its justification in painless orthodoxy.

All research costs money. Large or small, grants provide money. Skills in identifying and attracting grants become necessary and important. Special research projects are designed to become more favorably viewed by grants-givers. Hence a whole subculture emerges just to center on grants. "Grantsmanship," as this subculture is called, has become an indispensable ingredient of academic sociology. Ability to receive grants is valued often as highly as traditional scholarship itself. A sociologist's reputation often precedes him simply because he has attracted large grants from governments and foundations. The larger the amount of money involved, the larger his reputation as a serious sociologist. Vacancy announcements routinely include the desirability of grantsmanship among the scholarly qualifications. But getting grants is largely a salesman's job that is thrust upon the sociologist. Like any good salesman, the sociologist-salesman cannot possibly be any further removed from pursuit of the truth. He is so intent on his sales record that he naturally thinks like a salesman and acts like a hustler. The campus, on its part, richly rewards the salesman-hustler-sociologist as it routinely does in other fields. Once grants, where necessary at all, were used to produce scholarship. Now scholarship is used to produce grants.

All this points to an increasing standardization of the discipline. Not unlike other academic fields that increased in size during the preceding decades, sociology must be "democratized." Democratization allows a process in which scholarly excellence is made sufficiently routine to cushion the solitary effects of individual responsibility to scholarship. Democratic standardization reduces individual anxiety and encourages collective irresponsibility. More and more, sociologists find safety in numbers. According to an exhaustive survey of sociological scholarship, professors Steve McNamee and Cecil Willis found that not only has the frequency of multiple authorship increased over the last two decades or so, but the number of authors on each article has also increased steadily over the same period.[1] In typical democratic thinking, two heads are considered better than one; three better than two; four better than three, and so on. Significantly, McNamee and Willis's findings also indicate that there has been a gradual shift, however imperceptible, from theoretical papers to more quantitative researches among the multiple-authored. This trend allows an assembly-line notion of the work process in which many persons carry out their assigned parts. The result is that everyone is satisfied and no one held responsible.

Standardization naturally has a strangling effect on originality. All individual truth is by definition original as long as it is pursued and concluded individually. But standardized production lines, however subconsciously, tend to stifle and discourage creative thinking. Only "established" lines of research will be accepted by "established journals;" only those who respect orthodoxy will be admitted to the ranks of tenured seniors. Yet, originality survives as a tribute recognized largely as lip service. To do so, the meaning of originality is taken out of the context so that anything can be "original" if it has "not been done before." If it has been done before, then it is a "replication." In this way both ends are covered. Ingenuity passes for originality; size replaces profundity; safety in numbers nullifies individual truth and responsibility. Everyone in sociology either is creative or replicates with his research. Few recognize that "originality" must mean a new interpretation of the *orthodox*, a new way of looking at what is thought settled—not trying something bizarre or odd that no one has tried before. But this new definition of democratic originality makes everyone happy.

However, celebration is premature. This democratized, party-line, mass production of scholarship has its drawback. The scholarship thus produced predictably lacks individual imagination, passionate truth, and simple human interest. Hence it is boring and pedantic to read, uninspiring as ideas, and singularly monotonous as an exercise of mind. No honest and independent scholar, much less the public, can possibly pay serious attention to what is produced in sociology. The sociologist claims to be knowledgeable about society and humanity as his subject matter, yet little or nothing he ever writes is about them. It is more about how a sociologist does his research (or how other sociologists do *their* research) than about society or humanity.

Specialization is a favorite technique for elaborate irrelevance. Once specialized, the rest of the whole—community, society, humanity—ceases to exist for the specialist. Specialties primarily serve the limited and practical purposes of hustling specialists. They do research, publish results, organize meetings, circulate newsletters, and so on entirely for themselves and no one else. Each specialty is so isolated from reality that it is difficult to say exactly what results from these specialties add to new knowledge. It is an elaborate game that only insiders can play, and not surprisingly, the specialty-players often resemble participants in a secret brotherhood rather than a community of public scholars.

A small group of sociologists label themselves "theorists" and use concepts as their primary tool. The word "theory" does lend them a measure of authority and dignity. But results are equally empty of significance. Some confuse theory with hypothesis (as in "a high correlation coefficient between variable X and variable Y"). Others confuse theory with truisms (as in "human behavior tends toward maximum reward"). But none relate it to the search for truth. The first type trivializes theory; the second type wastes it in redundancy. The emptiness of their theory is increasingly made up in phony elaboration of "conceptualization," "operationalization," and "empirical valida-tion." In this emptiness of meaning, their enterprises accord well with the prevailing ethos of routine research. Theory inspires research; research acknowledges its debt to theory. Honor is thus upheld among thieves. In this, few realize that theory is nothing but one's own truth about community, society, and humanity well-stated. As usual, scholars overcomplicate their tasks to death.

Where substance is absent the solution is obviously found in packag-ing. Everyone is engaged in furious competition for name-recognition. Publishing in "established" journals and under more widely publicized big-name publishing houses, dropping names of more recognizable professionals in the field, attending professional meetings to keep one's name in circulation, and so on are well-respected methods. The standing of a sociologist (perhaps more than in other related fields simply because sociologists love to study sociology) is normally determined by how many times his name appears in the works of other sociologists. An elaborate, computerized numbering system keeps track of this contest. Many big names have become big names primarily through improved packaging.

Given this reality, being neither a functionally useful practitioner nor a respectable dealer of ideas, sociologists as a whole constitute a pathetic lot. They are found scurrying here and there for small favors and recognition in the community of scholars. They sometimes appear as a marginal appendage, as second-rate technicians, to the more prestigious scientific institutions and agencies. A few successful salesman-hustler sociologists are elevated to the rank of professional Horatio Algers. They can be no other. Sociologists as a whole are often criticized for being extremely dull by educational socialization, undistinguished in intellec-tual endowment, and uninspiring as a cultural force. And the criticism cannot be more deserved.

This state of sociology may be understood more accurately in a comment made by one of its official apologists, Herbert Gans, president of the American Sociological Association in 1988: "Too many people still dislike sociology or, worse still, are not interested in it. To be sure, often they react to caricatures of sociology, but the very fact that they are not motivated to go beyond caricatures is itself depressing. In effect, we play a smaller part in the country's intellectual life than we should."[2] Gans urges his fellow sociologists to make greater efforts to speak to the lay public.

In spite of its occasional highlights and bylines in the mass media, and perhaps because of them, sociology in the public eye rarely amounts to more than mere street-curiosity or the image of a second-rate intellect. Whatever sociologists may attempt to achieve by playing with the computer, statistical models, or scientific jargon copied from the functional sciences, theirs is no more than adolescent fascination with modern gadgetry and neurotic self-absorption with themselves. They are greatly assured of peace of mind, knowing that whatever they do or say would make no important difference in the ongoing affairs of society. This nonexpectation frees them from any public responsibility with the consequences of their work. Hence, their work by and large begins and ends meaninglessly. They fail to tackle their work seriously and ambitiously. Hence, the department of sociology is almost always the first casualty in financial crunches. It has been eliminated in many schools (e.g. at Saint Louis University, Washington University, and the University of Rochester) or threatened with elimination (e.g at the New School for Social Research and Duke University).

Such public indifference and neglect—if not contempt—for sociology is largely self-wrought, and its present predicament or possible demise, in spite of its flashes of brilliance, is to be blamed only on itself. On a larger scale of things, sociology also represents by its own failure the sad predicament of the American intelligentsia.

As sociology has made research into a game of sorts, philosophy has developed its own equivalent of a game to play. It is called "argument." It is an elaborate game for gentlemen, to be sure, but no truth is likely to emerge from it. As research is fun in itself for sociology, argument is an endlessly fascinating game of words, wits, and strategies for philosophy. Most happily for participants in the game, argument on any subject is unfailingly without consequence. Philosophers (with the rare exception of Marxists) assiduously avoid as their subjects of argument anything that is relevant or potent for action. Thus, the problems of philosophy are fairly similar to those of research in sociology and other social sciences. They have largely succeeded in elevating emptiness and irrelevance to an art form. But aided by its own ingenuity, philosophy wastes and endangers the special meaning of academic freedom and truth.

Many people still associate philosophy with the august circle of human wisdom and justice, personified by Socrates, firmly established in their mind. The discovery of truth through dialectical discourse, a critical method of arriving at a wise and just conclusion, has been transformed into the "methodology" of philosophy. This methodology, represented in argument in a fashion familiar to social science's "research," in time has become the very purpose of philosophy as well. Philosophers largely occupy their time nowadays arguing with each other for the sake of argument, sophistry in its most extreme form. They live to argue as social scientists live to do research. Their own peace of mind, like that of sociologists, is guaranteed by the fact that the result is totally devoid of consequence.

Philosophers' argument assumes by necessity an environment, both political and logical, in which Supreme Order reigns. No inconsequential argument is possible unless this social environment is presumed to exist. The order is inviolate. Hence, no argument is normally presented to question that supremacy. All argument begins and ends with that reality. A slave in chains cannot, of course, assume this to be true. And in all likelihood he would not present any argument to his master about the injustice of slavery, any more than the philosopher would about the Supreme Order. The parties in an argument, like the players in a game, must believe that Supreme Order (or the umpire, the referee) is objective, impartial in its judgment of merits and demerits. In reality this Supreme Order is ultimately (but not always in open admission) in the form and substance of the United States Supreme Court, for that is where all arguments are eventually resolved.

If the environment is such that participants believe it to be rigged in favor of a predetermined party or class or agent, as in the case of the slave, no argument can indeed be possible to conceive and enact as a gentlemen's game of words, wits, and strategies. Robinson Crusoe might have used such advantages of a civilized mind in subjugating Friday, but his musket was also handy just in case that Supreme Order had to be invoked. But even a rudimentary inspection would show that *no* social or political or even logical environment is impartial or objective. For every social order is of a particular kind and is established and maintained with a musket at the ready.

Today, the model of environment for argument is that of the Enlightenment. More specifically, it is contemporary American society with all its political and economic assumptions. (For sociology, it is Talcott Parsons's conception of society.) In it basic substance does not change much, but elaborate procedural argument is allowed to take place in the margin. While empty of substance, it safeguards the appearance of intellectual freedom for philosophical argument. It is precisely John Rawls's kind of society (favorite of many philosophers and social scientists) in which "justice" can be argued and is believed able to be implemented by the sheer merit of its argument. But this Enlightenment model (with its attendant "market society") is only assumed, not explicitly stated by the participating philosophers. This assumption may be admitted, if at all, only after relentless prodding. It is a tall assumption indeed. It assumes that the Enlightenment model is so impartial and objective that only the best argument can affect the economic distribution of wealth, political power shifts, war and peace decisions, and other inconvenient issues. That the environment might favor arguments that favor the model itself does not seem to bother philosophers at all. Nothing facilitates one's peace of mind better than assuming the very best. However, to assume the very best is to assume the very best in the status quo. When a parent gives the appearance of an objective, impartial hearing to his child's argument, he still retains his undisputed authority. The authority will not allow the merit of the child's argument to interfere with itself, any more than would the master concerning his slaves. Simply, there is no such thing as an impartial, objective authority, institution, or society. But this small truth greatly inconveniences the gentlemen's game, and so it normally remains forgotten.

The appearance of ferociousness in philosophical argument is not to be confused with the seriousness of the issue. If it is to be argued, it cannot possibly be urgent or critical. After all, it is a gentlemen's game. Passion must be reined in tightly, any appearance of interest in truth avoided, and the inconsequentiality of the issue duly respected. No urgent or critical matters—such as wealth, power, war, and peace—are ever settled by argument. Nor is an argument on such issues even allowed unless it is pro forma. Peace is normally attained after the bullet has been spent. No wealth ever changes hands at the ballot box. No real power is ever given up on argument. No revolution has ever been held illegitimate in history. Indeed, the beauty of all philosophical argument is that participants need not come to a definite conclusion (truth) or to the inevitability of direct action (consequence).

Affirmative action is a good case in point. It is inconceivable that blacks, women, or other minorities can actually replace the white majority or take over a significant part of the status quo in society by the sheer merit of their argument. (Who will argue for them?, would be the first problem.) For neither slavery nor its counterpart, affirmative action, ever materialized as a result of argument. The argument came *after* slavery was already in place as an institution, and affirmative action came only when the forces, not argument, pushing it became irresistible as a historical process. That Congress debated the affirmative action issue is irrelevant. It was essentially an argument between two contending historical forces, neither gentlemanly nor inconsequential. No slave owner ever gave up his slaves or male chauvinist his privilege because he was compelled by a gentleman's "argument." Both gave up and are giving up their privilege simply because they *must*. It is a political, historical process neither can resist. Under the inconveniences of reality, argument, however eloquent, simply becomes irrelevant.

The way philosophers argue an issue follows the more established format of functional science. In it, by necessity all historical, political, and moral conflict is reduced to logically neat, semantically simplified, and practically manageable propositions (equivalent to "hypotheses"). Examples normally given in argument are either toally abstract and hypothetical in the sense that they could apply under any circumstances; or, if taken from actual historical facts like slavery and affirmative action, are so reduced to what-if propositional terms that their historical concreteness becomes lost or is made irrelevant. Affirmative action, then, is argued as a neutral principle of "compensation": how much compensation Party A deserves as a result of the action of Party B, which is no longer identical with Party C, and so on. Only the most reductionist mind could possibly conceive of slavery's cost in terms of compensation. Only the most naive person would assume that the outcome of affirmative action can be determined by argument.

Using compensation as a neutral measure of value and as a rule of argument assumes that all parties involved are essentially "rational" and all human deliberation is rationally conceived. For irrationality cannot be arguable. The notion of rationality in the Enlightenment model, or John Rawls's "self-interested" man, is almost wholly based on the model of "economic man." This is precisely the model of man used in the marketplace. Human decisions can be rationally made in an economic society with a free, open setting for argument. In it, self-interest is always rationally calculated to reflect one's economic advantage. This rational model, while neat and comfortable for philosophers, makes it impossible to make use of history, culture, and politics, the three most "irrational" repositories of human deliberations and actions. The problem is not that philosophers argue too much. Rather, it is that they do not *believe* in what they are arguing with any passion at all.

Such irrational forces obviously cannot be reduced to argument, for no two historical, cultural, and political phenomena are alike. One can

try for an intelligent comprehension of the forces. But reducing them to
logical propositions or hypotheses subject to argument would be so
simple yet so risky that only the wisest or the most foolish would attempt
it. The Enlightenment model of man and society as rational and self-interested, although immediately contradicted by tenure and academic
freedom, applies only in the West. All the philosophical merits and
demerits in argument based on this model would become instantly wrong
and irrelevant if applied in the Amish community or in Saudi Arabia. In
order for any argument to be possible, the issue must be reduced to
certain logical forms that contain equal alternatives with equally "arguable" properties in each alternative. This is all very good for philosophy.
But it is this very reduction that makes the very argument irrelevant. In
other words, what makes philosophy possible as a field of employment
is also what makes it irrelevant as an academic field in pursuit of the
truth.

Lest we be too easily convinced, let us drive one more wedge of
dilemma into philosophical argument: the dilemma between tautology
and value. All arguments result in tautology unless value intervenes
somewhere along the line of argument. But value does not derive from
logic. It derives from experience. Arguing that one kind of experience
(say, capitalist) is superior to another kind of experience (say, socialist)
has nothing to do with the merits or demerits of the experience itself.
Nor does the apparent superiority of one experience upheld by some (say,
apology for capitalism) have anything to do with its logical superiority
over the other (say, Amish socialism).

One common logic textbook by a philosopher gives the following
example of prototype argument: "If either cancer is caused by smoking
or cancer is caused by air pollution and cancer is not caused by air
pollution, then cancer is caused by smoking."[3] Of course, this is a
tautology in its most elementary form. If cancer is caused either by X or
by Y, then it is obviously caused by one of the two. If such were the case
in all arguments, there would be hardly anything to disagree. But neither
slavery nor affirmative action is such a tautological proposition. Nor can
it be reduced to one without making it wholly irrelevant as an issue of
truth about human value. Neither can be argued out "philosophically"
unless it is reduced to a tautological form or something fairly close to it.
Once so transformed, it becomes a meaningless game of words, wits,
and strategies. If not, the philosopher has to find a way to slip his own
value-experience into the tautological formula without being detected.

Assuming that philosophers are not devoid of value-experience, I
would venture to guess that this latter skill is what constitutes 99 percent

of an argument. The dispassionate philosopher after all may be a passionate human being fearful of openly confronting the truth about his own value-experience. How can he argue for or against affirmative action without seemingly favoring one position or the other? This is the dilemma of philosophical argument, and all arguing philosophers are fatally vulnerable to it. If it is worth arguing about, it is worth being committed to as one's truth. If it can be argued without such commitment, it must be a gentlemen's game without consequence. Anyone can predict what position a philosopher would take in an argument by asking him about his family's socioeconomic standing, his religion, what schools he attended, what kind of higher education he received, who his personal heroes are, how he voted in the last election, and a few other facts. Unless, of course, the issue is so irrelevant as to be a simple game of words, wits, and strategies.

There is much comfort in continuing philosophical argument, as much as there is comfort in social science research. It has the appearance of considerable creative ingenuity, of scholarly substance, and of orderly social progress through discourse. All one has to do now is reduce to neat arguable propositions the issues of happiness and misery, Central America, nuclear armament, teenage pregnancy, drugs, what to do about MTV, wealth and greed in market society, poverty amid affluence, and the decline and fall of Western civilization. To do so, the social scientist will invariably ask for more research and the philosopher for more argument. They are not too different from the university professors at the Grand Academy of Lagado that Gulliver encountered during one of his travels. Our academic freedom and truth in the meantime will have to do their best to survive without them.

Relevance or its absence is the best measure of game-like quality. In that sense Psychology is also a perfect game. Behaviorists and cognitive psychologists alike indulge in endless experiments and theories that are of no serious interest to anyone but themselves. Clinical psychologists play their game with each individual problem as it comes along. But each problem is different, since generalization of all Dear-Abby's is logically impossible, and each problem is a nice game to play. Their experiments are too general to be of any specific use, applicable to specific problems. Their clinical individual problem-solving is too specific to be of any general use, applicable to generalization. And these two aspects of psychological enterprise rarely cross each other. Psychology thus conceived primarily serves itself. Of course, this self-serving tendency could be said of any other academic field in today's university. Peace of mind that comes from larger irrelevance is paramount in all of them. In the meantime they all look for the next subject for research or problem-solving.

The typical university is a busy place today. Much goes on, or so it appears, with academic professors. They are busily engaged in this or that research, this or that lecture, this or that book-writing. But the appearance is highly deceiving. They work hard, to be sure, yet their hard work is without passion. They are productive by academic standards, yet their productivity is without significance. They occupy a position of intellectual prominence in society, yet their prominence is without any real influence.

However, a myth persists that sociologists study society as a whole, that psychologists understand the human mind, that philosophers possess philosophies of their own, that historians comprehend the sweep of history, or that writers agonize over the great American novel. Nothing can be more false than this myth. They as a whole know very little about their own field, much less the field of the entire human condition. They have little or nothing to say about society as a whole, about the human mind in general, about their own philosophical belief and commitment, about their own historical vision, or about their conception of their own great American novel. Almost without exception, they specialize in a totally obscure and therefore "safe" fragment of their subject matter and blithely announce their authority and knowledge in that specialty. Their formal educations have failed to teach them to think within the grand tradition of Western thought and beyond. Their personal experience as human beings has failed to produce any lasting (and tragic) impressions in them about the human condition that surrounds them. In a way, a Mother Teresa can speak about humanity more profoundly and with greater simplicity than can all those pretentious professors combined.

Not surprisingly, academics remain by and large shallow-minded people. On the whole, their average learning is not very impressive. Nor do they make up their learning deficiencies with the improvement in practice. With rare exceptions on any campus, they neither *think* very deeply about the human condition nor *feel* the moral passion that reflects their personal experience. Deep thinking and moral passion—the two cardinal forces that drive a scholar and define his scholarship—are largely absent in their work and lives. Ever since Socrates, it has been obvious that "good" truth is produced by "good" human beings. However, in virtually any academic department, those who can be morally and intellectually counted on make up only a fraction of the tenured seniors. As usual, the current academic mode of operation encourages adaptive relativism and mercenary cleverness among academics, and it severely restricts the number of good human beings in academia by denying them tenure.

Intellectually and morally, the seniors are drifters and schemers without principle. Sometimes they act "liberal" if it suits them; at other times they act "conservative" if their own self-interest is at issue. Lacking any conviction as individuals and scholars, they drift and scheme according to the purpose of the moment. In the meantime, their shallow thinking and feeling is ferociously shielded by their disproportionately abundant arrogance in claiming importance and in demanding perks. In all this, their model of life is closer to that of habitual liars and mercenaries than to that of saints, martyrs, revolutionaries, or artists, with whom they share the basic framework and origin of selfless service.

NOTES

1. Steve McNamee and Cecil Willis, "Taylorism in the Periphery: The Decentralization of Research Productivity in Sociology" (Paper presented at the 1986 Southern Sociological Meetings, New Orleans, LA, 9–12 April, 1986.) I must report, however, that our interpretations of the data, which are still being updated, are slightly at variance, although not mutually exclusive.

2. Herbert Gans, "Sociology in America: The Discipline and the Public" *American Sociological Review* 54 (February), 1. Yet, more graphically contradictory to his concern than anything else, the articles that follow his comment in the same journal illustrate the totally "scientific" approach to social analysis even the educated public finds so irrelevant and ridiculous, especially on a subject about which they all feel they have some personal knowledge. In diametric opposition to the spirit of Gans's comment, the last article in the same issue (Randall Collins, "Problems of the Discipline," 124–39) basically confirms the essentially "valid" scientific status of sociology.

3. Robert G. Olson, *Meaning and Argument: Elements of Logic* (New York: Harcourt, Brace & World, 1969), 171.

Part II

Truth and Academic Freedom

Chapter 5

Of Truth and Facts

Professors as a whole are rather ambivalent toward truth. More often than not, the term scares them to death. They admit that tenure and academic freedom exist in exchange for the ideal of "pursuit of the truth." Yet, confronted with the ideal as a real task, they tend to fall back on either false modesty that they would not presume to know what truth is, or simple relativism that everyone is doing his thing in pursuit of it. Of course, neither position serves us well at all. If academic professors expect tenure security and insist on academic freedom as preconditions for scholarship, then their scholarship must be predicated on what they claim to be its purpose: pursuit of the truth.

If they cannot adequately define it, they had better come up with a definition pretty quickly or give up tenure and academic freedom as irrelevant and truth as impossible. Nature abhors a vacuum and fills it with its own wonders; society exploits a vacuum and fills it with its own evil design. If professors are *not* pursuing the truth for one reason or another, they must surely be pursuing the *untruth*. For no society voluntarily fills itself with truth. A professor with no clear idea about what he is doing and why is only doing the devil's work.

Neither false modesty nor relativism, while convenient for the professor, will serve truth at all. The first position confuses scholarship with The Truth (the final mythic resting place where all human conflicts and differences converge into a perfect, unified whole—both Platonic and utopian) and the second position is simply a defense of irrelevance. No professor is ever expected to accomplish the daunting task of discovering The Truth. It is a misconception of presumption. Nor does the everyone-doing-his-thing model ever result in serious scholarship. It is a misconception of purpose. Both misconceptions are the product of a false self-image among academic professors. They think too much of themselves and their perks, yet too little of their tasks. They are never asked to save the world by finding The Truth. Yet many feel they are. Some escape it with a Truth-is-impossible clause, others with an everyone-on-his-own clause. They forget the simple rule of life that, as in all things, we must define the task within the limits of our best ability and get on with it.

Most professors simply diffuse the issue by asking almost rhetorically, "What is the truth?" Of course, no answer is forthcoming. No one has been able, although many have claimed, to propose a definition satisfactory to all. That fact serves their original rationale: the task must be considered impossible and the question itself irrelevant. So why bother with it? But as a matter of practical concern, virtually every university statement of policy on tenure, promotion, and academic freedom mentions "truth" as the ultimate condition for such privileges.[1] *That* aspect of job description no professor protests as too impossible or too irrelevant. No tenure has ever been returned and no academic freedom ever refused by a professor because his task in exchange is impossible to achieve or too irrelevant to consider.

Surely, no reasonable professor will claim that he knows the truth. There is no contradiction in agreeing with this denial as a recognition of reality. But not knowing the truth in its *final form*, which is what this denial normally implies, is no handicap for our task. For our task has never been the discovery of the truth in its final form. We have to define what truth is in the way it makes sense in our practical reality; then clarify to ourselves and others how we should go about pursuing it; and finally, convince ourselves and—more important—the larger society, that it is necessary and beneficial to community, society, and humanity. The first two will be discussed in the present and following chapters. The third, obviously a more difficult task than the first two, will occupy much of Part III of this book. Through it all, an honest scholar will have no trouble in dealing with truth.

We may not know what truth *is*, but we may know what it is *not*. Truth certainly is not *fact*. The contrast between truth and fact will be the first step toward our definition of truth. As mentioned in an earlier chapter, definitions, classifications, contrasts, comparisons, and so on, are imperative intellectual devices and we ought to use them as they become useful to our purpose. Our purpose is defining truth (not *The* Truth, I must repeat), and we shall make use of facts as its counterpart in the task.

In the latter part of the twentieth century a man named Buzz Aldrin returned to Earth a conquering hero, having been the second man ever to set foot on the moon. He was a man of science's dream. With a graduate degree in physics, he was perfect in every possible way. His mastery of space science was complete; he was a physical specimen molded to perfection. As he related later, he had often thought of himself as a real-life superman. He had been born and bred in scientific knowledge, and no one was considered better in the mastery of scientific facts. Upon returning to Earth following his space exploit, however, he crashed. During the next ten years or so he became a regular customer of drug and alcohol rehabilitation centers all over the country. Eventually becoming a celebrity spokesman for Alcoholics Anonymous, he confessed the awful truth about himself. What he knew in scientific facts, which was enormous, he said, was "kindergarten stuff" compared to life on Earth. Scientific mastery, which he had embodied to perfection, had nothing to do with life on earth. In the truth of life, he was but an ignorant child.

Some twenty-five hundred years before our times, there lived a man in Athens who was virtually an ignoramus in scientific facts, at least by our modern standard. He was only faintly aware of and interested in the development in medicine, astronomy, mathematics and other scientific fields then fashionable in his time. He paid practically no attention to matters scientific. The fact of sun rising in the east and setting in the west, or that gravity pulled things down, held no meaning to the man. He was about as ignorant of scientific facts as any man in his time. However, this did not deter him in his pursuit of the truth. In spite of his ignorance and disinterest in science, he knew all the truth about life. He was declared the wisest man in Athens by the oracles of Delphi. The greatest philosopher of all time, Plato, called him "the wisest, and justest and best."[2] His name, of course, was Socrates.

In an age of scientific facts, no man could personify the virtues of science better than Buzz Aldrin. In the service of truth, no man could demonstrate greater facility than Socrates. Yet Aldrin was but a child in truth, as was Socrates in facts. Their ignorance in one, however, did not deter them in mastering the other. They operated to almost perfection (as a great astronaut and as a great philosopher) in one area without having the slightest notion of the other. No examples can perhaps better illustrate the distinction between truth and facts than these two men and their respective tasks.

The discomfort we may instinctively feel in separating truth and facts will have to be overcome in consideration of the service such a distinction performs for us. The general axiom in academia tends to favor the idea that truth and facts are one and the same. Truth is based on facts; facts, accumulated and tested, become truth. Contrary to this campus axiom almost unanimously upheld, however, as the Aldrin-Socrates illustration demonstrates, they are two totally separate categories. Yet our campus orthodoxy and conservative inertia insist that they are inseparable.[3] In fact, our present complacency regarding truth is served well by this comfortable assumption. Since we regard truth as unattainable or impractical, we can always produce facts in its place or insist that truth is naturally entailed in facts.

Nothing is more vehemently resisted than an idea that will force a change in one's attitude. That truth and facts are mutually exclusive categories is a moderately unconventional idea for academics, and it will be questioned and resisted. But we will go on with the idea in consideration of its greater serviceability. As with all other comforting ideas, truth-as-facts does not serve us at all; we cannot go forward with it.

Facts are well known, and their well-knownness is always equal to the total amount of human knowledge at any given time. Truth is always *yet to be known*. Unlike facts, all known truth could be false. Facts also have consequences, but they are *entailed* in them. Facts about nuclear war are well known, as much as science allows us to know. Facts about it are a matter of scientific knowledge. What is *unknown* about a possible nuclear holocaust is the truth about human decisions. That both the Soviets and Americans have nuclear arsenals of enormous destruction is a well known fact. The truth about their intentions is utterly unknown. What makes World War III so pivotal is not the awesome destructive power of nuclear weapons; we are well aware of that part. It is the awesomeness of human decision, about which we are as infantile as anyone. Facts about nuclear destruction are commonly known and available. Truth about ourselves is virtually unknown. World War III, if it occurs, will not happen because of the nuclear arsenal. It will happen by human follies or by lack of knowledge about ourselves. Facts build nuclear weapons. Truth tells what we will do with them. The former is well known; the latter is virtually unknown. How the well-known facts about the nuclear arsenal may lead to the discovery of truth about ourselves is the most daunting, and I would say impossible, task that academic orthodoxy must face.

Truth has consequences that are *created* by it. Facts have consequences entailed *within* themselves. Truth's consequences can exist only when the truth is spoken. They exist as a *result* of the truth being created. Facts cannot create consequences that cannot be foreseen within the facts themselves. When a group of scientists contemplate building a new weapon, surely the consequences entailed in it are what have prompted their effort. That it might have other unanticipated side effects only shows the inadequacy of their knowledge. That its consequences may be morally questionable is none of their business to worry about. Scientists deal with facts, both known and entailed. Only truth creates consequences never foretold or expected. Truth itself exists because it is created. Its absence, in consequence, is never missed. Yet-unknown scientific facts are always missed. The worth of truth is measured by the magnitude of its un-anticipated consequences in human behavior. The worth of facts is measured by how well the consequences conform to their expected performance.

The consequences of truth are always observed in the knower's behavior. By knowing certain truth, the knower's behavior changes. Large truth alters behavior in a large way, as in revolutions. Small truth does it in a small way. Large or small, truth affects human behavior once it is known. We do not learn *about* truth; we learn *from* it. There is no such thing as truth known that does not alter the knower's behavior subsequent to it. Truth *is* change in human beahvior. It does so by first altering the attitude. Facts never do such a thing. Facts do not alter human attitudes or behaviors that are not already entailed in them. Only an insane person would drink poisonous water to quench his thirst, even knowing that it would cause his death. (On the other hand, those who do not wish to leave the Soviet Union even when openly invited to America are not necessarily insane.) A course in philosophy may alter one's view on life and death forever. A course in biology may enlarge one's knowledge about the cell; but that in itself will hardly affect his view on life and death. Truth alters one's ideas. Facts enlarge one's knowledge about things.

Truth is always *personal* knowledge. It begins as personal knowledge; it is transmitted as personal knowedge; it is accepted or rejected as personal knowledge. It is a matter of personal belief. Hence the crucial role of the knower in it. Facts are always *public* knowledge. That it begins as personal knowledge, as in the discovery of gravity, is purely accidental. All natural science knowledge is public, for it conforms to everyone's experience that can be instantly verified or accepted. A hermit will know nothing about "idealism," "capitalism," or "socialism" if he does not hear about it personally. But the hermit, on his own, will share a large body of facts, such as gravity, seasons, growth, and decay, with other persons whom he has never met or with whom he shared such facts. No one will accept an "ism" unless he personally believes it or someone whose opinion he blindly accepts. One will easily accept scientific facts as long as they are undisputed *as* facts. Only the pathological will insist on his own personal facts even when proven contrary to public facts. Methodists, homosexuals, Communists, men, women, rich or poor, or any other socioeconomic categories can cooperate as scientists in pursuit of facts in perfect harmony. But the same group would find it impossible to converge on a single truth.

Truth, if rejected, is found to be false. Facts, if rejected, are found to be incorrect. False truth is personally, vehemently, unforgivingly opposed, and the opponents will see no salvation in considering false truth any further. Incorrect facts merely wait to be corrected with more correct knowedge about the matter. There is nothing personal about a wrong measurement or count, for either way there is no *personal* belief at stake. (That there may be pathological scientists who take their tasks personally is a separate issue.) To a believer of capitalism, a communist is not simply incorrect with his ideas; he is totally false. No false truth can be corrected by further knowledge. No truth has ever been changed by applying further knowledge. Many a fact, however, has been discarded when proven incorrect. Truth is determined by the *inquirer's* intention; facts by the *inquiry's* outcome. In truth, the outcome depends on the inquirer; in facts, the outcome depends on the inquiry. Many untenured professors have discovered, to their lasting sorrow, that tenure outcome has nothing to do with evidence. No evidence will change the senior's simple belief in the truth that one is unfit for tenure.

It is easy to see why the academic fields are particularly sensitive to the issues of tenure and academic freedom as preconditions for truth. Their whole subject matter deals with truth, although they may see it as "facts" for their own temporary convenience. They envy their brother professors in the functional fields in science, business, nursing, physical education, or whatever, where a "false" idea once misspoken by a junior member is rarely the cause for trouble. One is easily forgiven for producing incorrect knowledge; one is rarely forgiven for a false idea. Scopes's trouble was with the authorities, not with his colleagues in biology. On the other hand, Marxists in an environment unfriendly to Marxism are always on the brink of being accused of possessing false knowledge.

Truth must be persuaded to be accepted, for no truth is so self-evident as to be acceptable on the grounds of being there. All persuasion is carried out by words used logically, historically, metaphorically, even factually, or any other way that fits the occasion and purpose. In truth there are no equations to demonstrate, no "things" to show, no tangible results to anticipate. It is almost exclusively the workings of one human mind upon another. Persuasion, though difficult to effect, is the only arsenal of communication at the academic professor's disposal; the pen is still his chief weapon, and words still his magic bullet. This difficulty of communication, however, tends to drive him to the lures of concrete numbers, statistics, and results in his persuasion, more in the fashion of his counterpart in functional fields in presentation of facts.

Facts must be demonstrated to be effective. Often a fact's being there is enough to achieve its desired effect. The awesome destructiveness of a weapon needs no persuasion to a weapons buyer. The demonstration is enough. What could *persuade* him that such weapons should never be used on human beings? Or that the money would be better used in some other endeavors? The destructiveness itself requires no persuasion to be established as an effective means of violence; altering the buyer's attitude toward its use is subject to persuasion. The force of destructiveness would have little or nothing to do with the outcome of persuasion. It could harden his resolve as easily as it could alter his whole outlook on life and death. For the latter, the cry of a small girl could do just as well, or just as ineffectively, as the demonstration of awesome destruction.

The desire to unite academic fields with functional fields, generally in terms favorable to the latter, is irresistible. Professors know that the functional fields are where all the action is. Functional professors generally receive a higher salary; they use more forceful methods of "science"; they enjoy a higher public esteem; they occupy newer facilities and more spacious allocations; their fields are popular with students in their career decisions. It is with extreme envy, if not slavish imitation, that academic professors look to their colleagues in functional fields. As a way to be treated with more respect, the academic professor sets his model after the more successful functional professor. With that comes the desire to see himself as a useful, functional scientist. He then sets out on his facts-production in the methods and fashions of his functional colleague. Thus, when he really means truth, he speaks of facts. When he really describes his belief, he speaks of scientific objectivity. When he really expresses his intention, he speaks of "the conclusion from data." When he should really do the persuading, he speaks of facts "speaking for themselves."

The academic professor is greatly inconvenienced by the fact that truth has nothing to do with facts. It is neither advanced by facts, nor in need of facts to be properly established. When facts are presented in support of a truth, the same facts could be used for the opposite truth. Nor does fact inspire people in a particular way. It is a well-established fact that racial discrimination exists in America, but the fact hardly alters anyone's mind about it. Unmoved by fact, it goes on as before. Facts about discrimination are numerous and indisputable; the truth about them no one really knows or wants to acknowledge. The academic professor may produce facts after facts, but hardly with any effect as truth. Truth affects people; facts do not. Since truth is independent of facts, one deals with them only because one must. In order to make a persuasive case about racism in America, for example, one may be somewhat facilitated by facts. But no one would say that Martin Luther King, Jr., was effective with his persuasion because he mastered the facts about discrimination.

Facts are convenient; truth is not. The academic professor has decided to go with public convenience at the expense of private inconvenience. In his desire to avoid private inconvenience he acts and thinks more and more like his colleague in producing publicly convenient facts. His overriding emphasis is avoiding conflict with the status quo, while emphasizing his entitlement to tenure and academic freedom in the name of private inconvenience.

Academic professors, when they imitate science, and functional professors produce two slightly different sets of facts, however. The former produce "social" facts, those relating people to other people. The latter produce "material" facts, those relating material things (including the human organism) to other material things. Commonly, people are both at once: they are a material thing to their surgeon, and they are people to the surgeon's bill collector. For the academic professor, even minor social facts may stir up trouble. He learns to say nothing to violate the principle of public convenience, or to say it in such a way that it is totally obscured. Professional jargon often takes care of that problem. Through it all, he takes great pains to avoid inconveniencing the existing people-to-people relations. So he normally ends up saying nothing important that could be misinterpreted as speaking his mind.

Material facts have no relevance to truth. Social facts are only potentially or marginally useful for formulating truth or untruth. Whether we make use of them or not, material facts exist and have always existed by themselves. Gravity, black holes, mathematical relations among things exist by themselves. Social facts, such as racial discrimination, exist only if we make use of them or if they serve public convenience, such as laws and customs. Material facts lead to more material facts, to more material facts, and still more material facts. Social facts, if pursued intellectually beyond the limits of public convenience, could lead to the discovery of truth about discrimination. Gandhi could have simply moved to the car that he belonged in when he was thrown out of the white-only coach. But the incident led him to discover an important truth about humanity. If he had been an engineer checking on the safety of the train, he might have invented a safer wheel for the train.

It may be possible that a man can jump from material facts to truth, but the jump is not inherent in the material facts themselves. Scientists generally believe that scientific education will lead to a greater public awareness of environmental hazards. What they do not know is that the awareness is a form of truth that no amount of scientific information will discover. A man who is surrounded by filth, pollution, poison, and the latest encyclopedia of science may never discover the simple truth that he needs to change his consumptive habits to solve the problem. The misconception of facts and truth is so entrenched that we cannot overstate the simple axiom that facts do not advance or make up the basis of truth.

There may, for instance, appear to be a connection, especially in advanced societies, between possession and happiness. Thus, it may be thought that more money or more things will make a man happier. But this connection is an article of faith held valid under certain circumstances; it is neither analytically true nor universally believed. That a man would rather have more than less, given scarcity, does not help the connection. As a social generalization, possession increasing happiness correspondingly is fairly worthless. For not every society is a "modern" society, and not every man connects possession with happiness. It does help as a practical instrument of motivation for modern people in their performance of production and consumption. But it does not establish a connection between truth about happiness and facts about possession. The effort to enlighten difficult truth with easy facts, nevertheless, is relentless even among academic professors.

The academic professor who tries to relate truth to facts obviously endangers truth itself. He tries to make useful what is essentially useless, and in the process, he nullifies what he claims to cherish—namely, truth. Facts are about nature, including the human organism, and are pursued for their benefit to the life process. Useful facts make living easier and more comfortable for the organism. To that extent, facts are functional. But truth is about society, the abstract totality that makes up the psychology and culture of human beings. That each human being is also an organism is about as irrelevant as that each human being has four limbs. But the academic professor turned semi-functionalist ends up denying social truth as relevant. He is fascinated about human beings as quantities, as models, and as predictable actors, all in the methods of functional fields.

The functional professor simply asks how the organism can be made comfortable. The academic professor in pursuit of truth ought to ask *which* organism should be made comfortable and which not, and *why*. For the functional professor, it is enough to consider the human organism simply as an organism just like all other organisms. For the academic professor, each organism is a person in society, belongs to a class, earns a specific income, marries and raises children, goes to war and gets killed or stays home and lives, has a job he likes or hates, is black or white and is treated as such. The organism may have made enormous progress toward his comfort in technology, but the same may not be said about his society. Truth must be about his society, not about his bodily state.

A. M. Rosenthal has similarly observed that scientific progress from the Wright Brothers to Apollo 8 is entirely "discernible" because it follows a predictable turn of events. Only the details may vary slightly. But the "tone and texture of society" cannot be predicted at all. "That is quite an open question," says he, "because it is one thing that does change, and it involves a number of other interesting matters: What will be man's values, standards and goals? What will he consider worthwhile and what will he consider dispensable? What will be his style of thought?"[4] The questions Mr. Rosenthal is asking are of course the questions of truth as distinct from material facts.

The very nature of truth makes it impossible to produce it in a factory fashion, with division of labor, or in specialized task assignments. Truth is searched *alone* and its discovery is always a solitary act, although the same truth could be discovered by many at the same time, arrived at independent of one another. Truth-pursuers have always been lone individual scholars in constant dialogue with other scholars dead or alive. Hence all truth bears the name of the individual scholar who discovered it and is spoken of in his name. Without Plato (or Socrates) there would have been no *Republic*. But without the Wright Brothers there would be planes; without Newton the law of gravity; without Edison the electric light bulb. Unlike truth, facts are the culmination of the work of many people and many generations forming different links in the chain of unceasing material progress. All must be there for the next step or development to become possible.

We "search" for truth. The method is uncertain, the outcome unknown, and the benefit dubious. Every man must determine how to search for the truth, for what. There is no such thing as ten easy steps to truth. If truth is searched, facts are *researched*. Any modern research can be—and often should be for the sake of efficiency—carried out in a factory fashion, involving many specialists assigned to do different tasks. When done, each part fits into the overall design to form the whole. One need not know what the whole design looks like as long as he does his part well. Much of the work done in functional fields is carried out in this way. Every functional professor is a specialist in some minute field of competence.[5]

Truth, on the other hand, is always a whole and is conceived as a whole. There is no such thing as truth about freedom or justice for blue collar workers, ages 35, having been Democrats but now switching to be Republicans, earning less than $25,000 a year but more than $15,000, living in the eastern section of some city, and so on. Even if such were possible, how many different truths for how many different groups would be needed to say anything about freedom and justice for community, society, and humanity? While there is no sure way of arriving at truth, facts are produced by step-by-step methods, piece by piece, through trial and error, sometimes expected and sometimes revolutionary, with time and repetition as the ultimate ally. All facts are produced, one way or another, by time and repetition.

In Chapter 2 I contended that marketability makes the issue of tenure irrelevant for functional fields. Functional professors derive their worth from their usefulness, which is translated into corresponding market value. Because they do not necessarily depend on the university for a living, their tenure is to that extent irrelevant. That restated, we are now in a position to say that tenure does not apply to them in another sense. They do not need tenure because they do not need academic freedom. They do not need academic freedom because they have nothing to do with pursuit of the truth. Pursuing facts may require money, but certainly no tenure or academic freedom. Functional fields simply have no business with truth. Hence they need not exercise academic freedom or require tenure protection.

As noted, tenure is not a reward for a job well done or a badge of economic security. Normally people get paid for a job well done and they become economically secure by amassing wealth. For functional fields, reward is their salary; job security is in their usefulness and marketability. What truth is embodied in Physical Education 102 (Golf), librarianship, Chemistry Lab 101, Income Tax Law 202, Introduction to Spanish, or coaching basketball? Why would the instructors in these and other such functional fields need tenure? Tenure is a principle, not a reward, and must apply to those who need it on the grounds of principle. Functional fields do not deal with truth and therefore do not irritate or challenge popular opinion. Job security is a good thing to have only when one's job security is in some way threatened or is in doubt. Physicians do not have job security but they expect to work. Their job security in tenure, when they intend to work normally, would be meaningless. This is the reason the public school teacher's tenure is only lightly taken. Like the physician, with or without tenure, the schoolteacher still has to work every day.

For the academic professor, what he must do every day *is*, in pursuit of the truth, what puts his job security on the line. The only way his job can be secure, without tenure and academic freedom to protect him, is to make himself somehow useful like those in functional fields, or to grovel by trying to please the powers that be. The former would serve the market well, and the latter the dictator well. But in its infinite wisdom, American society has decided that such would serve neither the professor nor his society well. Hence tenure and academic freedom provide a way of guaranteeing truth.

The professor of functional fields teaches what he *knows* to be facts. The professor of academic fields teaches what he *believes* to be the truth. It amounts to a fraud if an academic professor teaches his students something he does not believe to be true. For there is no such thing as neutral truth or meaningless truth. It is his *belief* that needs to be protected, not his job. The functional professor's job is safe as long as he does his job reasonably. A chemistry professor or a librarian is almost never dismissed or denied tenure for the reasons academic freedom is established to protect. Doing his job reasonably does not help the academic professor. Doing his job, reasonably or otherwise, itself—pursuing the irritating truth—is *always* in jeopardy, all the more so if he does his job well. Academic tenure is created to protect the truth embodied in the belief, which cannot be expressed without endangering the believer. (By the same token, the academic professor who teaches something he does *not* believe to be the truth or who has no such belief should not be granted tenure and protected by academic freedom. This should be so regardless of how well the professor does in other areas of his work.)

One can teach facts as one knows them. But one cannot teach truth without believing in it. One cannot believe in the truth unless one has learned *from* it. All academic knowledge, sooner or later, leads to self-knowledge. Self-knowledge, thus gained, is ultimately the bridge between self and the world, between subjective and objective, and between moment and history. There is no way an academic professor's personal belief can be separated from his work in teaching and writing. That he presents his material in a "balanced," "objective" way, as it is fashionable to say on campus, is a matter of style. One still has to teach what one believes, and what one believes must be the truth. There is no other way that an academic professor, under tenure protection and in academic freedom, can justifiably act or think. A philosopher must ask himself why he teaches philosophy, not some other subject, and why philosophy X, not philosophy Y. A chemist need not. An academic professor who does not believe anything cannot teach anything. Society does not grant him tenure and academic freedom for nothing. For truth is always something.

Facts are important either in biological survival or, in a more advanced state, if desired routines are established in society. Facts improve material life but do not improve society's moral substance. In fact, there is enough historical evidence to argue the opposite. "Primitives" generally display greater moral values and humanitarianism than do the "advanced." Truth is imperative if society's concern is neither biological survival nor routinized life, but change for the better. Static societies, either political or theocratic, would not allow tenure protection or academic freedom to induce change. As we shall see, truth itself *is* possible only if social change is deemed desirable. Material fields have nothing to do with *social* change, nor truth, nor academic freedom, nor, ultimately, tenure. Their proven usefulness and market value speak for themselves. Applying tenure and academic freedom preconditional to truth in these fields is largely a waste of principle.

NOTES

1. As a fairly standard model, the handbook for the University of North Carolina system defines "Freedom and Responsibility in the University Community" as "To seek and speak the truth." Board of Governors, *The Code* (The University of North Carolina, August), 1988, 19.

2. *Dialogues of Plato* J. D. Kaplan, ed. (New York: Washington Square Press, 1957) p. 16. These famous words occur at the end of the dialogue.

3. A typical one is Arthur DeBardeleben's definition: "Truth, in the academic context, is concerned with facts, because of their significance, their relationship within a system of knowledge." See Arthur DeBardeleben, "The University's External Constituency," in *Dimensions of Academic Freedom*, eds. Walter P. Metzger, (Urbana: University of Illinois Press, 1969) 73.

4. A. M. Rosenthal, "Key to the Tone of Society's Future," in *In Defense of Academic Freedom,* ed. Sidney Hook (New York: Pegasus, 1971), 21–22. This book is a collection of articles in opposition to the political turmoil of the 1960s at American campuses.

5. In an interesting study conducted by J. D. Memory and his colleagues, we find that in academic fields (such as philosophy) single authorship prevails, and in functional fields, notably chemistry and physics, the number of authors per article

goes up to almost four and five authors respectively. See J. D. Memory, J. F. Arnold, D. W. Stewart, and R. E. Fornes. "Physics as a Team Sport," *American Journal of Physics* 53, no.3 (March 1985): 270–71

Chapter 6

Ways to Truth

How does one pursue the truth? Or, to put it another away, how does one *avoid* pursuing *un*truth? Once the second question has been resolved, the first one will take care of itself.

The academic professor should not be sloppy with truth by trivializing it into his routine facts-production. Nor, on the other hand, need he be overawed by his task. Pursuing the truth, like all things in his life, must accord with his academic reality. He is not asked to walk on water or carve The Truth in stone. Neither trivializing nor panicking over it, the academic professor should confront the pursuit of the truth primarily as an academic task. It is an enormous task, to be sure. But the difficulty, it will be evident, is not with the task itself. It is the difficulty of overcoming his own untruth. It is neither impossible to accomplish nor especially different from other such tasks. Its difficulty is on the scale of a priest's job, rather than of a scientist's, for his is a matter of internal struggle, not of external substance. Truth is *pursued*, not produced, and *how* to pursue it is all that counts.

Truth itself is nothing special. Pursuing it is. Truth itself may not be as important as avoiding the very conditions that make the pursuit itself impossible. How to pursue the truth is in this sense really a question of how to avoid untruth.

Tenure privilege for the academic faculty reveals two startlingly contrasting facts about American society: one, the noblest and the other, the ugliest. The noblest is America's unique impulse to grant its professors tenure and academic freedom to do as they wish. The ugliest is also American: the academic professor's impulse to take the money and run.

Just now we must assume that the noble impulse is yet to be rediscovered in the tenured faculty. Truth must be pursued by the academic professor who is tempted, by the unique arrangement of his economic security, to take the money and run. Can this man who is fixed for life be persuaded to rise to the noble height of academic freedom and truth? Assumption is a powerful tool of academic analysis. Much scholarly thinking is based on assumption, and without it academic speculations would be hard pressed and perhaps impossible to carry on. We must assume once again that reason and good sense will prompt the comfortable senior to action in pursuit of the truth. Not to assume this is to acquiesce to the worst.

Truth is no great secret that is revealed only through tortuous processes and mythic revelations. *Some* truths have been formulated that way, but ours is of a more ordinary kind. Consider the fact that innocent children can easily speak the truth. So can deathrow inmates in their "moment of truth." So can artists through their artworks. To be sure, the truths spoken by these are not "great truths." But great or small, they are taken as truth. Truth can be and is thus calmly revealed through rather common channels of ordinary life. Why do we take the utterances of innocent children, deathrow inmates, or artists as truth?

No one really knows what truth looks like when it is spoken. But one is inclined to believe that when a person speaks his mind *truthfully*, what comes out must be the truth. When great persons speak, naturally, great truth comes out. When we think of the truth spoken by great minds we tend to readily confer our agreement upon certain well-known persons: chronologically speaking, Socrates, Jesus, Thomas More, Abraham Lincoln, Gandhi, and many others. Great and small, what makes their utterances true?

Truth recognizes reality as it is. But reality has many shades. What a fool sees is different from what a sage sees. But *what* makes a fool's truth so unreliable? What makes him a *fool* in the first place, as far as truth-seeking is concerned, that makes him see the *un*truth? It is much more difficult to know what true reality is than to know what would *prevent* one from seeing it as it should be seen. Therefore, we shall follow the second and more manageable route to truth: that is, trying to discover what would make it difficult for one, like the fool, to see reality as it is.

Truth is spoken, as a description of reality, when one sees reality truthfully. To put it another way, truth is the end result of seeing reality as it should be seen. The task now is how to see reality truthfully. This can be reformulated as a question: *What makes it impossible or diffficult for one to see his reality truthfully?* We can get one step closer to the answer by stating that in order to see reality truthfully, one must be *free* to see it as one should. Free from what? Consider children, deathrow inmates, artists, Socrates, Jesus, More, Lincoln, and Gandhi. What freedom did they have that makes their descriptions of reality so true so that we do not doubt their truthfulness? It is no secret that they are deemed to be free from *themseves*, or more specifically from their *self-interest*.

Children's innocence is free of concerns for the consequences of its action; deathrow inmates at the moment of truth have nothing to gain or fear any more from their confession of truth; true artists reveal only their true feelings, however ambiguous or disagreeable, through their art-works. The great men and women of history have been elevated to their exalted positions largely through their freedom from themselves. Once freed from themselves, their vision is clear. Reality appears uncluttered when self-interest is overcome. Truth is merely the end result of this process.

It is self-interest, then, that distorts. Truth is easily spoken when one's vision of reality is no longer distorted by the consequences of one's vision. Whenever we suspect someone's self-interest, we suspect falsehood in his description of reality. Thus, what truth is can be easily resolved by *how* it may be searched. Virtually in all cases, search for the truth ends up being search for freedom from self-interest. As always, one leads to the other. This freedom may be attained in some by virtue of their social situations (children, deathrow inmates, artists), or in others as a result of their private quests (Socrates, Jesus, More, Lincoln, Gandhi). But the result is the same nevertheless. All speak the truth. Freedom from self-interest—economic being the most overriding one—is thus the precondition for pursuit of the truth. Therefore, truth is present always *proportional* to the absence of self-interest. By the same token, it would be nearly impossible to expect a distortion-free perception from a self-centered man. Hard as he may try, self-interest makes distortion inevitable in whatever he says or does.

Self-interest is perhaps one single most important ingredient in con-temporary American life. This is all the more remarkable in view of tenure and academic freedom in academia conceived primarily as an antidote to self-interest. In a wholly self-interested market society, tenure-based academic freedom, which liberates the academic professor from his self-interested concerns, stands as the most puzzling contradic-tion to itself. It takes no great cynicism to observe that self-interest makes everyone basically a thief. It is said that opportunity makes a thief, but self-interest takes advantage of an opportunity. Thus, self-interest and opportunity eventually create a world of thieves. Yet it is also the same world that creates in the university a sanctuary of freedom from self-interested thieves just so that the free professor may do whatever he wishes with his freedom. To underscore this remarkable phenomenon in American society more fully, we need to appreciate self-interest itself more fully.

What has impressed many observers of American society in the postwar decades (C. Wright Mills, David Riesman, Richard Sennett, Christopher Lasch, Andrew Hacker, William Whyte, John Kenneth Galbraith, to name the well-known few) has been the robust and assertive emergence of self-interest as the single most telling characteristic of American values.[1] In daily subconsciousness as well as in national political themes, in cultural anecdotes as well as refined legal structure, in the images of heroes and villains as well as children's tales and moral allegories, self-interest has overshadowed all other values. What began as an explanation for economic exchange at the marketplace is now the driving force of an economic society, which easily surpasses even the deepest of religious and political commitments. All may be disputed in America, but one dare not dispute the merit of self-interest. It transcends religious conflicts, unifies political differences, and unites divergent intellectual models of human behavior. Subcultures, ethnic diversities, and social classes come into perfect unity and harmony in the upholding of self-interest.

The casualty of self-interest is as all-encompassing as its commitment is all-consuming. It unbinds human bonds; it negates personal loyalty; it authenticates commercial intimacy; it renders God expedient to whims; it replaces reality with fantasy; it derides high-mindedness and personal virtue; it corrupts public life; it makes everyone suspicous of everyone. The list is endless. To summarize it in one succinct statement: self-interest makes truth impossible. For the academic professor, the battle line is easy to draw: It is self-interest, including his own, on one side, and academic freedom and truth on the other. Tenure privilege can be used by either side. It can further self-interest by justifying sloth and syco-phancy. It can serve academic freedom and truth, and by extension the larger society that grants it, by protecting him from the consequences of his truth. It is a bitter battle, and only the professor himself knows for sure which side he is on.

If truth is selflessness in thought, then naturally justice is selflessness in action. Truth entails justice whenever it is acted upon. Thus, truth and justice make up the complete whole of selflessness. Whenever a truthful person acts, justice results. If self-interest is represented in the market-place, selflessness is represented in the university's academic freedom and truth. More significant, if functional fields (e.g., chemistry, account-ing, physical education) can be said to contribute to self-interest in comfort and pleasure, academic fields stand as the constant reminder of the higher virtues of community, society, and humanity. That functional fields sometimes claim to the higher virtues, or that academic fields sometimes succumb to market temptations should not obscure this basic distinction. Functional fields are deemed useful and marketable precisely because they enhance self-interest. Academic fields are often neglected and avoided precisely because, albeit sporadically and weakly, they point to the higher virtues. As the academic professor must struggle against his own self-centered tendency, defeated more often than triumphant, he must also find himself an adversary of his brother colleagues on campus.

The reach of self-interest in America is enormous. As a force of individual motivation, it never sleeps, rests, or diverts. As a determinant of social relations, one self-interest is always pitted against another. As a social guide for individual conduct, it causes an endless war in each person between selfishness and moral decency. Intellectually, all the more so for the academic professor, self-interest necessarily miniaturizes a man's world into the narrowest sphere of the here and now. His decisions are shortsighted, self-centered, and balanced precariously between con-flicting impulses. His focus becomes specialized; his intellectual purpose can concentrate only on one thing at a time. No longer free from the consequences of his thought and action, he is forever on the lookout for his possible losses and gains.

A self-centered man is also a rational man in the economic sense. The moral commitment that may have guided his earlier purpose is now entangled with the more immediate economic balance sheet for him. A man facing the possibility of gaining or losing something economically dear to him must weigh his thoughts according to the probability of gaining and losing, however insignificant. The academic man is espe-cially vulnerable to this because his gains and losses are so small. And this very smallness is what summons the best of pettiness and meanness from an academic man. Among academics one easily finds the noblest and the ugliest of the human species. Rationality motivates him to the meanest of human spirits in defense of self-interest. Thus, rationality is predicated on self-interest. No rational person, therefore, can pursue the truth, disregarding his possible gains and losses.

Inability to pursue the truth does not end with the simple absence of truth. The absence of truth is always accompanied by the presence of untruth. A self-interested man is not only incapable of speaking the truth; he is also a habitual lover of untruth. Self-interest is best protected by deliberate untruth, or lies. Since the academic professor's self-interest is small in quantity, his lies are also small in quality. This makes him, when he is a small-time liar, the most pitifully despicable tyrant over students, juniors, and secretaries. Once guided by self-interest, the academic professor's lying habits do not end when he gets tenure. As he climbs up the ladder of academic hierarchy, his lying increases correspondingly. Thus, untruth increases as self-interest increases, and self-interest increases as one's economic success increases. There is no lie more honestly told and believed than a lie fortified in elaborate intellectualism.

As an untenured junior member he may be a small-time liar and petty tyrant. But by the time he becomes a full professor, his entire day is a continuous succession of untruth solely in defense of his self-interest. Dishonesty becomes his way of life: he may pretend to pursue the truth by writing books and articles of absolutely trivial significance; he may pretend to give fair consideration in a junior's tenure decision while playing the worst kind of politics; he may pretend to be a serious scholar by resorting to incomprehensible jargon; he may pretend to disdain committee work while thoroughly enjoying routines; he may pretend to respect academic freedom and truth when his sole concern is his petty self-interest against the academic freedom of others. By then, he has become the worst enemy of all that is dear to academic truth and, by extension, to the larger society that has extended him an unconditional tenure privilege.

Self-interest seriously impairs the academic professor in yet another way. It deters his progress as a free scholar. As a philosopher, a social scientist, a writer, an artist, a man progresses in scholarship only if his mind is free to grow. But once possessed by self-interest, he becomes stupified by its effect. Books he has read or lectures he has heard cannot broaden his intellectual horizon if he is enslaved by self-interest. His self-interest makes him so blind that he cannot see anything clearly. His factual knowledge may be impressive; he may display potent intellectual talent. Yet, all that is for naught when he is overcome by self-interest-induced stupidity, the kind that afflicts academics in the worst way. No man is more impossibly stupid than a self-interested educated man. He cannot think like a free scholar and he cannot see things with clear enough vision for his scholarship. Everything he says, writes, and does is distorted, with or without his own knowing about it. He is forever enslaved by the all-consuming passion of self-interest. He uses all his learned ingenuity and cleverness to disguise, defend, and diffuse his self-interest and stupidity. Few are in a better position to carry on with all this than an academic man. His whole life's education has prepared him for that deception.

To the extent that one is possessed of self-interest, the academic man tends to display all the familiar characteristics of insanity. (Rational insanity may be a contradiction in terms, but not in the way self-interest is rationalized in contemporary American society in general and on campus in particular.) As with the possession of power, which I shall discuss in a later section, self-interest makes it impossible to listen to reason and to comprehend reality. Reason and reality give one a sense of proportion and perspective, potential ingredients for truth. But self-interest deprives him of this essential faculty as its intrinsic power. A self-interested man, to the extent of his conviction, thinks and acts in complete self-absorption that is observed more commonly in the mentally insane. As life in academia is normally more insulated from reason and reality for the professor, this personality trait in particular stands out for easy observation. Thus, nothing is more pitiful or contemptuous than the insulated professor playing the insane game of self-interest oblivious to reason and reality.

This state of mind for the academic professor is especially difficult to forgive because he enjoys a privilege no one else in his society enjoys. Tenure is *designed* to free the professor from his self-interest. His society has guaranteed lifetime economic security so that he may pursue the truth to the fullest benefit of his society. Yet, any cursory observation of the Ivory Tower confirms the worst kind of economic behavior. Professors who are fixed for life are no different from those in fierce market competition, from which they have been absolutely and unconditionally liberated. They have been liberated from the economic burdens of life precisely for the society's *salvation* from such market behavior. Appointed to this role, the academic professor behaves worse, primarily moved by his petty rewards, than those whose moral life he is entrusted to uplift. From society's point of view, not only is it a poor economic investment on professors, but the economic largesse itself has created only more viciously economic animals in those professors.

Tenure has been granted to academic professors to remove the self-interest that blinds ordinary people. With it, the most—if not only—important reason for self-interest has been nullified. Society has legally guaranteed his decent livelihood forever. There seems to be no reason why their souls should still be troubled by petty economics. While untenured, they tend to think of tenure as a great liberating experience. But the long-awaited liberation is entirely the wrong kind. Instead of liberating him from self-interested concerns, it merely frees the professor from his primary responsibility. That is, pursuit of the truth as a wholly free man. Instead, he is now free to concentrate on furthering his economic interest.

A tenured professor, according to academic tradition, is responsible to no one but his own conscience. His own conscience is the sole arbiter of what is true and untrue. Every university handbook affirms this. But his conscience is hopelessly beholden to his own economic interest. Everything he does is bound to his self-interest. After being freed from basic economic concerns, now he concentrates his energy on getting more economic rewards. By awarding him tenure, the university has only freed the most ferociously determined economic animal from his cage. What was designed to nullify his economic interest has only fueled it by granting greater freedom to his energy and cunning.

Doing the minimum in the most routine way on campus is easy. Under the protective umbrella of tenure, many academic professors moonlight for still more money. Some work as poll-takers for commercial firms, using their offices as headquarters; this somehow serves them as a scholarly activity as well. Others sell real estate on the side, now that they have ample free time on hand. Still others do "consulting" work as hired hands for whomever will pay for their service. What these professors indeed *teach* their students is anyone's guess. What is certain, however, is that they serve neither academic freedom, by abusing it, nor truth, by distorting it. By temporarily serving their self-interest they ultimately destroy everyone's interest.

Surely, in pursuit of the truth, the professor is not asked to walk on water. Pursuing the truth is as simple, or as difficult, as telling what one believes *honestly*. This honesty is greatly facilitated for the professor by tenure and its economic privilege. Apparently, tenure privilege has not adequately liberated the American professor from his inner economic struggle, as it was once thought, to demand honesty in his thought. It has only intensified it. And in the process truth has been unceremoniously dismissed as an afterthought. Tenure is given to nullify economics for the benefit of truth. Yet, it now nullifies truth for the benefit of economics. Society grants that not every professor can be brilliant. But it expects every professor—by virtue of his economic freedom—at least to be truthful.

Supposing, however, that tenure and academic freedom did indeed liberate the professor from his self-interest, could it mean that every academic professor would be doing the *same thing* in pursuit of truth? There is genuine fear among college professors that they might end up doing what somebody else is doing. It is like the fear of a woman who goes to a party only to find, to her horror, that someone else is wearing the same dress. Professors simply take pride in doing their own things. They go to great length to avoid doing the same thing. Thus, the idea that everyone should pursue truth disturbs them greatly. But this concern is entirely overwrought and groundless. There are two reasons for saying so. One is that what passes for diverse activities on campus only covers up their essential lack of true diversity. The other is that pursuing truth is actually a process that requires diverse modes of thinking.

It is the unwritten code of academic conduct among professors that everyone must do "different things." No one likes to be crowded in his specialty by other researchers. Staking out one special area is crucial to one's well-being and prosperity. Departments are careful not to hire people with overlapping specialties. But, as they are freed from their self-protective cocoons through the offices of tenure, how would this freedom affect their "research," "writing," and "teaching"? Would they end up doing the same thing, since truth-pursuit is essentially the same for everyone?

Nothing makes academic professors obsolete as fast as specialization. But that everyone is doing different things—which department chairmen like to point out to impress visitors—is the best way to ensure their continuing relevance. However, every academic professor doing "his thing" normally means that what he does has no connection with what anyone else does, or with the larger society. In a typical university, everyone is doing his thing in total oblivion and in utter irrelevance to anyone else or anything else in society. Since what he does is so specialized, no one outside his narrow specialty can make any judgment about it. By doing different things, professors are guaranteed their independence from qualitative judgment. No one has to explain the logic or reason behind one's research involvement because outsiders are expected to know little or nothing about it. It amounts to carte blanche in the hands of a thief. This privilege inevitably invites silliness in thought and encourages laziness in the academic professor's behavior. It is no wonder, then, that professors cannot communicate with one another, for no one knows or cares what anyone else is doing. This lack or impossibility of communication liberates the professor from any sense of responsibility for his action. In a world where everyone does his thing, no explanation is necessary. That one is doing his own thing is sufficient.

On the other hand, pursuing the truth as a singular purpose of scholarly life does not necessarily mean that everyone does the same thing. In the world of ideas and freedom in the truest sense of the term, it is impossible for two people to think alike. In fact, it is much more difficult to duplicate someone else's thought in freedom than in the world of superficial diversities. Freedom from self-interest allows true divergences of thought about truth. Truth and freedom encourage creative responses to given reality. Self-interest encourages stock responses to stock definitions. In our contemporary reality, however, professors doing seemingly different things display greater conformity in thought and action than one normally suspects. Their differences—the so-called "diversities"—are so strikingly superficial and shallow that one might say all their research activities have been produced by the same mold. In many ways, they have. People driven by self-interest tend to choose similar social structures and act alike in a given situation. Truth deeply and imperatively diversifies human thought; self-interest necessarily and inevitably prods people into conformity. Thus, there is little reason to fear conformity in the pursuit of truth.

NOTES

1. Their literature is now familiar to all: C. Wright Mills, *White Collar* (New York: Oxford University Press, 1959); David Riesman, *The Lonely Crowd* (New Haven: Yale University Press, 1950); Richard Sennett, *The Fall of the Public Man* (New York: Vintage, 1974); Christopher Lasch, *The Culture of Narcissism* (New York: Norton, 1979); Andrew Hacker, *The End of the American Era* (New York: Atheneum, 1969); William H. Whyte, *The Organization Man* (Garden City, N.Y.: Doubleday, 1957); and John Kenneth Galbraith, *The Affluent Society* (New York: The New American Library, 1958).

Chapter 7

The Academic Imperative

Pursuing the truth hardly ranks among the more urgent businesses of life. It is motivated by what Thorstein Veblen called the "impulsion and guidance of idle curiosity" for what is a "profitless quest of knowledge."[1] A society otherwise actively engaged in the business of survival would not expend its precious time and money in the indulgent pursuit of the truth. Such a task has always been among the preoccupations, many not so honorable, of the idle class. It requires a considerable reservoir of unused energy and resource, not the kind that the less well-endowed of society can spare. Truth may be a noble thing to pursue. But bread and butter, among other facts of life, are more urgent.

For a society to create an entirely *new* class of people to be wholly subsidized by the state just for pursuit of the truth requires an extraordinary surplus of resource as well as a foresight to match it. This state-subsidized pursuit of the truth is possible, then, only in the most advanced of societies that cherish truth. The state, as we know it from historical evidence, likes to suppress truth rather than encourage it. It harasses the truth-pursuing process rather than comforts it with subsidy. It pressures truth-pursuers toward self-serving falsehood rather than liberates them with unconditional freedom.

It is indeed remarkable that contemporary American society, as the only nation-state that is such an exception, expends its considerable resource and indulgence for what may surely seem to many an "idle" and "profitless" pursuit of the truth. It cannot be overstated that this is so in a society of perhaps the worst kind of market greed and self-interest the world has ever seen. Truth guaranteed by tenure exists neither in

Great Britain (where the current system originated) nor in the Soviet Union (which has been our ideological rival) nor in Japan (which is our economic competitor). Among the allegedly and more often admittedly trashy artifacts of American culture, this free pursuit of academic truth stands as one shining beacon of incongruity.

The academic professor cannot insist upon unconditional academic freedom through tenure unless he serves truth unconditionally. He cannot demand tenure and academic freedom unless he *needs* it. He does not need it unless his pursuit of the truth threatens his academic freedom. Tenure is thus inconceivable without the very *threat* to his livelihood that is the price of his academic freedom.

Tenure and job security are two different issues. In tenure, truth is imperatively demanded. Without truth that justifies tenure, tenure degenerates merely into job security. All academic fields being basically without practical function, however, tenure without truth as its precondition for being has no reason to exist. A philosopher who no longer pursues the truth, yet who has secure tenure privilege, has a sinecure for life. A scholar on an easy street is an ugly thing to behold, for he becomes slothful with his performance and yet pretentious with his claim. For the academic professor, there is no such thing as job security. What he is committed to is no job. What he pursues is no security. For he is committed to and pursues the truth, and nothing else. Truth is the end and livelihood the means. When livelihood becomes his end and truth his means, we witness potentially the most corrupt transformation of a noble idea. In it, the professor uses truth to serve his economic interest. Tenure has been established to ease his conscience. Yet, used as a means, it only corrupts him thoroughly.

Job security, on the other hand, applies to the normal run of social functions. Chemists, librarians, accountants, physical education teachers, and any number of functional professors can enjoy their job security simply on the continuing demonstration of their competence. Their job security is their functionality. As long as they remain competently functional, their job security is assured. Unlike the academic professor, functional professors are burdened neither by an extra-job requirement—namely, truth nor by the meaning of academic freedom. Theirs neither requires freedom to exercise nor is strictly speaking "academic." The usefulness of their job demands only that they work normally and competently. A chemist must know chemistry, a librarian books and videotapes, an economist the workings of the marketplace, an accountant accounting rules, and so on. But neither their society nor their institution insists that they pursue the truth, exercise academic freedom, or go for tenure in a do-or-die manner. Tenure or no, academic freedom or no, truth or no, their work remains fairly routine and uneventful. No discoveries made by functional professors in modern times have ever threatened or irritated the status quo enough to cause the issue of truth to flare up. The possibility of a nuclear war is not blamed on physicists for having invented the bomb, but on political and moral leaders for not having eliminated its threat. A dirty environment, even when chemically caused, is not the fault of chemists, not any more than of the truck drivers who helped transport the chemicals. Chemists like everyone else are an instrument used in a specific series of events that are simply beyond their control. In their routine tasks chemists are no threat to anyone. Neither are librarians. Neither are accountants. Neither are Spanish teachers. Their job is doing what they are *told* to do by the funding agent. Why should they worry, in the fashion of academics, about tenure, academic freedom, or pursuit of the truth?

Service to society takes two common forms: material service and "moral" service. When a society as a whole values one service more, the stock of one goes up while that of the other goes down, or vice versa. Often when society is uncertain of its own purpose, the two tend to be mixed and confused. When society has one strong preference in place of the other, then the strong tends to overpower the weak. The world of the Middle Ages valued moral service; our contemporary world, especially in the West, values material service. Because of the emphasis on spiritual salvation and meager scientific and technological development, material service used to be an insignificant factor at a medieval university. Today, at a typical American university, moral service survives at the special grace of society while material service thrives. In spite of this relatively insignificant role in contemporary American society, the university faculty primarily devoted to—or specialized in—moral service has been retained in the current academic structure as philosophers, art teachers, writers, sociologists, historians, and others in the liberal arts curriculum. Whether by foresight or as lip service to moral values in society, the moral faculty is protected by tenure and coexists with its more prosperous material faculty.

In one capacity or another all functional professors are engaged in the production and maintenance of material service. In spite of its seeming complexity, the production and management of material service in society is a relatively well defined, if not entirely simple, task. The complexity of manufacturing a nuclear bomb is simple compared to the task of deciding *whether* the bomb should be manufactured at all. Every functional faculty member, whether a chemist or an accountant, works in a capacity that contributes to the production and maintenance of material service. Providing this service is an end in itself. No chemist would ever agonize over why he must do this or that chemistry work. One particular task may be more personally interesting or involving, but the distinction is minute. The functional professor does whatever he is trained and told to do. The seeming complexity of technological production in material service is the complexity of *organization*, not of technology itself. It is the invariable fact of human nature as an organism, however, that functional professors must take this work fairly seriously, and as a whole they have done well.

Academic professors engage in moral service as their primary task. As a task, it is an entirely different order of things. It approximates the Pandora's box more closely than a task. For moral service is really none other than the promotion of happiness for community, society, and humanity. The complexity of the task is so enormous that there is no way it can be adequately described. The academic professor confronts in his reason for daily being the sum total of events in human history: man's wars, heartbreaks, sorrows, suffering, witchhunts, tears, wrongful deaths, tragedies, art, culture, ideas, arguments, politics, laws, thievery, violence, greed, injustice, untruth, treachery, betrayal, deceit, corruption, conquests, slavery, servitude, waste, and so on, intermittently graced with short reminders of happiness. In view of this, it would be the height of absurdity to think that an academic professor should insist on his expertise in this or that specialty. He is engaged in discovering reasons for, explaining, describing, attempting to prevent or reduce, these events for the sake of human happiness. That he happens to be a philosopher, a sociologist, an artist, or whatever, working in different academic departments, is entirely irrelevant. As a professor, he deals with either material comfort or moral salvation. There is no other choice. That his task is too large or too difficult is his practical problem, not a problem of definition. He must deal with the whole or nothing. Dealing but poorly with the whole range of human happiness is still preferable to doing one tiny special task well.

A material scientist's accomplishment is measured by the result; an academic scholar's by his effort. The former's task, if done properly, bears results; the latter's rarely bears such fruit. The former's is rewarded in market value; the latter's in tenure, academic freedom, and truth.

That the moral issue of happiness is difficult to deal with, or that there can be no clear end result in one's effort to deal with it, is precisely the reason why there exist tenure, academic freedom, and pursuit of the truth. Otherwise, the issue would have simply been relegated to the material professor, as it is threatened often by the philistines among us. The ambiguity of the academic professor's task today is inherent in the ambiguity of his own existence: he must convince himself and others, especially his functional colleagues, that happiness is a moral issue, not a material one.

The task may be simply stated, but its difficulty is enormous. I say he must convince *himself* first because it is perhaps the most daunting task he faces himself. It is daunting because he must think and act *as* an academic professor, not as a material scientist. It is obviously easier said than done. Once this is accomplished, the second problem takes care of itself. The inferiority complex that the academic professor must overcome on campus on a daily basis, in relation to the more prosperous and somewhat pompous functional colleagues, needs no reiteration. In a startling reversal of tradition in a predominently materialistic world, it is now the academic professor who must scramble to find a niche for himself in the university community and society at large. Often he feels he does not belong. So he does what comes naturally to him: he *imitates* his functional colleagues by thinking and acting like a material professor. He borrows their language of science and business, their frame of mind, sometimes donning a white coat if it helps, and identifies subconsciously with *their* issues. In his wretched state of inferiority, like Veblen's footman imitating his master, he subtly adopts the mindset of a groveling Yahoo rather than that of an independent and free scholar. He offers his pitifully limited or nonexistent market skill, such as poll-taking for a new local bakery or bank, for a pittance thrown his way. Thus, his honest uselessness, which liberates him to pursue the truth, becomes dishonestly useful in the most pitiful and despicable way.2

Supposing that this almost impossible self-conquest is accomplished and that the academic professor recognizes his primary task in moral service, he must now convince the world that happiness is a not a material issue. The first task is really a spiritual struggle against oneself, preparatory to the second. The second is the substantive, intellectual one of taking one's case to the world. This task is much more urgent to the academic professor than it appears. Once the present belief in identifying happiness with material service is accepted—which is increasingly likely nowadays—the academic professor's whole reason for being disintegrates. He exists in tenured comfort only because a smattering of resistance to that idea still remains. But the avalanche of the materialist interpretation of happiness is irresistible as a historical force. Evidence is everywhere that moral service, after all, may be material service well performed. But persuading the world otherwise is not only for the survival of happiness as a moral issue. It is also for the survival of the academic professor himself. Once material service and moral service are thought one and the same, the academic professor has seen the last of his own existence. His job is nothing less than convincing the world that happiness is to be found in truth, not in materialism. He has no other choice: tenure has been granted to him for that task and nothing else; academic freedom has been declared unconditionally for that task and nothing else; pursuit of the truth has been mandated for that task and nothing else. If not, he must quit his academic post and join a bureaucracy or a corporation, or start a new career as a functional professor.

The primary instrument in the pursuit of truth is, of course, *ideas*. As opposed to *things*, ideas are defined by other ideas. Ideas arise from other ideas. Ideas are ultimately defended or disputed by other ideas. Ideas exist in the company of other ideas in history. Things do not change society; ideas do. Computers do not change society; the human purpose (bigger profits, more effective war-making, greater comfort and ease) to which they are put does. Money does not determine human behavior; the idea the human being attaches to it does. No matter how seemingly complex, things are resolved by time and repetition. But ideas do not evolve naturally from simple to complex. Nor are they resolved by time and repetition. Things are replaced by other things naturally, through evolution and obsolescence. Ideas are replaced by other ideas socially, through revolution and force. From the smallest routine in the daily socialization of a child to the most brutal tyranny, struggle for ideas goes on.

The most profound ideas are those that would create the most profound changes in human attitudes and actions. It is these ideas that the unjust authorities fear and suppress. It is these ideas that a free society requires for its own evolutionary benefit. It is these ideas that tenure protects, academic freedom explores, and truth mandates. In an unfree society academic professors are pressured *not* to deal with such ideas; complying, they become the subservient tools of tyranny. In a free society academic professors are *guaranteed* the freedom to deal with such ideas; complying, they become free guardians of truth and moral service.

Under the present habit of mind both functional and academic professors converge on a method in pursuit of "the truth," namely, research. It is through research that the former maintain their claim to accustomed authority and the latter their tenuous status in the scientific community. But functional research and academic "research" are two entirely different things. Even the term "research" is borrowed by academic fields from functional fields to appear useful, scientific, and functional. By being busily engaged in one kind of research or another the academic professor seeks his possible link to prestige, higher salary, and self-fulfillment. Of course, this not only makes him thoroughly useless for pursuit of truth and moral service, it corrupts him as well. But the desire for research is pervasive among academics. What is indeed this thing called research, and how is it related to the academic imperative of truth?

Research carried out by functional professors—whether in science, business, or literacy tests—is geared to produce useful facts. The degree of usefulness determines the willingness with which research is facilitated. All research costs money, and money becomes available or tight depending on the potential usefulness of the facts so produced. Thus, in functional fields the very existence, the very function, of research is tied to its usefulness. Its usefulness is determined in the marketplace or in the national interest for survival. Funtional researchers have often been criticized for serving such obviously utilitarian ends.[3] But it is their job. It is eminently unfair to critize them for doing what they are supposed to do. All research in functional fields is subservient to the purpose and the cost that dictates its existence.

By the same token, there is no such thing as an autonomous functional professor, for he is tied to his field, which is tied to the usefulness of the marketplace. The current lierture on tenure and academic freedom routinely, and quite erroneously, includes research freedom among the freedoms of academia. Research freedom is not academic freedom and cannot claim the immunity the latter can. Society may value all science, but it watches what costs. There is no such thing as freedom if it involves somebody else's money. (The freedom guaranteed in tenure and academic freedom is for truth, not research, and is an entirely different issue. For it involves principle, not utility.) All research is carried out to produce specific results as against cost, and its utility is a matter for the investor to decide, not the researcher. As far as the cost analysis is concerned, the researcher is but a functional tool. He who pays the piper calls the tune, unless the piper is a free artist. No functional researcher is a free artist.

Assuming for the time being no distinction between functional research and academic "research," to the extent that the latter imitates the former, we may observe certain pertinent points about research in general. Any knowledge produced by research cannot determine its result in advance. Whatever the outcome, it must be determined by the research procedure itself, not the purpose intended by the researcher who assumes on probability or his investor who hopes on possibility. Although the origin of a particular research project (the first atomic bomb, the feasibility of another bakery in town) may have been conceived by a specific purpose, the result is helplessly dependent on the research procedure itself. An unsoundly built bomb will not go off; a poorly started bakery will not prosper. Most researchers, both functional and academic, have adjusted to this fact of life. They may be elated or disappointed with the result, but only in terms of what they expected *within* the hypothesis of research procedures. Alchemy and voodoo have no place in modern scientific research. The researcher is prepared to accept any outcome, and indeed he must. By the same token, a researcher who interjects his personal views into his research—say, a stock analyst who favors a particular outcome and therefore deliberately mishandles his research—will not have the opportunity to handle another research project.

Naturally researchers, whether functional or academic, display little or no personal attachment to their current research projects. Since every research project costs money, they must select those projects from among the possibilities within their specialties that are most likely to get funding. No personal favoritism need apply here. When a chemist wishes to do research on the calcification process of crabs but is persuaded by his granting agency to do it on oysters, he is not going to be terribly disappointed. After all, he has no (and should not have any) personal attachment to crabs as opposed to oysters. It is not quite like asking an aspiring philosopher to become an accountant. As any outcome is acceptable to the researcher, any research topic is also acceptable as well. When a man is passionately committed to an idea, it is unlikely to be advanced by research or money as its primary factor. Nor is he likely to accept the outcome that negates his commitment. Research is thus neither committed to nor predetermined by its outcome. With minor quibbles over detail, one research project is pretty much like another, and one outcome pretty much like another. From the investor's point of view, all reseachers are interchangeable. From the researcher's point of view, all outcomes and projects are interchangeable. If all research projects were abolished from campus, it is doubtful anyone would go insane. They would have to find some new hobbies to fill the time.

But academic "research" is slightly different, or ought to be different. Whereas functional research is carried out, and its outcome produced, primarily through the investment of money, academic research is carried out in pursuit of the truth. But research and truth are unrelated for the reasons I described above. Truth is a personal commitment that cannot be altered by funding preconditions, scientific procedures, or contradictory facts. An economist of the market orientation does not abandon his field because the market economy is found to cause social misery. No commissar of a centrally planned economy abandons his belief because of some inconvenient facts. Both capitalism and communism are ideas, and they will only be persuaded by another idea equally or more powerful. Truth is a belief, not a fact, and no amount of research will affect it. It is never found through research; it is never abandoned through research. It is likely to emerge through the most unscientific of all sources: heroes, grandparents, preachers, fictions, movies, propaganda, upbringing.

A sociologist may think of himself a scientist and act scientific, but what made him a sociologist in the first place is no science. That, not science, has determined how he subsequently fares as a sociologist. Whatever he thinks of himself in the accepted image of a scientist has nothing to do with the validity of his thinking. An idea that depends on the outcome of research is, of course, no idea. Not only are ideas unrelated to research outcomes, but they also *direct* the outcome of research if research is ever involved. In the service of ideas, facts are insignificant. It is therefore inevitable for us to separate functional research from academic "research." For what may be called academic research, carried out by academic professors, is sham, apology, or trivia. Not only that, academic research is easily the worst offense to academic freedom and truth.

Truth in ideas becomes irritating to orthodoxy only because it bears the mark of a particular person or group. Research, whether functional or academic, bears no such personal identity. The outcome is solely the function of the research procedure, which is the function of the very nature of science. Science, not the scientist, produces the outcome. Whether one likes it or not is beside the point. Only in the most barbaric of ages was the messenger killed for bringing the message. No scientist is ever blamed for having produced a certain research result. But every academic professor who has been in trouble with orthodoxy has been blamed personally for having espoused the idea. No self-respecting academic can simply blame his "research" for the unpleasant outcome.

Now I am prepared to reach a conclusion on the basis of what has been said: Anyone who does conventional research, either in a functional field or in an academic field, in the mold of material science and in the cause of material service, stands to forfeit tenure and academic freedom and ultimately renders himself irrelevant to truth. Why would a research professor need protection from tenure and academic freedom when his utterances are wholly the product of his research, not his own? Why would any reasonable orthodoxy be upset when new facts are entirely the procedures of the orthodoxy itself?

There is no such thing as research freedom in the same way there is no freedom *in* research. For every research project operates under conditions that are not the researcher's own making. Consider that (1) every research project costs as against its benefit, (2) every research outcome is independent of the intention, and (3) every research project produces facts, either useful or not so useful. Tenure protects academic freedom, and academic freedom pursues the truth. No truth pursued, then no academic freedom is needed. No academic freedom exercised, then no need for tenure as a principle applied to academic freedom. Researchers may indulge in any research project their skill and money would allow, and they may accept any outcome their procedures would produce. But they may not claim tenure privilege on the account that theirs is in pursuit of the truth that requires special protection against orthodoxy. Why, they *are* the orthodoxy.

Academic freedom is freedom of mind, not of material resource. An academic professor is granted the freedom to use his mind any way he wishes in the interest of truth. Use of material resource is a decision for the allocating agency: citizens, government, industry, donors, universities, whatever has a stake in the outcome. The academic mind, now freed and protected to pursue the truth, only belongs to the academic professor himself. When he engages in research, however, he negates this very agreement and in consequence forfeits that very privilege. Then he is subject to the judgment of the market value his research may bring in, not under the false assumption that he is in pursuit of the truth by honoring tenure privilege in academic freedom. Not in the moral service of truth, whether the professor be functional or academic, tenure is in demand by the professor only as protection for his sloth, incompetence, or self-interest. The principle is too precious for that sort of misuse. One does not throw pearls before swine.

There are no grants or fundings to produce truth. There is only tenure for that. What does truth cost? For the society, tenure and academic freedom. For the individual academic professor protected by tenure and guaranteed freedom of thought, nothing. It is normally argued in favor of the professor's right to academic freedom that "It is irrational and unjust to employ a person to do a thing and then to prevent him from doing it."[4] It is equally irrational and unjust to insist upon that freedom only to waste it. Any sign that this absolute privilege may be misused or, worse yet, unused is cause enough to argue for the abolition of tenure altogether.

NOTES

1. Thorstein Veblen, quoted in Richard Hofstadter and Walter P. Metzger, *The Development of Academic Freedom in the United States* (New York: Columbia University Press, 1965), 452.

2. Confusion has been the rule, not the exception. In the same paragraph defining truth, Arthur DeBardeleben mentions "facts," "observations," "investigations," "cogitations," "things," and "concepts," among others. See Arthur DeBardeleben, "The University's External Constituency," in *Dimensions of Academic Freedom*, eds. Walter P. Metzger, Edmund L. Pincoffs (Urbana: University of Illinois Press, 1969), 72–73.

3. One of the classic criticisms of material research is in C. Wright Mills, "Two Styles of Social Science Research," in *Power, Politics, and People: The Collected Essays of C. Wright Mills*, ed. Irving Louis Horowitz (New York: Oxford University Press, 1964), 553–67.

4. Judith Jarvis Thomson, "A Proposed Statement on Academic Freedom," in *The Concepts of Academic Freedom*, ed. Edmund L. Pincoffs (Austin, TX: University of Texas Press, 1972), 264. A fuller argument is in Hardy E. Jones, "Academic Freedom as a Moral Right," in Pincoffs, *Concept of Academic Freedom*, 47–48.

Chapter 8

The "Great Truth"

Facts are established tautologically. Truth is established historically. Facts become factual by being in agreement with given reality, either in nature (material facts, such as gravity or mathematics) or in society (social facts, such as black-white income difference). All truth becomes true only by becoming *historically* true. That all men are created equal is neither material nor social fact. But it is held true historically. There is nothing wrong with disagreeing with this truth. The man who disagrees with it would only be historically wrong. He might as well be in another historical era. That all men are created equal, like other such "truths," is held true only as a *living* truth, continually reexamined, debated, and renewed as living doctrine and social policy. An academic professor's job exists essentially within that tradition and nowhere else. For society improves and civilization moves forward only through such processes.

In the preceding pages we have seen ways to avoid untruth. In the following pages we shall complete our progress by searching for ways to find the truth.

All truth, historical or otherwise, begins as a personal vision, an idea, a problem to be resolved. By the same token, all true scholarship begins with the scholar himself. Material facts march on unceasingly as collective events, through some revolutionary breakthoughs, but the scholar's truth always begins as a solitary act. His only companion and guide are other scholars past and present. It is lonely and solitary. But the first words, concepts, or articulations must emerge from the scholar's own mind. Material facts may be helped by laboratories and computers; the scholar is on his own with his ideas to be shaped into truth, and eventually into historical truth.

All historical ideas are made up of the sum total of these processes. The mysterious ways in which history seems to materialize to our contemporary neatness have to do with its sheer size. The history of ideas is too large for a single person to dominate or control, and it tends to overwhelm even a well educated person. But it is not impossible to simplify, and no understanding is possible without simplifying.

First, the subjective element (the scholar's idea) begins the process by discovering a problem, a conflict to be resolved. The realization of a problem requires that some aspects of social reality (moral, political, economic, whatever) must be reformulated into words, concepts, and thoughts—or to put it another way, ideas. Although the "problem" originates in the mundane world in which humanity resides, for the scholar the mundane world is several times removed from what is generally observed in everyday life. A slave owner may be concerned about the rising or falling price of slaves; the scholar thinks about the system of slavery or, more removed, the very character of human nature.

What triggers the scholar's mind may be anything that defies immediate, easy solutions within the established routines of society. No serious scholar will trouble himself with automobile fatalities on the highway or with a more efficient operation of a factory. These are problems that can be resolved, as far as they are materially possible, within the available solutions of society. These are not "scholarly" problems. The scholar's problem is no less *real* than the mundane world's. But his *reality* is many times removed from that of the mundane world's, ideally as close to the root of things as possible. To the mundane, such problems seem remote and irrelevant, and the mundane mind would not trouble itself with scholarly problems. That is why tenure and academic freedom are not made available to bricklayers or bankers. Of course, there is a fine line between a scholar wrestling with a real problem in a removed way (political discontent, cultural issues, economic injustice, artistic inspiration, psychological strains in a historical, theoretical way) and a scholar who is removed from reality (either in extreme scholasticism or equally extreme scientism). At any rate, aroused by the problem, the scholar first begins to define his own thoughts, examines the thoughts of others before him, and considers the interrelations among these elements. He thinks, reads, and talks about the problem. At a certain stage, he has completed his subjective inquiry into the matter and has come to a definite conclusion. He has found the truth—large or small—about the problem. Thus, the subjective period of an idea ends.

Second, the scholar's definition of a problem and its solution—or his "truth"—now enters its "objectifying" stage. He states his "truth" as he has found it. A successful idea—whether a philosophy or an artwork—leaves its audience in a dilemma. To go on with conservative inertia is to confront the illogical. A powerful truth would make conservative inertia, though a natural reaction, too painful to adopt. Thereby successful and powerful, the new truth will now be recognized by others around him, in the larger community, society, and humanity as it becomes known as worthy of wider recognition. His truth may find its way to supporters, followers, and even zealots who are persuaded to think about that part of reality in the symbolic and theoretical way the scholar has described it. The idea is aired and shared, and desirable actions (for ideas always require actions) are mapped out and initiated. They attack the problem by gathering strength, winning battles of ideas over opposition or changing their own opinions. Their triumph now becomes a new reality, which either alters or replaces that part of existing reality. New thoughts are formed; new social policies are initiated; and new habits of mind emerge as naturally as old habits of mind in their own time and place. Thus, subjectivity has become objectified through the workings of ideas and persuasion.

Large or small, every new idea gains its status as a "truth" in this way. Force or chance has no place in this, for neither is an idea. Slavery requires no idea's persuasion; it only requires force. Nor does gender, for its determination is purely by chance. Only a false scholar, like a dictator's pet apologist, would support anything associated with force or chance. Force and chance are the antithesis of ideas, thoroughly repugnant to the scholarly mind.

Not all battles of ideas go as smoothly as described above. Inertia of the mind and of social habits cannot be underestimated. Eventually, new ideas become stronger than any force of inertia. But the new ideas are not received kindly just because they are new. New ideas that alter or replace known reality are always critical to it, and they are likely to be unpopular. Irritated or threatened, the authorities may go to extreme lengths to punish the idea and the idea-creator. Scholars and heretics have suffered no less than defeated soldiers and vanquished tribes. (Thankfully, in our more advanced state of things, scholars and heretics are given tenure and academic freedom just to guarantee the sanctity of such unpopular truth.) The new idea has to contend not only with old institutionalized habits, or conservative inertia, but also with other competition. Semitruths or untruths abound in any society and era. Often respectable scholars subscribe to such notions. There are hypocrites, liars, sycophants, false prophets, hangers-on, and simply corrupt individuals among learned men and women. Universities have their share among their academic professors. More likely than not, they occupy powerful positions as controllers of ideas and resource. They set up the gauntlet, in tenure evaluation and publication decisions, that junior scholars must go through as the most difficult part of their scholarly survival. Be that as it may, an easy life for a scholar would not require tenure or academic freedom to protect it. Popular and inconsequential ideas may be easily accepted. But they are just as easily dismissed and forgotten. No scholarship is more easily dismissed and forgotten than that which is irrelevant to reality or redundant in daily experience, however popular it might have been at the time.

Finally, some ideas survive, prosper, and solidify as uncontestable historical facts. That all men are created equal, once a heretical idea, is almost universally accepted as true. This universal acceptance is of course an historical acceptance. As history changes, the acceptance changes. But such changes are uncommon. As revolutions are rare, truth endures, even through some revolutionary changes. They are so entrenched historically that only the most foolish or iconoclastic would consider it possible to challenge such established historical truths as "democracy" in the modern era, or "the marketplace" in a capitalist society, or "socialism" in a socialist society, or Beethoven's "Fifth," or Shakespeare's "Hamlet." Even those who may disagree with any of these ideas cannot dispute the universal existence of these "truths."

These and other such ideas are so universally accepted and recognized that disputing them would be like disputing $2 + 2 = 4$, and that, more seriously, nations will go to war to assert them. But like all such ideas, each began as a subjective idea in someone's mind, fought its way through resistance, and gained acceptance.[1] Now as historical truth, to deny it is almost as irrational and contradictory as denying gravity or mathematical equations.

But the certainty of market economy's superiority is not like the certainty of gravity. Nor is the certainty of socialism's triumph on the same level as mathematical certainty. These ideas are accepted and established only *historically*, meaning temporarily, artificially, and arbitrarily. This distinction is simple but significant. Scholarship would be impossible without its recognition. It is with the recognition of this simple truth—that all historical truths are temporary, artificial, and arbitrary— that scholars define their task. History and ideas give scholars their work to do: transforming their own private vision into historical truth; examining all existing truths honestly and independently; modifying and altering them wherever necessary and inevitable; and disseminating to students, other scholars, and the public what they regard as cardinal truths beneficial to community, society, and humanity. More than anything else, scholarship is nothing short of history-making, and scholars nothing short of history-makers. For history is ideas. In this way the scholar creates and reshapes history and the world.

But all historical truths eventually either corrupt, adopted by the interest of the status quo, or are taken for granted, thereby made irrelevant as a historical force. All men may be created equal, but equality corrupts in reckless competition or becomes irrelevant in mindless repetition. Every idea must be renewed, re-examined, or discarded. Doing it is scholarship. Not doing it is either sloth, sycophancy, or mediocrity, or most likely all these.

Not all truths are equally beneficial to humanity. Not all selfless pursuits result in historically important ideas. Some are better than others. In every school of ideas there are leaders, supporters, and followers. Not every scholar creates ideas. Not every idea merits equal consideration on the continuously changing stages of history. Into the cruel graveyard of history many ideas once great and memorable have fallen and been forgotten. Those that survive and still exercise their influence upon the later world are called "great ideas." It is history's way of sifting contending ideas and preserving the very best for posterity. Pursuing the truth, therefore, largely consists of learning about and from these great ideas. A good scholar is one who is familiar with them and has incorporated them into his own private vision.

Average minds can and do participate in the ongoing production and research of facts. Scientific geniuses or brilliant accountants contribute to the progress of material facts and comfortable life. But theirs is almost instantly superceded by the later, more advanced facts and progress. Modern telephone company laboratories have no use for the technology that Alexander Graham Bell created. Nor is modern cinematography anything like what Thomas Edison envisioned. Students of modern telephones need not study Bell any more than need the modern mathematicians study Sir Isaac Newton. In every scientific field and research laboratory, the founder is made irrelevant and forgotten by the march of time and repetition. Even the most prized scientific discovery, such as the double helix, races against time and repetition, for many others are similarly close to its discovery. If it is not one person, it is another. Sooner or later, all are resolved, if they are resolvable at all, by time and repetition.

But such is not the case with historical truth. The greatest truth is always exactly as the original mind has created it. No one will say that Plato has been made irrelevant by the later generation of Platonic scholars. Unlike the laboratory technician, the student of idealism studies Plato. Without Plato, there is no Platonic idealism.

Average minds search and create average ideas. Great minds search and create great ideas. Average ideas are dismissed and forgotten. Great ideas endure. It is doubtful if any of the professional journals and books produced today by scholars would remain as historical documents, and the truth embodied in them as historical truth. More likely than not, they are forgotten as soon as they leave the printer's hand. This chilling thought should give our modern-day scholars pause for their meaning of life. Good scholars have read about great ideas and are comfortable in the presence of great minds. Poorly prepared scholars are in general not very well read beyond the professional "literature" in their specialities. Their vision tends to be narrow; their personal character deficient; their interest mostly self-serving as a result.

Material facts rely on average minds for their production and consumption. But in truth, *average truth* is thoroughly useless as moral service and irrelevant as social guide. An average chemist or an average accountant is all chemistry or accountancy requires. But truth must be good, useful, and relevant, or it has no reason for being. Few things are more unmemorable than a truth superceded by average experience. Functional fields are made up of average facts produced by average minds; the very nature of material facts produced in these fields necessitates the imperative of averages. But in truth, average truths may as well not exist. There is nothing as meaningless or useless as an "average" philosopher or sociologist. Their average truths would be no more useful or forceful than the utterances of a man at a local bar spouting his philosophy or social commentary. Normally it is this average scholarship produced by academics, instantly superceded by the man at a local bar, that invites public ridicule and derision.

As average truth is no truth at all, average scholarship is no scholarship at all. Either one deals with important truth or one becomes irrelevant. Truth simply cannot tolerate average truths. Routinely conducted research projects, duly published in established journals, officially recognized as one's professional contribution, and placed on one's curriculum vita as an achievement, are simply destined to the dustbins of history at the moment they are produced. Not only do these professors produce no truth at all, but they are searching for it in the *wrong* place. Great ideas have already been produced, sifted, and preserved for them in history.

A scholar will benefit much more by spending one hour with a great mind in the library than one year with an average mind on an island. The scholar learns much from a mind better than his; he learns nothing from a mind like his own or lower. The scholar learns the most from the best historical mind. There is no reason to look elsewhere than in history's well-preserved great ideas. Only a shallow scholar and a still shallower man will presume that his new research results replace or supercede the ideas of the giants in his field who preceded him. Much of good scholarship thus involves getting acquainted or reacquainted with such great minds.

Good scholarship is made possible, although it hinges on individual subjectivity, by a strange tendency in history. There is a tendency among great ideas to converge. All great ideas tend to be similar. There is good reason to believe that the Good Society, and Happy Life in it, envisioned by Socrates, Jesus, Lincoln, and Gandhi is really the *same* one. All have identified self-interest as the enemy of the Good Society and Happy Life. All have valued honest and independent truth as essential to human salvation. Likewise, all honestly and independently pursued truth tends to converge on a simple set of principles. And these principles tend to be fairly similar, if not identical, to one another. All honest and independent minds tend to admire other honest and independent minds and learn from one another's honesty and independence of mind. Great minds produce great ideas as their response to the problems of their particular age. Although the particulars may be different, their problems have always been the basic problems of mankind: how to build the Good Society and Happy Life. Honestly and independently pursued, the truth they arrive at tends to converge on fairly simple rules of life. The problems of society and life today are no different from those of earlier eras. The truth that modern scholars must pursue is no different from that of those periods.

Contemporary professional scholars tend to think of their knowledge as fairly unbiased in character and rational in acquisition. Their confidence is so great, in fact, that they rarely question the character or acquisition of their present frame of mind. Every academic professor carries on with his academic routines blithely ignorant of his own bias. Economist Joan Robinson has said that it is as difficult for a man to realize his bias as to smell his own breath.[2] Nothing is more difficult for an academic than to try to pursue the truth when he has no ideas about what he already knows to be true. There is no need to invoke the authority of Socrates, for he has made it absolutely undeniable truth that truth begins with self-knowledge. By the same token, we must also admit that all true knowledge is self-knowledge. What one discovers about the Good Society and Happy Life is, after all, about oneself. All truth one pursues leads sooner or later to truth about oneself. Self-interest instinctively protects one's bias. That is why a selfish man rarely learns anything valuable in life. Repeated experience, still protected by self-interest, can teach him nothing new.

There are only two ways one can have one's own frame of mind as it is. It is acquired either by default through upbringing or by conscious persuasion. Contrary to their self-image, most academics' minds are made up already by default. Their early socialization has already determined what they are and what little philosophy they may have about the Good Society and Happy Life. By and large, what they know is what they have been taught when they were young. Education, especially graduate education, may affect them slightly but not much and not everyone. With rare exceptions, they remain throughout their adult lives exactly as they have been as children. Their later, more articulate defense is simply a professionalized refinement of their earlier bias. Prevented by the protective shield of self-interest, they normally see no reason why they should examine their own beliefs and lives. It takes no genius to realize that this is so. Most scholars at American universities think, act, and are *American*. Only the most outrageously alienated American scholars, such as Thorstein Veblen and C. Wright Mills, have been able to overcome this burden. As a result, most American scholars remain exactly as they are expected to remain, basically as they have been brought up as children. These children grow up to be nice, "conservative" average American scholars.

The persuasive route, like the one taken by Veblen and Mills, is an exception to the rule of socialization. Here, the scholar makes a heroic attempt to liberate hismelf from the orbit of his earlier childhood bias, which consists of his parents, his preacher, his teachers and professors, television commercials and political appeals, and most of all, his own self-interested inertia. He examines himself thoroughly; he questions orthodoxy, even that of his own professors; and he overcomes his worst enemy, namely, his self-interest. American Marxists, without Marxist upbringing, are good examples of this. They have embraced Marxism, good or bad, because they have been persuaded by Karl Marx's ideas. In doing so, they have had to overcome all that they have believed, known, and liked, in fact everything that made up their whole being. They smelled their own breath and, for one reason or another, they did not like the smell. In this and other similar instances, one takes his significant step toward truth. Honesty and independence of mind require that one be free from oneself. But self-denial is extraordinarily difficult to accomplish. Most people, scholars included, prefer to remain dishonest with their bias and dependent on existing reality. Hence, most scholars prefer to remain dishonest and unfree by default.

When these dishonest and unfree professors write textbooks, they establish the "substantive" orthodoxy of the field. Many untenured teachers are dismissed for not covering such orthodoxy adequately. There emerges an agreement among these professors on what such orthodoxy should be, which is then gradually solidified as the field's substantive knowledge. One quick look at all the textbooks in any academic field makes it obvious that they are all cut from the same mold. They are the manifestoes of professors who write down their bias by default as truth. They are what they have learned about the Good Society and Happy Life as children. Fundamentally, what they think or say as professors is no different from what they would have babbled as children, only more refined and articulate. These professors of orthodoxy then expect all untenured juniors to follow their orthodoxy or get axed. In this way, they make an honest and independent pursuit of the truth impossible for everyone.

But of course in all academic fields there is no such thing as substantive knowledge or orthodoxy. An economics textbook assumes the market model as the good thing because economics professors have been brought up to think that way. A sociology textbook assumes American society as the model of all societies and goes ahead with its description of what all societies must look like. A moral philosopher discusses John Rawls while being imperiously ignorant of the assumptions in his model of justice. Assumptions are unnecessary in functional fields. A chemist accepts the nature of things and goes on from there. An accountant only counts money according to the rules of money-counting that his society has established for him. He does not and should not question the rules of money-counting any more than does the chemist the rules of nature. Not questioning them does not make the chemist or the accountant incompetent. Not questioning, however, makes the economist, sociologist, or philosopher dishonest and unfree, and makes the "truth" he speaks and teaches the incompetent babble of a child. Once the rules are questioned, the game may not go on as usual, and it is a quite inconvenient for him. The dishonest and unfree professor of orthodoxy thus sacrifices truth for his little routine convenience as a safe but inconsequential parasite blithely living off tenure and academic freedom.

Since there cannot be substantive orthodoxy in any academic field that does not verge on fraud, textbooks should be explicitly banned from all academic fields in the interest of truth. Textbooks are possible only when the field's knowledge and knowledge-production can be standardized and routinized. That possibility has historically coincided with the process of professionalization. A field becomes a profession only when the possibility of standardization and routinization exists. All functional fields exist as professional fields because of this very possibility. After all, chemistry is the same both in the United States and in the Soviet Union. So is counting money. But the imitation of functional fields by academic fields has created standardization and routinization as substantive knowledge in each field. And it is written into textbooks as orthodoxy. Obviously, this task cannot be accomplished without academic fraud. But when everyone is guilty of fraud, the honest and independent becomes the guilty. Fraudulent textbooks pass for the field's manifesto of truth. Not surprisingly, textbook-writing is normally undertaken by the most average of all professors in each field.

One of the common assumptions that comforts the professor in his pursuit of the untruth is that academic business is neutral. In this he obviously confuses objectivity with neutrality, and truth with orthodoxy. One must be objective enough to see reality as it is. But this objectivity is not the same as detachment, the idea that one is not really involved personally or otherwise with the object of one's thought. Objectivity is achieved through *dis*interest (or selflessness), not through *no* interest, which is what is meant by neutrality when the professor uses the term. Instead of pursuing the truth actively, now the professor assumes that if he just stays neutral, truth will be obtained naturally in the way things are done through standard and routine procedures. In this way his lack of interest in objectivity is covered up by "neutrality," and his inability to pursue the truth by his reliance on orthodoxy, which is in turn a product of professional standardization and routinization.

However, no truth is neutral. Nor is society itself ever neutral. Truth states a specific belief. Society represents a specific system of beliefs. All truths must contend with other truths, as all societies must with other societies. An objective scholar, not a detached one, overcomes his own self-interest and his own upbringing in pursuit of the truth. A neutral scholar is overcome by the conservative inertia of self-interest and socialization and, in the name of neutrality, does nothing. By doing nothing he accepts the conditions of society and humanity as they are and partakes in the perpetuation of untruth in the name of professional orthodoxy. There is no moral incompetent quite like a neutral professor. He is guaranteed economic security for life and academic freedom for thought so that he may speak the truth as he sees it. Yet he sees nothing and speaks nothing. As a neutral man he cannot pursue the truth because no truth is neutral. In the pompous comfort of tenure privilege, however, he is shielded by dishonest neutrality and protected by untrue orthodoxy. Thus, by making a mockery of the meaning of academic freedom and truth, the corrupt professor succeeds in living out another day of parasitic existence. His academic field, useless to begin with, fails once again to make itself useful in pursuit of the truth. Tenure and academic freedom are, needless to say, also wasted in the process.

A neutral professor not only fails to teach the great ideas that have survived historical judgment. He teaches false truth as truth by relying on orthodoxy. An honest and independent professor makes clear to himself and to his students what his basic beliefs are. Only by becoming clear about his own beliefs can he protect himself and his students from his own bias. One who pretends to be neutral and objective invariably calls on orthodoxy—namely, the textbook—as his source of truth. Thus, he fools himself with false objectivity and deceives his students with untrue orthodoxy. All the time he prides himself on taking the "objective approach" in his teaching and derides his juniors for being biased.

The dishonest and unfree professor is also a scrupulous observer of "scientific" methods and "rational" discourses. But he altogether fails to realize that whatever is produced by scientific methods and rational discourses *cannot* be truth. For science and rationality, understood in this context, only produce what is perfectly harmless and neutral fact, whether material or social. Facts produced by a scrupulous observation of scientific and rational procedures cannot possibly be offensive to anyone, much less threatening to the authorities or causing popular discontent. It takes money to produce facts, not tenure or academic freedom. Only passionately held views, when voiced as one's truth, get in trouble and therefore need tenure protection and academic freedom for expression. Professor John R. Searle perhaps innocently calls for "methodological and rationalistic" assumptions for valid knowledge "as opposed to dogma or speculation" to define academic freedom.[3] He would certainly be surprised to hear my argument that methodological and rationalistic procedures only produce facts (which is perhaps what he has in mind), which hardly *requires* the kind of academic freedom he sincerely advocates.

In the imitation of functional fields, many academics find comfort in scientific methods and rational procedures. As long as they pretend to be useful scientists (they hope), the rest will take care of itself. But this is, of course, not only erroneous as a concept but also a dangerous self-delusion. With rare exceptions, so rare as to be nonexistent, all the scientific researches carried out, all the books written, all the journal articles published, all the papers presented at professional meetings by academics in recent decades put together would amount to *almost nothing* as a contribution to science. As a contribution to truth, *absolutely nothing*. (I mean to include in this estimate the generous portion contributed by psychologists who are certainly more advanced in "science" than other academic specialists.) In scientific and rational fields, the professor cannot possibly use academic freedom even if he *wanted* to. What freedom can a physicist possibly use in his scientific and rational research? He cannot operate against nature as matter in motion even if he wanted to, not any more than can a free accountant create his own rules of money-counting. Tenured physicists and untenured physicists, academically free accountants and academically unfree accountants, would have to conduct their business exactly alike. But there is a world of difference between a tenured, free sociologist and an untenured, unfree sociologist, *if* truth is the goal. But then, without truth as the goal, we need no sociologist.

Why, then, is truth so important? We will tackle that question in the next few chapters.

NOTES

1. I have used this concept concerning art in Jon Huer, *Art, Beauty, and Pornography: A Journey through American Culture* (Buffalo, N.Y.: Prometheus Books, 1987), 83–85.

2. Joan Robinson, *Economic Philosophy* (Chicago: Aldine, 1962), P. 41.

3. John R. Searle, "Two Concepts of Academic Freedom," in *The Concept of Academic Freedom*, ed. Edmund L. Pincoffs (*Austin, TX*: University of Texas Press, 1972), 88.

Part III

Truth and Society

Chapter 9

The Imperfect Society

Truth through tenure prospers the best in a Gesellschaft-type society. Contemporary American society is its most fitting example. By the same token, there are other societies, especially the Gemeinschaft-type, where tenure-guaranteed truth fares relatively poorly. They have their own ways of getting the truth. But only in American society do we find the peculiarly legalistic, contractual way of getting the truth.

Of the Gemeinschaft societies, three types come readily to mind. The first is the "utopian" societies by design. The Soviet Union until recently, the Amish and the Hutterite communities, and the feudal societies of Europe may belong to this group. Their social system is deemed perfect, either by divine conception or human ingenuity. Truth in these societies *is* the very social system. They would consider it odd to designate a particular segment of the population as having the responsibility of pursuing the truth. For the truth is by tradition equated with their very own way of life.

The second type consists of "totalitarian" societies, theocratic, hereditary, or military. Neither Saudi Arabia nor military dictatorships in Latin America could afford to guarantee an independent pursuit of the truth by their professors or anyone else. Anything they might find would easily be considered a threat to the regime. The fortunes of professors in Latin America, for example, are so intimately tied to the rise and fall of regimes that an independent professoriate is impossible to fathom.

The third type is the "natural" Gemeinschaft society best exemplified by Japan. There is no tenure system in Japanese universities. Yet, no professor seriously worries about his economic security. Upon entering university service a faculty member *assumes* that his job is for life, and the university shares a similar assumption about its employee. It is an assumed rule of conduct. And there is nothing quite as powerful as an assumed rule in restraining human conduct. In this environment, truth cannot be conceived as an objective entity isolated from the whole of society that can be pursued and analyzed through rational investigation. The professor's comfort is thus secured in exchange for his complete surrender of independence. As long as he remains a docile member of the community, on and off campus, he is comfortable and secure. Vigorous social criticisms, therefore, normally come from writers and journalists in Japan, not from the professoriate.

All of these social types share one thing in common: they *believe* theirs is a *perfect* society. The kind of skepticism and uncertainty prevalent in a more open, competitive, voluntary society, a Gesellschaft in the mold of contemporary American society, is deemed neither necessary nor desirable. Hence the absence of tenure, academic freedom, truth, and all their legalistic, rationalistic trappings in these societies.

What would a voluntary, open society do if it wished to improve itself, or perhaps perfect it if possible, according to the ingenuity of human mind and the desire for happiness? On a moment's reflection, a few things are universally obvious.

First, it would select and educate the best and the brightest among its population. These people would be exposed to the best that the heritage of human civilization has preserved. Through this education, they would become *wise* in the way of human nature; *knowledgeable* in the way of actual management of society; and *free* in the way of self-interest that might compromise them. In this way the best and the brightest of the lot will be molded into "super citizens" specifically charged with the task of improving and perfecting their society.

Second, it would specify their task: namely, seeking truth and only the truth that the society *needs* to improve and perfect itself. No lies, no flattery, no false image, no routine orthodoxy. Nothing short of absolute honesty would do. Conformity to human weaknesses may go a long way for a salesman, but it would be contrary to the very purpose of the best and brightest in society. Their job is to improve and perfect their society, not to perpetuate its flaws. And to that end, only the truth about society would do. By definition, however, anything said in order to improve or perfect society is *necessarily a criticism against society*. Nothing will improve in society unless it is told what is wrong with it. That constitutes their "social criticism," and they are the best people to know what is wrong with their society. Social criticism, however beneficial to society and happiness, does not please everyone. This simple fact puts the best and brightest in some jeopardy against public opinion and authority. They might be pressured to compromise the truth. Truth requires courage, and courage entails personal sacrifice. But personal sacrifice for the benefit of truth-telling is not welcomed by everyone, not even by the best and the brightest.

Third, the improving and perfecting society comes up with a solution. It *guarantees*, by the force of law as well as the structure of custom, that *absolutely no harm will come to them for telling the truth*. It would call such an arrangement "tenure," its guarantee "academic freedom," and its ultimate purpose "pursuit of the truth." Now the best and the brightest would freely enjoy their pursuit of the truth without fear of popular pressure, economic insecurity, or compromise of conscience. The guaranteed employment takes place in a specially protected environment called the "university." The task is to think along with history's greatest minds, teach the next generation of the best and the brightest, and write one's conclusions freely and critically. For everyone concerned, society and individuals alike, this arrangement surely is the best of all possible worlds.

Of course, this hypothetical society is none other than contemporary America States and its best and brightest the tenured professors. All is well with this scenario—except one small deviation: professors now begin to abuse the privilege granted by their society with sloth, flattery or apology, and self-interested corruption of mind. Perhaps the most ingenuous and noblest system of self-improvement and self-perfection thus becomes threatened by self-destruction.

Burton Clark identifies the professor as "a special kind of professional man, a type characterized by a particularly high need for autonomy . . . to be innovative, to be critical of established ways."[1] This need for autonomy is rooted in none other than his need for truthful criticism. It is not only the professor's educated and innate urge to tell the truth. It is also his society's *demand* in exchange for the privilege he enjoys in security and freedom that his society grants. It would be a violation of both his own intellectual instinct and his social obligation not to tell the truth that is honest, independent, and by necessity critical. Since it is granted as a special privilege, it entails special preconditions. The professor cannot simply take the privilege without fulfilling its preconditions. In a bygone era of hereditary privilege, the aristocracy could enjoy its privilege without fulfilling its attendant obligation. The French aristocracy, an extreme example of this kind, Alexis de Tocqueville tells us, was eventually destroyed by a populace aroused to this discrepancy.[2]

Much closer to home and our time in American society, many legislators, egged on by their constituency angered by certain professorial conduct, have introduced bill after bill designed to abolish tenure.3

There is a subconscious reluctance on the part of the professor to criticize, for fear that the system granting tenure privilege might *withdraw* it if sufficiently provoked. There are many instances, especially in the 1970s, to remind him of that. But the fear is grounded in his inability to distinguish tenure and academic freedom used properly from those abused. It is the abuse that the populace and the authorities, both in legisture and in university administration, reacted to negatively. As we shall see, *how* to pursue the truth and tell it is as important, if not more, as *what* truth is pursued and told. This fear is as meaningless and self-defeating as saying that protests in South Africa would only hurt the blacks. A free and equal society would be good for blacks *as well as* South Africa itself. Protests serve that function. It is incumbent on the professor to *persuade* his society that truth, however painful at the moment, will benefit all in the end. This persuasion is what constitutes the totality of his scholarship.

A society that cannot afford truth cannot afford tenure. A society that has instituted tenure has obviously decided that it can. A professor who would not render that critical truth does not need the protection that tenure affords and does not deserve the security that tenure accords. To repeat Byse Clark and Louis Joughin's statement so casually ignored: Tenure exists for "the benefit of honest judgment and independent criticism."4 No more than lip service is paid to it simply because the professor is not reminded enough of its significance. As we have seen above, a society that does not need or want the truth does not grant tenure to its professors.

That all societies are imperfect and are in need of critical truth in order to improve or perfect is one thing. That these societies *want* to improve or perfect is quite another. It is no coincidence that American society is perhaps the first, if not the only, society that declared a "perfect union" as its ultimate purpose. A less-than-perfect America is simply unacceptable. In 1894 the Board of Regents of the University of Wisconsin similarly declared in defense of a professor that "We cannot for a moment believe that . . . the present condition of society is perfect. We must therefore welcome from our teachers such discussions as shall suggest the means and prepare the way by which knowledge may be extended, present evils removed and others prevented."5 A professor's timidity of mind, slothfulness in work habits, or apologistic flattery in place of critical truth not only hurt his society that asks for the truth but also harm the professor himself in the long run.

"Truth" that accords well with popular taste and political climate is by definition false. No existing society or institution is perfect, and none is served better by apology. It is entirely possible that our present tenure system is but a window-dressing to calm the volatile discontent among the intellectuals. But this is self-flattery in the extreme. The present tenure system was instituted and solidified at the height of America's political stability and economic prosperity. If anything, the academic professor was at the lowest point of his utility to society. Neither its political stability nor its economic prosperity will suffer without the academic professor. To be sure, present tenure policy may be a noble experiment that only a free, mature society in search of its own perfection can risk. Only the critical truth from the professor will fit into the experimental scheme.

Ultimately, truth improves and perfects society by serving *justice*. Whenever truth is searched, justice is pursued. Whenever truth is spoken, justice is achieved. Truth is criticism, criticism justice. Justice is the ultimate end in the professor's progress to get tenure to be secure, to exercise academic freedom to criticize, and to pursue truth to perfect his society. Our civilized reflection simply demands justice, not injustice, for human happiness. Thus, whatever the professor does is to bring about human happiness in his community, society, and humanity, concretely expressed as justice. Nothing short of this aim justifies his existence in the comfort and security of the Ivory Tower.

All academic fields owe their existence to the simple fact that by and large almost all society is imperfect and almost all humanity unhappy. No scholar can presume to study the conditions of mankind as they exist without some notion of what they *ought* to be like. Most scholars habitually fear the notion of "ought," linking it with some ultimate absolutes that simple humanity cannot comprehend. This is not only absurd as a practical question, but it is also illogical because it is a clear contradiction. Consider the fact that professors are the most complaining members of society. Every complaint materializes simply because, according to professors' perception of things, what *is* is not to their liking. Every complaint is thus evaluated against what *ought* to be. The academic professor presumes to be studying society and human conduct only if he *knows* what he is looking for. A corrupt professor will find it in something already "legitimate," or in something popular, or in something considered orthodox in his profession. An honest, independent, and critical professor will find it on his own and in his own conscience. The former goes for falsehood, the latter for truth. That the "ought" is the guide to all their scholarship, whether false or true, is simply unquestionable. The only question to settle is *where* to locate it: in prefabrication, or in one's own searched truth.

The business of academic truth is always found in the gap between what society *is* and what it *ought* to be. It is the range between best possible and worst probable. A society may improve or perfect itself only if it knows the difference between the two. Pointing out the difference is the task with which the academic professor is specifically charged. Academic fields, especially philosophy and sociology, have always been most dynamic and creative when society was deemed most imperfect. The academic mind has been most galvanized when it is compelled by discontent and the urge to reform and progress.[6] The *whole* of academic mind is and ought to be involved in the ebb and flow of social, political, and cultural development. A chemist will do his lab work either in a capitalist society or a socialist regime, in a stagnant period or in a reformist era, with but a minor adjustment. A philosopher or a sociologist will not and cannot. Depending on the mood of society, his whole life is alive with possibility or is crushed and buried in obsolescence. Consequently, few fusses over academic freedom have ever been raised in functional fields. Almost exclusively the issues have affected the academic men and women, and it is mostly for them that tenure and academic freedom have been instituted. The chemist may deal with imperfect nature but he can do nothing about it. The academic man or woman deals with always-imperfect society, which requires his critical analysis. The former is safe and routine; the latter is fraught with danger and peril.

Whatever may be good for society's improvement and perfection, however, is not always welcome. For all truth, however truthful, hurts. It is often regarded as subversive, "utopian, impractical or pernicious."[7] It may be roundly denounced and ridiculed by moralists or threatened with retaliation by populist politicians and nervous authorities. But this is what is expected of an academic's career. Doing it otherwise, just to be safe, would serve no good at all. It is too bad that a nation once thought most subversive of all, most revolutionary, most forward-looking, is now so weighed down by its own conservative inertia born of long stability and high prosperity. But this is all the more reason why the professor's role in American society is just now so critically important. Most professors would rather have a nice office, teach a few classes, publish inconsequential articles, and stay out of trouble until they retire. But this is not the purpose of tenure and academic freedom, either from the society's viewpoint or from the professor's.

The professor's job is simply to improve and perfect his society. The reason is equally simple: society improves only in direct proportion to criticism leveled against it. A society never criticized—say, under a dictatorship—never improves. A society mildly criticized improves mildly. The improvement will progress to the same degree of the severity of criticism against it. The most severe criticism—say, a revolution—will improve society to the ultimate degree. Without being prompted by criticism no society, no institution, and no individual will improve. It is the very nature of conservative inertia that no system, large or small, contains within itself a mechanism for its own improvement. All "improvement" it wishes to make is generally in its own self-interest, which is no improvement. When AT&T "improves" itself, we know it has become bigger, more profitable, and more dominant. That's no improvement *of* AT&T, although perhaps *for* it. No system ever improves itself voluntarily and *against* its own interest. (This point will be discussed more fully in Chapter 10.)

By the same token, each system improves only to the *extent that it is aware of its own imperfections*. It becomes aware of its own imperfections only to the extent that it is criticized. The professor's job is simply to point out these imperfections in the course of the pursuit of truth. But again, the professor whose truth describes these imperfections in society must also know what a perfect society looks like. Without this knowledge, one cannot know what an imperfect society looks like. Without it, the professor plays straight into the role of a cowardly apologist, an ingratiating flatterer, and, worse, a slothful nonentity, all the while praising what a great society we have.

Social criticism is thus impossible without self-criticism. The validity of criticism, the force of persuasion, and the benefit of ideas would rise or fall exactly at the same rate as the rise and fall of self-criticism. Social criticism without self-criticism is hypocrisy of the worst kind, and it is often the cause of intellectual inaccuracy as well. Self-criticism is impossible without self-examination, and unexamined ideas invite falsehood. As always, the best way to examine oneself is to examine the thoughts of others greater than our own. In the end, all self-knowledge comes from the reading and internalizing of all great ideas. They are the very best that humanity bestows on posterity. In the end, all who criticize what is, for what ought to be, are utopians in search of a more perfect society.

The temptation to produce harmless, inconsequential nothings in the name of professional productivity bears relentlessly on all professors. Controversy may be secretly envied by some, but it takes some nerve to court and withstand controversies, even an academic one. For most professors it is more prudent to avoid controversial issues. Most teachers would rather not mention Marxism in class than risk unpopularity. But avoiding unpopular truth, which all social criticism must ultimately be, is not easy for the professor. For him, doing nothing means doing something ill. While unpopularity may be avoided, what is actually *done* in fact has to be *something*. What would be noncontroversial? Anything flattering and ingratiating to the system would be noncontroversial. But, if truth is in criticism, then surely falsehood must be in flattery and ingratiation. Any idea that is advanced in conformity with established orthodoxy, causing no disturbance in its wake, is therefore *false by definition*.

To paraphrase Thorstein Veblen, praising imperfection is not only false, it serves no good purpose for a society that strives to improve and perfect itself. Tenure is not established to help maintain the status quo; nor is academic freedom protected for false flattery and ingratiation; nor is pursuit of the truth mandated to produce falsehood. Politicians flatter the voter; commercials ingratiate the consumer. But they are not interested in improving the political system or perfecting the economic habits. No moderately sane person would say that the truth is to be found among politicians or commercials.

Since no system improves itself voluntarily against its own immediate interest, its willingness to encourage self-criticism is often the best indication of the state of its freedom. No capitalist would voluntarily improve capitalism against profit-making. Nor would a commissar voluntarily denounce socialism against its centrally planned economy. But capitalism and socialism, for that matter any "ism," improve only thanks to their critics. American professors love the Soviet dissidents because they speak out against their system, risking great personal peril while doing it. The dissidents are regarded as the epitome of an unbridled conscience, an uncontrollable urge of freedom, and an uncorruptible expression of the truth. But America's academic professors are our equivalent of the Soviet dissidents, without the monumental threat of exile to Siberia.

The differences between the two types of truth-speaking are great. The American "dissidents" are comforted by economic security, protected by academic freedom, and distracted by no other concern than the sole purpose of pursuing the truth. Yet what they profess to admire in the Soviet dissidents they do not do themselves, although under immeasurably more favorable conditions. What these Soviet dissidents really think about their American counterparts, the secure and free academic professors who claim to admire them, is unclear. But the cowardice, sloth, and ingratiation that American professors live by will naturally repulse the courageous, truthful, and critical. In fact, to them the American professor's comfortable falsehood would seem nothing less than repugnant.

Nothing argues more forcefully for the abolition of tenure than tenure unused. Tenure protects the professor's livelihood because it is easily imperiled. It is easily imperiled because the professor, in line of duty, provokes the powers-that-be. But the threat must be made *real*, not just possible. Tenure protection exists because the professor's livelihood is *actually* threatened. But this happens *only if* the professor does something that would invoke the wrath of society. When he does nothing, his livelihood is no longer threatened enough to require special protection. If his livelihood is hardly disturbed because he does nothing to cause its peril, then he needs no tenure protection at all. Therefore tenure, now made irrelevant, must be abolished.

Tenure cannot protect something that needs no protection. In order to invoke tenure protection and justify academic freedom, the professor must make such protection and justification *necessary*.

Our present society is vulnerable to criticism. It is fraught with crumbling social values that require the most thoroughgoing examination. The extent of modern market society—money-consciousness, avarice, individualism, philistine hedonism, temporalism, mass entertainment, high-tech culture—has never been so ripe for social criticism. No field in the modern American university deals exclusively with social criticism as its subject matter. Social criticism is rare or severely muted, while everyone manages to stay busy. Academic professors by and large waste their days teaching and writing standardized routines that are thoroughly inconsequential. On the other hand, by the very nature of their enterprise, chemists, physicists, mathematicians, Spanish instructors, physical educators, accountants, real estate experts do their routines in the lab, on the computer, and in the classroom, oblivious to the goings-on of society. There may be topical, sporadic, and isolated highlights of this problem or that among more liberal-minded academic professors, but no sustained commitment to truth about the whole society and its permanent values.

One way for the academic professor to get around the dilemma is through "constructive criticism." Here, criticism takes the form of a gentlemen's game. It is constructive criticism if it hurts no one in particular, yet is delivered in the format of criticism—to be politely applauded and instantly forgotten. It is conveniently ignored that all criticisms must be destructive, for what is criticized against what it could be. Present habits and structures must be destroyed in order for them to improve in a way that is a true improvement. The more radical a change, the greater the improvement. Perhaps what grates on people when they are subject to criticism is the manner in which the criticism is made. Often, critics appear pompous, egotistic, and insincere with their criticism, thereby upsetting the sensibilities of those whose change is desired. Such criticism is different from a hard-hitting and vigorous one, as all criticism should be. But, to be effective, criticism must not be delivered in a manner suggesting that the critic takes himself more seriously than his task. Yet the task itself, as honest criticism, must be unsparing and total. There is no such thing as a palatable truth; nor is there a partial commitment to the truth. It must be either all or nothing. Partial truth may make the professor's comfort more comfortable and his audience's peace of mind more peaceful. But it is surely corrupt comfort that he enjoys and dishonest peace of mind that his audience delights in at the expense of truth. Society needs critics, not sycophants. Tenure demands truth, not platitudes.

During tenure crises, suggestions are often made to maintain professorial job security more on the model of civil servants than on tenure. Since many professors work in public universities, this model has reasonable appeal. In it professors can enjoy the security and permanence accorded the civil servants. But this is a deplorable idea. Nothing could be more absurd than for professors to adopt the behavioral model of civil servants, even subconsciously. For no two groups in society can be more different. The differences are instant and unforgiving. Civil servants must be subserviant; professors subversive. Civil servants do what they are told; professors follow what their own conscience dictates. Civil servants practice unquestioned obedience; professors must question society's major values. Civil servants do not criticize their society; professors must criticize it as their daily routine.

But when tenure is unused, the civil servant model emerges as an attractive alternative for the professor. For, in many ways, he is more of a ritualist civil servant at heart than an independent professor. In this model the professor can find the servile comfort and predictable irrelevance as a way of life—but, of course, without doing the civil servant's honest day's work.

NOTES

    1. Burton Clark, "Faculty Organization and Authority," in *Professionalization*, eds. Howard Volmer and Donald Mills, (Englewood Cliffs, N.J.: Prentice-Hall, 1966), 286.

2. Alexis de Tocqueville, *The Old Regime and the French Revolution* (Garden City, N.Y.: Doubleday, 1955).

3. See, for example, Robert M. O'Neal, "Tenure under Attack," in *The Tenure Debate*, ed. Bardwell Smith (San Francisco: Jossy-Bass, 1973), 178–99.

4. Clark Byse and Louis Joughin, *Tenure in American Higher Education* (Ithaca, N.Y.: Cornell University Press, 1959), p. 4, paraphrasing Fritz Machlup.

5. Quoted in Arthur DeBardeleben, "The University's External Constituency," in *Dimensions of Academic Freedom*, eds. Walter P. Metzger, Edmund L. Pincoffs (Urbana: University of Illinois Press, 1969), 69–70.

6. See Richard Hofstadter and Walter P. Metzger, *The Development of Academic Freedom in the United States* (New York: Columbia University Press, 1965) 416–17.

7. Criticism of a professor's book by the Board of Regents of the University of Wisconsin, quoted in Metzger, *Dimensions of Academic Freedom*, 87.

Chapter 10

Paradox of the System

Two melancholy laws, neither of which is flattering to humanity, operate significantly in our argument. The first is "Gresham's Law," which states that the bad usually drives out the good. This law applies to the way tenure is actually awarded to professors, a matter we will examine in a subsequent chapter. The second belongs to Lord Acton, whose famous dictum holds that power tends to corrupt and absolute power corrupts absolutely. We will examine this presently. Both of these laws, perhaps truisms, have been tested repeatedly in human experience and have been found to be largely true.

The ancient Oriental king could safely ignore his truth-speaking scholar-critic whenever he wanted to. Undoubtedly he most often did ignore his critic. But the critic was a thorn in the king's conscience that he had to be mindful of. This was certainly a primitive and highly ineffective mechanism for checks and balances. Whatever its intention and outcome, the scholar-critic was a constant reminder of the dangers of unchecked power. To reapply Lord Acton's law, power corrupts to the extent that it can act free of checks and balances. If it can act without restraint, then it becomes absolutely corrupt. Therefore, all power is unjust power and all absolute power is absolutely unjust power.

This is still an assumption, although it is seemingly validated in actual experience. We need to be certain of the validity of this law. To be convinced of the importance of social criticism, we need to be persuaded that uncriticized power is surely unjust and that it imperils us all. We have seen that imperfection in society dictates the critical role for scholars. But going one step further, we may conclude that the extent of imperfection in society determines the extent of injustice that prevails in society. Then a society is unjust to the extent that it is imperfect. Where there is no countervailing force, the imperfect, unjust society, as absolute power, corrupts absolutely. If we can sustain Lord Acton's dictum in this reapplication, we can also sustain our own argument for the professor's critical role in social justice. Thus, our present task is a pivotal one.

"Power tends to corrupt and absolute power corrupts absolutely." So said the Cambridge history professor Lord Acton in the late nineteenth century. But why? Is there any logical or historical connection between the aim of power and the corruption of power?

All true power is ultimately either political or economic. The desired end is served by either. Political power can draft one into the military service; economic power can dictate whether or not one will survive in society. Politically, power means the ability to control persons, groups, classes, or even nations against their will; this control is both physical and ideological, involving body and soul. Economically, power means the ability to own, manage, or control someone's labor, intelligence, skill, talent—in short, the total economic assets of another person—and enlarge one's own economic rewards by means of someone else's economic assets. Both forms take place relative to the extent to which each society values politics and economics as its fundamental creed. In either case, power exists as a coercive instrument of society, as it must, to be true power.

As a logical progression, power always begets more power. Pure power, as opposed to instrumental power established to accomplish a specific task, knows only one thing: to enlarge itself by adding or multiplying the spheres of its influence. No power ever consciously tries to *reduce* itself, for the very aim of power is to become *powerful*, and the best way to become powerful is to try to become *more* powerful. In this progression, power reaches its zenith when it reaches a point *at which it becomes capable of self-defense*. All power grows up to the point of self-defense, and growing up to that point is the aim of all power. That aim is said to be achieved if it can defend itself against its enemies. In this sense, the ultimate aim of all power is simply self-defense, at which point power can self-perpetuate Therefore, a power that is self-defensible is also absolute power in society. As absolute power it can dictate its own terms without opposition.

While power at the point of self-defense need not fear opposition, there have been few societies and power-holders in which outright brute power was used to control their members and institutions. Even dictators and tyrants use elaborate forms and ceremonies to make their possession and exercise of power look right. They may establish a puppet cabinet, parliament, or advisory council; they may enlist high priests for seemingly divine ordination; they may even encourage the masses to display their loyalty and enthusiams, albeit after the fact, to justify their power. Even the advanced "democratic" society resorts to such means of public relations. In doing so, these forms and processes make it unnecessary to resort to brute force in order to demonstrate the effectiveness of power. This process is generally known as "legitimation," in which might becomes right. It makes power socially acceptable, commanding voluntary respect and obedience without the show of force. Every dictator loves such pomp and circumstance. Open democratic societies achieve legitimacy through constitution-writing, regular elections, terms of office, legal and administrative blessings, and so on. Either way, legitimacy is the very lifeblood of power. No office-holder worries about someone taking over without legitimate authority, and no money-owner fears that fortunes might be confiscated the next day. Social stability is largely affected by the degree to which power is held legitimate.

But no legitimacy confers righteousness on power unless power is there first. Power that exists requires legitimation to make it right, but legitimation does not create power. It always *follows* power. Power precedes legitimacy, which merely confirms the power's right to exist. But power must exist first, legitimately or not. By existing first, it acquires the right to *become* legitimate. That is the right of power. All existing societies were powers first, revolutionary or not, and legitimate powers next. But the moral right that legitimacy confers upon power is extraordinary: it determines what is right and wrong in society; it makes might right; it defines and dispenses with justice; it transforms the profane into the sacred, upon whose name life and death are decided. Once this legitimacy is secured, no legitimate power is ever considered unjust and no illegitimate action ever just.

No legitimate society or power, however, puts itself to its own judgment. The ends of all legitimacy are also self-defense. By virtue of legitimacy, the legitimating organ or process itself is immune from opposition. No legitimate power ever makes itself illegitimate by dissolving itself. The question of legitimacy arises only when the question of legitimate power's *ability to defend itself arises*. The last hours of all falling dictators, governments, and societies face the question of legitimacy. As long as power is capable of self-defense, there is no such thing as illegitimate power and the question is irrelevant.

All power, consequently, spends much of its energy in maintaining its own legitimacy through social order. To the extent that social order is maintained against revolution, legitimacy is upheld. To the extent that legitimacy is upheld, power's right to exist is affirmed. But no social order can be maintained without bringing the powerless under the control of power. The extent of social order is really the best indicator of how much power is used in controlling social behavior. At the same time, it is also an indicator of power's self-defensive ability. Hence, social order, legitimacy, and power's self-defense form the triad that sustains a social system and its institutions.

Every pure power exists *just to exist*. And to exist it must consume an inordinate amount of its own energy in maintaining social order. This is obvious: no legitimated power ever declares itself illegitimate as long as it still has the ability to self-defend, whether or not it is morally fit to defend. By the same token, no power ever declares itself undeserving of existence as long as it remains self-defensible in capacity. First and last, power's aim is to defend itself, and there can be no other aim for it to pursue. It is in the name of self-defense that power exists; it is to the point of self-defense that power naturally progresses; and it is on the issue of self-defense that power lives or dies.

What is, then, the *nature* of power that is self-defensible? Lord Acton says all power corrupts, and more power corrupts more thoroughly. Why does power corrupt invariably? We can now answer the question in this way: *All power corrupts by virtue of its self-defensibility*. Power is defined by its ability to defend itself against opposition, but power corrupts because of this very ability. If it cannot defend itself against opposition, it is not true power. If it *is* true power, it must be capable of self-defense. If it is capable of self-defense, then it must be corrupt. Our preliminary conclusion is inevitable: *Power must be corrupt to be power*. If self-defensibility defines power, so does corruption. In short, power cannot exist without being corrupt. How is that possible?

Since pure power has no purpose, and all society *is* pure power, the exercise of its legitimacy against opposition or in its own self-defense can serve no other purpose than itself or its self-interest. What is the purpose of making money in America? To make more money. Power exists to protect itself by becoming more powerful. There is nothing secret about this. It is the very nature of power in society. In our ordinary life, in which our conduct aims to attain a specific end within a specific time limit, we may try to make a certain amount of money for a specific aim. A vacation, paying an outstanding bill, repairing a car, whatever, will do. These are specific purposes for which our effort is predetermined. Once the aim is achieved, that part of our effort is no longer needed. When money is power, the question of what *purpose* the acquisition serves is irrelevant. Entrepreneurs do not want a vacation, do not have an outstanding bill, do not need to repair an automobile. Money for them is power, and power *must* grow until there is no more left to oppose it.

If money-making as a social philosophy is challenged, all the money in America will close ranks in its defense. In this, no reason in the world, no logic that exists between heaven and earth, no faith that can move mountains can dissuade the power of money from considering the defense of its own self-interest first and last. All holders of power (individuals, groups, corporations, classes, or nation-states) will justify themselves against their enemies real and imagined. Thus, *power's very ability to justify itself precludes all possibility of power ever becoming justifiable in itself.*

Every power is therefore extremely nervous and reactive. For no power in society is self-deserving or permanent in its existence. Its existence is solely determined by the fact that it manages to exist at all. Its legitimate existence lasts only so long as it is capable of defending itself. The shadow of illegitimacy follows in every corner of its existence. It sees enemies everywhere, to be identified, conquered, or co-opted. And every threat to its existence is magnified one thousand times. It is like talking to a banker about the evils of capitalism or a commissar about socialist failures. Power and reason make a poor mix. Naturally, all power perceives self-protection as its only obligation because of its innate *need* for self-defense. When something goes wrong, it is power's natural first reaction to cover up, not to expose or exorcise the wrong. Every holder or agent of power, from the head of state to a minor functionary, creates an elaborate defense perimeter around him and is ready to jump at the drop of a hat. (Dictators always have their escape plans handy.) The state thus exists for itself; wealth begets more wealth; every bureaucratic office becomes a fortress. None of these sources of power can tell why it exists at all, other than the nervous compulsion to exist and to defend itself. But what is *it* against which all power must defend itself? Why, of course, those who do not have it, the powerless of the realm. Everyone who stands to benefit from power begins to believe that power must be self-generating in the sense that its self-defense becomes as logical as its own existence.

It is precisely at this point of self-defense that power takes its first but inevitable step toward corruption. Thus, Lord Acton's absolute power begins to corrupt absolutely in direct proportion to its ability to defend itself against the powerless. *Anything power does in its own behalf must be corrupt because absolute power does nothing else.* All legitimate power, by virtue of its legitimacy, becomes corrupt power. For no legitimate power can exercise its power for anything other than its own self-interest. Absolute power has now become unjust power.

In order to do injustice to another person, group, class, or nation, one must be in possession of a *means* of injustice. In order to inflict injustice, one must have either a political means or an economic means, or both. One cannot hurt another unless he has the means to do so. There is nothing more effective and thorough than power as a means of inflicting injustice to the powerless. In fact, history proves time and time again that *having* a means of injustice is almost the same as *doing* injustice. In the idioms of contemporary American society the dictum might read, "Have Power—Will Do Wrong."[1]

Examples abound to show that the gap between power used and power abused is negligible. Since injustice is impossible without the means of injustice, power tends to be positively related to injustice. The larger the size of power, the greater the extent of injustice inflicted on the powerless. Superpowers do super injustice; medium powers medium injustice; small powers small injustice, all relative to the powerlessness of their opponents.

Every instance in history—or just around our workplaces—proves that it is closer to human nature to do wrong with power than to do right with it. It is always the powerful who do wrong to the powerless, never the other way around. It is always the majority against the minority; always the powerful and wealthy against the powerless and poor; always institutions against the individual. There is nothing more capable of injustice (often in the name of justice) than a legitimate power with full complements of the means of injustice—law and order, military, police, courts, and all other legal means at its disposal. Thus, legitimacy is always the greatest menace to justice. The menace takes place on all levels: animals under inconsiderate masters suffer; children under unloving parents suffer; people under unjust governments suffer; small nations under large nations suffer. The masters, parents, governments, large nations are all on the side of legitimacy, and they all possess the full means of injustice. And having the means, they will surely use it.

We have seen that power naturally leads to self-defense, which naturally leads to corruption and injustice. There is yet a historical, psychological explanation as to why injustice, rather than justice, is the natural result of the means of power on the more personal level. Why does power tend to lead to injustice rather than justice in the hands of those who possess its means? The answer is a ready one: doing right is always more difficult than doing wrong when doing either can be justified. Doing right requires the *sacrifice* of one's self-interest. Doing wrong requires the *assertion* of one's self-interest. And self-interest is always supreme. This self-interest is always supremely expressed through power and legitimacy. A master is under no obligation to treat his animals kindly. Nor is a company president under compulsion to be considerate to his subordinates. A tenured professor does not have to be just and fair to a junior colleague. Government bureaucrats need not be helpful to their public. It is almost always the case that injustice flows from the master to his animals, from the president to his surbordinates, from the tenured to untenured professor, from government bureaucrats to the public, never the other way around. Power and legitimacy make justice unnecessary and irrelevant. When relations are determined by power, one is not nice if he need *not* be nice. In it inertia prevails.

Power (or wealth) confers upon its possessor many privileges. One of the most popular privileges—in many cases the most exclusive one—is the right of the power-holder to be childish. The lost privilege of childhood to be irresponsible is restored with a vengence through the social privilege of power. The idea of irresponsibility is relentlessly irresistible. Since social responsibility is normally borne by the weak and poor in any society and no one enjoys the burden, consideration for social responsibility declines as one's power to be irresponsible rises. In interpersonal relations as well as in large institutional hiearchies, power and irresponsibility normally go hand in hand. Power increases one's irresponsibility and makes one's yearnings for childhood a reality. One with power can act like a child, a bad one at that, any time he wants and for any cause he chooses. Immunity to criticism is built proportionally into power and wealth. That is why power and wealth are universally pursued. Almost never does power improve one's personal character or private virtues. It is always the opposite. Given enough power and wealth, even a reasonable man soon reverts back to childishness. While absolute power corrupts absolutely, the way it corrupts is always absolutely childish. Nero, Idi Amin, Stalin, and many others like them exercised their powers in ways that, under normal circumstances, are exhibited only by children—and sometimes by the insane.

However, the most serious source of injustice is in power's inability to act against its own self-interest. By virtue of its self-defense and legitimacy, power becomes incapable of self-reflection, self-criticism, or self-analysis. These are fundamental to just acts. Never does a person, group, or society possessing the means of injustice also possess the means of counteracting its own means of injustice. The power of the scholar-critic for the Oriental sovereign is never equal to the sovereign's. One's conscience is never as powerful as one's power. A superpower's discretion is never a match for its indiscretion. The powerful do not feel the compulsion to moderate their own power or legitimacy even for the sake of justice. Those who assiduously climb up the ladder of power in politics or economics are not reflective men and women given to self-examination. Power can dictate its own terms of justice, legitimacy, war and peace, or anything else that matters. From small power to large power, injustice increases as the magnitude of power increases. For more power can do greater harm. At the same time, the greater the power, the less capable it is of self-criticism and possibly of justice, charity, or mercy. The powerful cannot reduce their own power any more than children can reduce their sweets voluntarily. Power must protect society from its *own* menace, which is like asking children to voluntarily protect their teeth from the menace of sweets.

A power strong enough to defend against its enemies by nature is incapable of stopping its own corruption or injustice. It is in power's nature that it is essentially deprived of its ability to self-regulate. Those who are capable of self-regulation are not found among the powerful. Those who are powerful are not interested in or capable of self-regulating. The irony is that power is inherently unjust, and justice inherently powerless. Neither history nor human nature has found a way to combine the two. Those who value justice are not likely to pursue power, a process made possible only by accepting the premises of power. Those who pursue power by accepting the premises are not likely to be interested in justice or capable of perceiving the need for justice. The wrenching dilemma is this: *power can be just and uncorrupt only if it has the ability to invalidate itself.* It is about as difficult as expecting normal children to have the virtues of a saint or a martyr. Self-denial is difficult even under the most favorable circumstances. Few have ever succeeded.

No power-holder ever relinquishes his power voluntarily, whether it be a political post or wealth. No power has ever been relinquished by the power-holder to be given to the powerless and poor without a severe prompting from a source equal or almost equal in power. Justice is rarely obtained without violence, as in the case of American civil rights and apartheid in South Africa, for legitimate power recognizes no other as equally legitimate. Power's greatest triumph would be to act against its own self-interest, but that is one triumph it is quite incapable of conceiving, much less achieving. It is always the powerless and poor who must compromise and do with less. There is no way power can exercise itself wisely—that is, against its own compulsion to self-defense and corruption on its own accord. A power capable of self-defense will never act on its own self-destruction.

All power leads to the point of self-defense, and sooner or later, self-defensibility leads to corruption and injustice. There is no way this cycle can be broken voluntarily. It is neither in the nature of power nor in the history of power-holders. No political control or economic wealth has been given up voluntarily when there is no reason external to power for it. Power means one's ability to force another person to act against the person's own interest. That same power cannot possibly be used by the power-holder against *his own* interest. In other words, power is logically incapable of acting against its own self-interest when unopposed by equal or greater power. And this is the reason why power corrupts and absolute power corrupts absolutely. Lord Acton has been explained.

Given power's inability for self-criticism, now we can see why tenure and academic freedom in American society are so extraordinary. It is the act of power repudiating itself, however small a measure in end results. A most crassly market-oriented society, where everything from votes to babies can be purchased, is willing to pay for a truth that is not only worthless in the market but is also the thorn in its side. For the first time in history, a system of power has given its most educated segment a legal and economic immunity to criticize the system itself. Through tenure and academic freedom the system has guaranteed the safety of an act whose sole significance is in telling the critical truth about itself. It is a paradox of power never observed anywhere before.

Not all criticisms may be willingly accepted, but making the criticisms persuasive enough to be acceptable is the professor's job. The first job is to truth, not acceptability. An unacceptable truth is always preferable to an acceptable flattery or falsehood. A professor cannot be too critical, for no injustice of power is too insignificant. American society, like all other social systems, is a legitimate power. Its first duty is to its own self-defense, and it is a simple cold fact of reality. No one person or agency has ever established tenure and academic freedom as a grand philosophical gesture for justice. It may very well be an accident of history. Whatever its intentions and origins, the fact remains that a legitimate power of immense self-defensibility has allowed itself a measure of redemption. This must be pursued to its fullest possibility. Only in pursuit of truth-telling about itself can a power save itself from its own relentless progression to corruption and injustice. The society calls for it, and the professor's own commitment calls for it. It is a magnificent gesture of society that must be answered only in honest, independent, and critical truth.

To squander it in sloth, apology, or incompetence would be an act of monumental stupidity against justice.

NOTE

1. When President Reagan ordered a bomb attack on Libya in retaliation for its terrorism in 1986, *U.S. News and World Report* titled it, "HAVE POWER—WILL USE." Similarly, a February 1989 *TIME* magazine article on gun-related deaths in America titled it, "Have Weapons, Will Shoot."

Chapter 11

Professor as Citizen

It is rare among tenured professors to be dismissed for unpopular "political" activities on campus. It is rather common among the untenured, however, to be denied tenure for allegedly unprofessional or uncollegial conduct. Sometimes it is their senior colleagues, at other times administrators, who find their activity of questionable quality. Especially prevalent during the peak of Vietnam protests in the 1970s, unpopular political activities of professors on and off campus have been an issue with respect to academic freedom. The issue itself is simple: should academic freedom protect professors in their political activities as well? Professors themselves are divided.[1]

I find myself agreeing with the opinion that it should not. But the reasons for my opinion are entirely different from those advanced by some on the same side. Professor William Van Alstyne, for example, contends that such a specially privileged protection would create elitism among professors, that it would delay legislation specifically guarnteeing academic freedom, and that there is no special protection for academic freedom guaranteed in the Constitution.[2] I argue simply that political activities by professors are not appropriate in the first place. Their political activities are largely partisan ones, which should not be confused with the pursuit of truth. Whether their activities should be protected by academic freedom is entirely irrelevant. They should not be involved in those activities in the first place. It is *not* part of their *academic* business.

Let us start with this classic division of American politics. On February 4, 1987, a strange but little noticed exchange took place between Senator Edward M. Kennedy of the Senate Judiciary Committee and then–Attorney General Edwin Meese. Displeased with Meese's record on civil rights, Kennedy told him, "This is the most anti-civil rights administration I have ever seen." Mr. Meese, responding to a similar charge from another senator, described himself (and his administration by extension) as "one of the foremost defenders of individual rights." The exchange was a non sequitur, of course, but, while speaking past each other, it highlighted an interesting dichotomy in American politics. Although one (individual rights) is given as answer to the other (civil rights), they represent two ideological opposites. Most professors in trouble have been caught under the crossfire of this exchange in action.

Individual rights and civil rights have a history of conflict in their mutual existence. Whenever and wherever one flourishes, the other declines. Civil rights cannot prosper, for example, unless they forcibly take issue with the unrestrained expressions of individual rights. It is correct, perhaps, to define one kind of rights by the extent to which the other rights are restrained.

Individual rights have their origins essentially in the development of the Enlightenment in all its economic and political implications, articulated for American society by the Founding Fathers. They are derivatives of the "state of nature" conception of human society expressed through market ethics and (classic) liberal politics. To attain and maintain individual rights, a free, solitary, and competitive expansion of private powers is considered fundamental. Civil rights, on the other hand, are of fairly recent origins, basically as a reaction to the preponderance of individual rights in both economics and politics. Unlike individual rights, civil rights are neither conceived nor practiced as a private endeavor. Both in theory and practice, they are expressed through cooperative, collective, and community-based activities. Whatever ultimate end it may seek, the civil rights movement lives or dies as a group endeavor.

Rooted in the original conception of private powers to oppose the aristocracy and divine right of kings, individual rights are the primary ideology of the "new classes," generally the rich and the upper–middle class, which perceive their rights in terms of *maximum* economic and political expression. By contrast civil rights—at least to the extent that their existence depends on moderating this concept of maximum privatized political and economic powers—reflect the *minimal* entitlements to basic human needs. In more popular terms of conventional politics, the difference often divides Republican "conservatism" and Democratic "liberalism." The role of government, passive or active, is a crucial factor in this push-pull contest. Both rights expand or shrink according to how this role is played. Obviously, proponents of individual rights want a passive government; proponents of civil rights an active one. Both know that where government is quiescent, the individual reigns supreme (and vice versa).

In this basic contest of two rights in American society, on *which side* should the professor enter? The popular perception that college professors tend to be more "liberal" on the side of civil rights is misleading. Only the "active" academic professors who so express their preference get in trouble. Many functional professors tend to be sympathetic with individual rights. Besides, even among academic professors, senior faculty are more conservative than their younger counterparts. Neither side, however, has any morally justifiable edge.

Individual rights find their supporters in Thomas Jefferson, Herbert Hoover, Ronald Reagan (and Edwin Meese). Civil rights have been voiced sympathetically by Abraham Lincoln, Franklin Roosevelt, Jimmy Carter (and Edward M. Kennedy). Both philosophies form the twin pillars of what Hans Morgenthau once called the American "purpose": equality-in-freedom.[3] With the closing of frontiers and the coming of a corporate market society, however, equality and freedom cannot be enjoyed in unlimited quantity. Now, individual rights prevail in the modus operandi of market rationality; civil rights in the backdrop of human service. Individual rights personify the New World of violent, masculine self-realization; civil rights reflect the Old World steeped in the short-comings of man. Every new American from the Old World is a civil rightist until he passes the Statue of Liberty. After that he becomes at least partially an individual rightist. Historically, individual rights found their nemesis in the aristocracy and divine king. Now, civil rights find theirs in individual rights, for whenever civil rights must fight for their minimal needs they necessarily encounter the long shadows of individual rights in every aspect of American politics and economics.

As such, neither side has any monopoly on American society. With rare exceptions, Americans regularly put individual rightists and civil rightists in the White House. Many states send both to the U.S. Senate as their representatives. Sometimes the governor represents one position, the state legislature the other. Both positions are legitimately American in their basic philosophy and are acceptable to American society in its practice. One's own position on this issue—such as the one exchanged between Kennedy and Meese—is a *partisan* matter. It is a matter of individual differences of opinion on an issue that is *neither right nor wrong*. My contention is that it is none of the academic professor's business to get into any of these partisan issues.

A typical partisan issue is one over which America is evenly divided. With few exceptions, all partisan issues in America have this sort of balanced division. From abortion to whaling, from animal trapping to taxation, most Americans tend to be divided in these issues. Such is the very nature of partisan issues. Americans argue, protest, and eventually go to the polls themselves or have their representatives cast the vote. One way or another, depending on how urgent they are, all partisan issues either remain contentious or are settled at the ballot box. Contentious or settled, at least temporarily until the next round of contest, they are part of the ongoing realities of American life. These issues themselves, or some of them, may attract the scholar's attention. But his attention should be paid to the *issue*, not one *side* or the other of the issue. For *both* sides are legitimate and American. And this is the crucial point for "politically" endangered professors.

In a partisan issue, one side tends to think that *its* side is the solution and the other side the problem. The other side tends to think the opposite. Both sides, given their evenly matched energy, skill, and organization, tend to have their days. One side or the other wins the battle for the day. Roughly one-half of them opposed George Bush for president of the United States. But Bush *is* the legitimate president of the United States for *all* Americans. It is the way a game is played. They may lock horns with primeval ferociousness and determination, and with a zealot's fervor. But it is still a game that they are playing. Rules must be observed; order must be minded; end-results, however disagreeable, must be accepted. It may sometimes appear more serious than that, as in the case of abortion where violence may be present. But it is still a game. The protesters go home after the protest, enjoy television, and go to bed feeling secure that they are not going to be attacked by the other side during the night. This applies also to so-called *bi*partisan issues as well. Two partisan sides do not the truth make.

An academic professor is in no position to get involved in this game of society as if his whole moral commitment is being tested. His moral test is in pursuit of the truth, where there are no rules, no order, and the end-result is never satisfactory. A typical academic professor, if in pursuit of the truth, tends to be uncertain and neutral on partisan issues, or if asked to give an opinion on a particular issue, will start thinking deeply about it only then. One has not honestly thought about the issue before, simply because the issue did not attract one's attention as a serious subject of scholarship.

If pushed, the scholar would first state that he had not really given that much thought to the issue. But he would, after some thought, give an opinion in an even-handed way *without being partisan* while still favoring one side or the other. That is an art of persuasion as much as scholarship. Persuasion is not in giving out statistics or demonstrating material facts. It is in affecting the reluctant heart of a partisan. In this the typical scholar is aware that in partisan issues *no one* is an expert because *everyone* is. The scholar's "expertise," which does not really exist in matters of opinion, is no more taken seriously by the partisan than *his* own expertise. No scholar ever wins a debate or scores a point on a partisan issue without being countered by the other side's own scholar. The scholar cannot win in partisan issues. One must, if one cannot avoid it, approach it as a scholarly subject. Given the volatility of any issue, discretion is as much scholarship as scholarly valor.

Let us take abortion, a rather touchy issue, as a test case for the scholar. Suppose he is asked to give an opinion on the issue in front of a fiery group of partisans from both sides. First, the scholar would highlight both positions. One side says life is sacred; the other side says freedom is sacred. Then, the scholar would calmly point out that those who are opposed to abortion because life is sacred should also recognize that American society is not a very life-loving society. The issue is much larger than the life of an unborn baby. American homicide rates, infant mortality rates due to poverty in the lower classes, hunger in children, disregard for life in other societies in support of dictatorship, and so on (and such facts are legion) are such that abortion is only a small, almost insignificant issue by comparison. The pro-lifer should set his sight on higher issues of life if sacred life is his main concern.

On the other hand, he points out that the pro-choice partisan must also be aware that the decision of abortion is made almost wholly on the basis of *self-interest*, or, one might say, of personal convenience. Overpopulation could not be the reason because American society is not overpopulated. But then there are economic, social, and cultural factors involved in every pregnancy that bear on the decision, which may be beyond the prospective mother's powers to control. Pregnancy as a social phenomenon, much larger than the individual's decision to have or not to have a child, must be pointed out to the audience. Now, if the scholar is successful in his discourse, the issue should then become something different. Taken away from the individual moral context, the issue calls for different questions and answers: Should—and can—American society support *all* children conceived in America to a healthy and happy future? Would the prospective mother be willing to set aside her own self-interest or inconvenience in this if given enough support from society? Can American society afford such a policy? If not, why not? It is always

"American society" that the scholar must point to in his effort to transcend partisanship. Otherwise, he will never get out of the partisan quagmire.

This sort of approach may satisfy neither side. But it may simply be an impossible task in the partisan atmosphere. Both sides want a confirmation of *their* own position. None is interested in discovering that its own position may be slightly shortsighted and narrow-minded. But it is the professor's function, if he can at all, to *elevate* their shortsightedness and narrow-mindedness. It would be both foolish and impractical for him to be involved in the issue as a partisan, for there is no satisfactory end to it. His opinion on the issue, if requested, is that of a scholar only interested in the truth. If there is no truth involved in the issue because of its insignificance (and there are many such issues by virtue of their game-like quality), the scholar should simply express his view that he does not think the issue is important enough for him to have any opinion on it. Either position is fine with him. It is easier to agree with one side or the other and arouse its already charged passion. It is also "safe" to support the "liberal" side because of the built-in support system. But as in all emotionally charged and safe issues, the consequence for the partisan scholar in partisan activity is personally unwise and intellectually meaningless. The best course of action is, therefore, no action at all on all partisan issues. What seems to be profitable in the short run almost always brings about long-term regrets.

All partisan issues are temporal and ideological. All truth pursuits are historical and universal. Both liberalism and conservatism are temporal and ideological; so is the issue of abortion; so are many such issues that divide the opinions of the day, however heated and fervent they may first appear. A professor getting involved in such issues merely adds one more voice, one more body, and one more partisan. No matter how authoritative, the professor's is just as insignificant to the opponent as all the others in that position. In matters of partisan politics, all experts are disputed by the other experts. In the end, the ballot speaks and settles all that. Such political activities are so *ordinary* that the special privilege of academic freedom in pursuit of the truth simply cannot apply without debasing that special privilege itself. When a professor leads or participates in a political protest with students or citizens, the activity cannot be any different from that of any other person present. In this, there can be no claim to immunity for a specially privileged scholar. Nor can the claim lend special privilege to an inherently ordinary cause. (Of course, a campus where professors are also activists makes for a livelier scene and gives the university a more dynamic and liberating ambience. This may have its own merit, but it should not be confused with the scholar's primary duty, namely, pursuit of the truth.)

Some professors take on a "high-profile" task, such as vocally and actively shutting out a guest speaker on campus (a common occurrence) or create "controversies" in the mass media with one thing or another (a more common occurrence). The controversy such acts court may be in the course of one's true scholarship. But it is more likely to involve a partisan issue than scholarship or truth. The very fact of controversialism indicates that it may be so. Truth rarely courts controversy in the way American society normally reports and deals with "controversies." The latter tend to be ephemeral, trivial, and faddish, and very likely forgotten by the next such controversies. Besides, all controversies by definition *are* partisan controversies, both sides having supporters and detractors. The controversial professor is merely a new player in the old game. "Controversies" have been raging over Plato ever since his time. Yet he is not a controversial professor in our present definition of the term. Truth causes painful pause and thoughtful reflection; a controversy stirs a loud, immediate, and partisan reaction. The mass media never report the Platonic controversies; the present-day controversial professor is a hot topic.

Since partisan issues do not justify the scholar's proper involvement, what *would*? All partisan issues, by virtue of their being an issue at all, are half-and-half issues, half supporting and half opposing. The scholar must carefully steer clear of such minefields. It is both foolish and impractical to get involved. But that does not eliminate all the relevant issues for the scholar. In fact, that eliminates for him all the *irrelevant* issues, leaving him to deal with *true* issues. They are the *all-American* issues that affect virtually all Americans and are generally agreed on by all Americans. Unlike partisan issues that are nullified by the other half, all-American issues are held by most, if not all, Americans as inviolate. They are not controversial issues at all, for virtually no one disputes their validity. They are not discussed critically because it is not a popular thing to do. They stir no particular interest as conversations and as media topics because they are taken for granted. They cannot be challenged or changed easily because they are deeply embedded in subconscious cultural ethos and folklore as well as in orthodox textbook teaching. They are sometimes called the "American Creed," or more popularly the "American Dream." These are, for the scholar, truly controversial issues of our time. They are the historical and universal tests of our community, society, and humanity.

What are these issues? In fact, such issues can be easily defined by the simple criterion that *they are supported by the absolute majority of Americans*. They are the "American Way of Life" They can be found wherever the absolute majority of Americans find agreement, conservatives and liberals, pro-lifers and pro-choicers, whatever one's partisan shade may be. They are in the marketplace where everything is bought and sold to the highest bidder. They are in the "Me Generation," the first fully self-interested generation the world has ever seen. They are in the appalling decline of moral life and in the proliferation of sleaze in high offices as well as in the ordinary habits of mind. They are in the DisneyWorld mentality in pursuit of fantasy life, get-rich-quick schemes, easy escape from realities. They are in the culture of mind-captivating but soul-depriving entertainment and thrills, television and sports. They are in the rise of material science and the decline of the arts and humanities, not to mention the bestsellers and attendance records. They are in the foreign policies of American government that support friendly dictators, which always end in sorry spectacles. They are in the greatest peacetime military expenditure the world has ever seen, which is still largely unabated. They are in the meaningless grinding out of work and life routines whose emptiness and alienation cannot be dissolved into easy prefabricated fantasy and short-lived thrills. They are in the pitiless neglect of children, turning them into unloved but spoiled savages who will inhabit America and determine its future.

All these and more considered *separately* may constitute partisan issues. But they are merely different facets of the same problem that historically confronts American society now and in the future. It would be futile to take up one facet at a time as an issue, or one issue as a lifetime commitment. It is indeed puzzling that the professoriate as a whole is not aware of, not alarmed by, and not outraged by this rapid deterioration of its society and its irresponsibility to the larger world in which it makes up the most powerful core.

To be sure, these are difficult issues for anyone to deal with. Not only do most contemporary academic professors find these subjects an unfamiliar territory for their own upbringing and education. But they are also difficult issues with which to persuade the public who must come to an opposite and painful conclusion about the most familar and imperative aspects of their routine lives. These are taken for granted by most Americans. These are also the most urgent and critical ingredients of American life that are to be truthfully debated and searched, as all such imperatives of society should. They are, in the absence of political tyranny, the new tyrannies of America's mind and soul. They demand absolute obedience, unquestioned acceptance, and permanent establishment in every American consciousness. They are the new "truths" about American society that are false, new fulfillment of life that is empty, new freedom that enslaves, and new pleasures that leave us forever unhappy.

These are, naturally and imperatively, where the scholar must find the truth for community, society, and humanity. The nation's entire creative, dynamic, and destructive energies are devoted to its consuming culture. What could be more compelling to engage a scholar? Every major ill of American society sooner or later leads to economics. Why is every scholar not attacking that very problem regardless of his own specialty? Every professor is afraid of stepping out of his own specialty, that nice cocoon that protects his job and ignorance. Attacking economics in America would be suicidal if one were unprotected by tenure and academic freedom. What one may find out in the process about oneself and one's society will not be pleasant. What one must do to persuade a public thoroughly in agreement with itself will not be easy. The farther truth is from the accepted wisdom of the day, the more daunting will be one's task of persuasion. But tenure and academic freedom have not been granted for a life on easy street. Some take the easy way of partisanship; others, more commonly, take the easy way of scientism, reducing the issues to lifeless subjects for *research*. There will be no lesser-of-two-evils comfort in this: both are simply escapist ploys for irresponsibility.

When the issue is truth in society, the conventional line of liberalism and conservatism, or left and right, or whatever other models of guidance that divide people—so crucial to partisans—fades into insignificance. What liberal dogma is there that cannot be countered by a conservative one, and vice versa, with equal logic and moral justification? But truth necessarily transcends these partisan lines of thought and action, and it indeed must to be valid universally and historically. Good scholars may be partisans, but great ones are difficult to classify. It would be absurd to pigeonhole Thorstein Veblen or C. Wright Mills into any of the conventional party lines. To them, the partisan split is fairly meaningless, too conventional and narrow for their utterly unbridled pursuit of truth in society. Partisanship serves some immediate convenience for those career-minded professors. But it further erodes what little effect they may have in the long run of truth and society.

In a competitive market society, there is nothing inherently "good" or "bad" in any definable sense. Advantages and disadvantages, good and bad, profit and loss cancel each other out in a push-pull contest of power and fortune. What is bad for one is good for another. If it is bad for men, perhaps it is good for women. Unemployment is bad for employees, but it is good for employers. If the Republicans win, the Democrats lose, and vice versa. In American society morality has no specific definition or tradition. What is good for oneself is all that matters. All things in American society become, in the end, a matter of who benefits from each instance of win or loss. But no society, no human community, can survive—and survive decently—in a moral vacuum. By this reckoning, American society is at the very threshold of a moral collapse, if it has not collapsed already. It is this moral imperative, more than anything, more than any partisan issue because the imperative is not a partisan issue, that must engage the academic professor. It is this moral vacuum that he must define and, if possible, endow with coherence and substance.

Justice, which is the end product of truth, is always a *specific* design. It cannot exist in a social vacuum, although many in America insist that it can. They call it "natural order" or "human nature." (If this were true, we would only have functional professors who make better medicine, machines, and toilet paper, but none of the "useless" moral endeavors.) The price of this morality of "no morals" in American society has become obvious to all but the most intellectually blind: the decline of national purpose, of industrial productivity and of good work habits, and most important, of the moral authority of America. The rest of the world may look to American affluence with envy, but its moral resolve is suspect. Many now recognize that morally, politically, and economically, America has become the *oldest* society in existence that stands still—immensely satisfied with itself—while the rest of the world is moving. Its continuing eminence as a world-idea is in grave jeopardy, as is the very notion of America's purpose as traditionally defined by it.

This is what faces the academic professor. Yet he sees nothing of the most obvious; he feels no anger at the human follies; his passion refuses to be aroused from its tenured and freely irresponsible slumber. In a morally vacuous society, the academic professor adds nothing and enlightens nothing because essentially he is also a man of moral vacuum himself. In the end, he allows injustice to prevail with his inaction or safe irrelevance in partisan activity.

Popular theories come and go in quick succession. Narcissism becomes popular; next, armament expenditure; next, the closing of the American mind. Next it will be something else that explains it all. Everyone is forever in search of a painless, piecemeal solution to a daunting historical problem. That the task may require much painstaking thoughtfulness for the scholar in pursuit of the truth; or that it is understood in the oath of a scholar's life, to pursue the truth and only the truth; or that sloth, apology, and incompetence cannot substitute the painful truth; or that American society cannot accept it, even if it rejects it on the surface, for the price of tenure and academic freedom that it has granted its professors; these are only dimly remembered, if at all. Our society demands the truth, the total and unconditional truth from its scholars. The scholar cannot hide behind easy controversies, safe partisan issues, or rote "science" any longer. The bill of truth has come due.

Tenure and academic freedom protect the scholar's thought, not action, and truth in ideas, not private opinion. Doing unpopular things is not necessarily scholarship. Nor is private opinion. (There is a huge difference between opinion and truth.) Thinking unpopular thoughts and expressing unpopular ideas constitute the essence of scholarly pursuit of the truth. The professor is an *academic* man or woman, not an activist. The university is a place of thought, not action. The scholar is the creator of thought that leads to desired action, not the leader of action. But the action the thought leads to must be universal and lasting, not a flash in the pan that flames the day's passion and adorns headlines for its partisans. The scholar is a free human being who has overcome his own self-interest through the freedom of tenure security and of academic thought. As a free scholar, he is beholden to no one and to no institution, but to his own free and honest truth. Society protects the scholar for this task and demands this task from him, nothing else. The scholar's mind is the best its society has, the scholar's thought the best its society needs. This is the proverbial scholar's life to which one has committed oneself and from which no one can escape.

By contrast, all partisan issues are self-interested actions. They may or may not be beneficial to all community, society, and humanity. By virtue of their partisan split, they are generally half-beneficial and half-harmful. When they are all-triumphant through political victory, they then become all-harmful. All partisan issues demand immediate, positive results over their opponents. As we have seen in the two types of rights, they tend to invalidate each other. Since their positions are always translated into action, theirs is a matter for the law, the legislative chamber, and the ballot to be counted. Partisans argue, write letters, picket, intimidate, demonstrate to get what they want. Their beliefs are particular, local, and fragmented, not universal or whole. Their aim is for direct, immediate impact realizable in the present, not for the future or posterity. Their goals are practical and visible, winning or losing the battle of the day. For them, nothing is permanent as long as the issue is alive.

When a professor is involved in partisanship, his presence affects only the small segment nearby. When an opinion on the issue is publicized, it only inflames the other side, who naturally questions the authenticity of his opinion. When the authenticity is questioned, it is no longer an issue of truth. Truth may be found disagreeable on the grounds of inaccuracy, but not on authenticity. When an opinion is found to be disagreeable, it becomes unauthentic. All partisan opinions are disagreed with on the grounds that they are unauthentic. Partisans win when their opponents lose, and vice versa. But all win when the truth wins. The scholar must leave no doubt that what he speaks is not a partisan truth, but a truth that will benefit all. In this, he must unscrupulously avoid all appearance of partisanship, even when his conclusions favor one or the other. As in the example of individual and civil rights, the scholar must invoke the earlier, more fundamental American commitment to freedom and equality, and he must persuade the partisans to take a higher road to truth that will serve them all better. It is the universal humanity that must be appealed to; it is posterity that the public must be reminded of; it is the better side of human instinct that must be aroused. It is much easier and safer to jump onto a partisan band wagon, but the result is almost always negligible and often regrettable. The academic professor's job is no less than building a just and truthful society, and no other job description is possible or acceptable. It is the very definition of true scholarship under tenure and academic freedom. Partisans win or lose, but true scholars always win. Partisanship and scholarship are thus fundamentally at odds with each other, and the scholar only sacrifices scholarship and truth when partisan approaches are adopted for partisan causes. In this they inevitably step out of the bounds of their scholarly oath and academic protection.

One of the frequent clashes on campus, therefore, occurs over the professor's right to free speech. Supporters invoke academic freedom and civil liberty for their cause. Opponents argue that free speech on campus must follow the same restraints applied to all other forms of speech. Both sides, however, commit cardinal error in this argument. The error is this: the professor's speech is *not really spoken speech*. That professors "speak" their minds or "speak" the truth is a figure of speech. They *think* freely and *write* freely. They do not actually *speak* freely. Their actual spoken speech must come under the restraint of all other spoken speeches. But their free speech is really their free thought (or ideas) expressed in scholarship. And their scholarship is basically expressed in writing. When he actually *speaks* to his colleagues at a professional meeting or to his students in a classroom, he is actually vocalizing his *thoughts*. His colleagues and students could very well learn of them by reading his writings. When a professor vocally interrupted an invited speaker at Northwestern University[4] and was denied tenure subsequently for her disruptive action, the professor had obviously confused these two types of free speech. Professors may speak or protest another speaker only as partisan members of the issue at hand, not as scholars, and should not claim academic freedom in that case. A scholar's audience is always the public at large, and his medium the writing of his thoughts and ideas. By vocalizing a partisan issue, he adds just one more voice to the many. This makes it ordinary, not special. The special privilege of tenure and academic freedom must be used in a special way for a special purpose. Vocal protests are no special way; partisan issues are no special purpose.

There will be immediate objections to the characterization of the free professor as our modern day "philosopher king." However, there may be fewer objections to characterizing him as a "super citizen." The new title is not undeserved. He is the best educated person; he is most knowledgeable in ways of human nature; he is the freest of all from self-interest that would interfere with his judgment. He is the best qualified among all in every way that our society has to offer. As a super citizen, his view of his society and fellow men is accurate, unbiased, and independent. As a member of that supercitizenry, together with other members of that body, he makes up the living "think tank" for his society. From this role, he dispenses his knowledge, wisdom, and truth for the benefit of his society. Is this too farfetched a view of the tenured professor in his most extended potential?

Let us look at the difference between ordinary citizens and the super citizen in an idealized, if slightly exaggerated, way to make our point. The difference, however idealized or exaggerated for contrast, cannot be over-emphasized. The ordinary citizen in a market society is conventional in his behavior, beholden to the norms of society over which he has no choice but to acquiesce. His thinking is wholly predictable—that is to say, sectarian and parochial. His views are almost entirely partisan and self-interested. He shares the usual amount of prejudice, bias, ignorance, bigotry of his fellow men. His economic imperative forces him to be servile and weak-minded. The cultural artifacts he must live with or crave make him gullible to mass persuasion and escapist fantasy. He shows little or no interest in the long-term implications of his present action. His taste tends to be physical, sensory, philistine. He is easily captivated by pecuniary motivation at the expense of personal loyalty, commitment, or passion. He rarely reads anything more overextending than the daily newspaper and speculates little beyond the next step. He is easily given to lying, deception, and propaganda effect. His every move, mood, and modus operandi is well studied and compiled to be used against him. He is constantly praised by politicians and commercials so that he generally remains juvenile in his self-appraisal and stupid in his social judgment.

In an advanced market society where surplus production must clear the dock at all times, the ordinary citizen as a consumer is a valuable commodity. It is his very ordinariness that makes him valuable for corporate plans and political campaigns. Great commercial or electoral failures occur normally when his intellectual capacity is overestimated. Time and again he proves that a voluntary citizen in an advanced market society is most susceptible to mental inertia. Things and ideas that appeal to him are carefully designed by the experts to arouse the least amount of his inertia, both physical and intellectual, yet maximum desire. Life in general has become too complex for him. His interpersonal relations are puzzling even in their most intimate setting. The world has shrunk into his living room, yet it is a wholly alien world, incomprehensible, remote, and unreal. His moods swing easily, capriciously and without genuine passion, but according to the plans that are set for him. In his utter predictability and ordinariness survives the very economic and political infrastructure of America's market society.

The only thing that stands between him and the world that controls him, body and soul, is the super citizen, the scholar, the truth-teller. In the super citizen, the ordinary citizen finds his greatest ally. In its perhaps unintended wisdom, America's market society has also created the super citizen, free from all the weaknesses and vulnerabilities of the ordinary citizen. He is educated and cultured to the finest degree at the best institutions of higher learning. He has read great books to broaden his mind and spirit. He is guaranteed for life to be safe and secure in the Ivory Tower, only to pursue the truth as he sees fit. He is the guardian of high virtues and lofty ideas. He is the hero for the coming generation and the carrier of the finest among human heritage. He is the super citizen to come to the rescue of the ordinary citizen in self-peril. America's future depends on his honest, independent, and critical judgment, which is nothing less than the truth.

The only thing that stands between this idealized version of his work and his degeneration into an ordinary citizen is the scholar himself. He can corrupt himself and he can redeem himself. American society has given him the choice unconditionally and absolutely. At no time in the history of higher learning has an individual scholar been given such a choice before now. The implications are as mind-boggling as its burdens are overwhelming.

Tenure unused is tenure irrelevant, it has been argued. Tenure misused is also tenure to be taken away. The society that gives tenure can also take it away. On balance, tenure underused does greater harm to itself than tenure overused in the right way. No society can have too much of a good thing, and no society seeking self-improvement and perfection can have too much truth said about itself. But the professor's job is foremost that of persuasion. Every device in the storage—emotional, historical, logical, rhetorical, polemical, scientific, even poetic—must be used in his persuasion. His job is neither to confront nor to destroy existing society. It is to persuade the society to improve and possibly perfect itself. To do the job, the professor will find that his own honesty of thought, freedom from self-interest, and defense of truth are among the best means of persuasion. No one likes criticism, but honest criticism is easier to accept than dishonest criticism. Tenure overused in this fashion can be forgiven. Tenure unused or underused in inaction cannot.

The super citizen-scholar should avoid being identified with a known partisan group or its dogma. That includes the Marxists, which brings up an issue of great import that I shall examine separately in the following chapter. The professor's criticism is validated only to the extent that it is *believable*. It is believable only to the extent that it is believed to be honestly and independently derived. Identification with a partisan group or a doctrinal ideology hurts its effect. The professor must demonstrate time and again that his loyalty is to the truth for the benefit of the largest humanity possible and for the longest posterity possible. He must transcend his own institution or own society if it conflicts with his larger aim. He cannot trivialize the meaning of tenure and academic freedom by misusing it for essentially partisan ends or personal gains. Why should a special privilege be given professors only to be used for ordinary ends when other citizens are denied the same privilege for pursuing the same goals?

There is yet another form of partisan scholarship, which I would call "localized scholarhip." Women tend to specialize in women's studies; blacks in Afro-American specialties; Asians in Asian-American communities; Europeans in European history or philosophy or sociology. When women are inspired by injustice observed in instances against women, the truth is in the injustice for all vulnerable persons in market society. The immediate localized scholarship will pursue injustice against women. More localized, injustice against that particular population of women under study. Blacks and Asians almost invariably make black studies and Asian studies their specialties. These are all localized scholarships serving partisan ends. Wherever women, blacks, Asians, or any other vulnerable groups experience injustice, it is injustice to all humanity. Solutions to one instance of injustice should be solutions to all instances of injustice. Solutions to one group may not apply to those of other groups unless the solutions are universally applicable. Subjective authenticity, which group experience inevitably strengthens in the scholar, must be transformed into some objective statement, or truth, about justice and injustice, humanity and inhumanity, and ultimately truth and untruth. Truth about injustice in a particular social system must be the aim of all such scholars. In the end, all truth converges on the whole system of power that corrupts or on the verge of corruption to the degree of its self-defensibility.

The self-defensible society that grants tenure and academic freedom in exchange for truth is often unaware of its own action regarding that very exchange. It gives the scholar his freedom yet binds him to an oath of loyalty to the state. Many a state university has dismissed professors, especially during the McCarthy era, for refusing to take the oath of allegiance to the state. A good deal of debate over academic freedom has been dominated by this particular issue. Should the scholar take the oath and keep the job or refuse it and possibly lose the job? It is a dilemma for the society as well as for the professor. For the society, it is self-contradiction; it grants freedom of conscience and yet binds it into an oath. For the professor, it is a choice between his conscience and suffering as a result of it. Luckily or unluckily depending on the point of view, this no longer seems to matter seriously nowadays. The state is not too insistent on its loyalty and the professoriate is not too rigid with its conscience.

My personal choice of action would be to take the oath as required and later write an article or a book pointing out the contradiction to either change the oath itself to a "scholar's oath" to the truth (as we considered in the beginning) or to have it dropped from practice. At any rate, the state no longer considers the professor a serious threat to either its conscience or its legitimacy. In view of the professor as guardian of the truth, this is altogether a bad development. It simply shows how far he has been removed from the ideal—and in many ways the only—model of scholarship and truthfulness that we have so far considered.

NOTES

1. Pros and cons of the professor's political activity can be found in Edmund L. Pincoffs, ed., *The Concept of Academic Freedom* (Austin, TX: University of Texas Press, 1972). See especially chapters by William Van Alstyne, "The Specific Theory

of Academic Freedom and the General Issue of Civil Liberty," 59–85, and John R. Searl, "Two Concepts of Academic Freedom," 86–96.

2. Van Alstyne, quoted in Pincoffs, *Concept of Academic Freedom*, 63–77.

3. Hans Morgenthau, *The Purpose of American Politics* (New York: Vintage Books, 1960), especially 63–77.

4. Committee A on Academic Freedom and Tenure, AAUP "Northwestern University: A Case of Denial of Tenure" (May-June 1988), 55–70.

Chapter 12

The Americanization of Marx

No discussion of social criticism would be complete without discussion of Karl Marx and academic freedom at American universities. Marx poses no small dilemma between academic freedom and social order. In the pyramid of academic hierarchy, Marxists occupy a precarious footing. In an ostensibly free, open society guaranteeing tenure and academic freedom, being a Marxist or being known to be a Marxist is still no small burden to carry. The way Marxist teachers are treated, often denied tenure for the sole reason that they *are* Marxists, threatens to make a mockery out of our claim to academic freedom and open society.[1] The celebrated case of Marxist philosophy teacher Angela Davis at the University of California, Los Angeles, readily comes to mind. Even where the truth receives more than perfunctory lip service, conservative inertia will single out the Marxist truth as different from the orthodox truth.

The position of both sides is fairly fixed and immovable. The university is an institution of higher learning in a capitalist society. The aim of capitalism is to make money, and it subordinates all its energies and components to advance this very aim. To claim otherwise, tenure privilege and academic freedom notwithstanding, would be tantamount to denying the very existence of American society itself. Marxism is also fixed in its own position. It has been feared by the capitalist order precisely because Marxism's existence makes capitalism's existence untenable. If Marx is right, capitalism is wrong. If Marxism asserts itself, capitalism must fall. It is the central tenet of Marxist thought that capitalism's days are numbered. This makes even mere mention of Marx a fairly eventful thing among capitalist believers. Marxism is perhaps the most anxiety-producing single word in the capitalist vocabulary. Nothing less than the total destruction of capitalism would do, and a good Marxist sees signs of this self-destruction everywhere in America.

Where a Marxist professor is concerned, academic freedom and the ostensibly free society that grants it get their most severe testing. More often than not, academic freedom and American society flunk the test and the Marxist is shown the door. But seldom would an individual department or an institution admit that one is denied tenure because he is a Marxist. The procedure always finds some other flaws making the professor unfit for tenure. Whatever other shortcomings the professor may have, his Marxist legacy is the most burdensome of all. And the American senior professoriate is fairly conservative toward Marxists in its midst.

The dilemma is obvious. No society will want to destroy itself by granting immunity of action to its worst enemy, at least not knowingly. It may be an open society to its own citizens, but not to its enemy. All things being equal, moreover, the rule of power's self-defense applies. As always, a power will not willingly reduce its own powerfulness. Granting Marxists free action would amount to, if all goes well for them, a capitalist suicide. That, common sense tells us, will not happen. Many Marxist professors survive, and even prosper, at American universities. But they are rather circumspect about their intellectual and pedagogical activities. Active Marxists are rarely given tenure without some struggle on both sides. This dilemma will continue, and no solution would be forthcoming to resolve the pains of ideas in conflict without some radical rethinking for both parties.

Every social system must survive in any way it can. No society has any other primary obligation than that of its own survival. But American society is not just a social system. It is *American* society. It prides itself on being the only society that grants almost wholly unconditional tenure and academic freedom to its professors. It is open to improvement toward a "more perfect union." But contrary to some past conservative reactions manifest especially during the 1970s, survival and perfection need not be mutually exclusive. American society *can* be open to infinite criticism for perfection *and* survive as a social system. In fact, America's adaptability to need for change has been cited by many as its greatest virtue for survival and prosperity. But this adaptability to change comes about only because of its critics. Other societies may silence their critics and live. But American society can liberate its critics, or even guarantee the safety of their criticism, and still prosper.

Obviously, Marxism is America's most severe and most formidable critic. Yet because of this very fact, Marxism also performs the *most beneficial* function for American society's own improvement and perfection. This very view of Marxism *for* America is the solution to the dilemma. Marx must be Americanized.

The worst one can do to one's enemy is to "improve" him toward one's own image. The Marxists can do just that by helping make American society move ever closer to their own image of America. To improve it toward a "Marxist" America is to score victory on American society. If reality conforms to claim, America will be more just, more merciful, more generous, more free, and less greedy and selfish. That this "new and improved America" may not wholly be a "Marxist state" is, at least for the immediate future, irrelevant. One bird in practice is perhaps more beneficial than two in theory. An improved America toward truth and justice is much preferable to a status quo America. To that end the Marxist critic must concentrate his energy and creativity, not to destroying it.

American society *is* perhaps strong enough to grant unconditional tenure and academic freedom to its critics. But it does not *feel* strong enough to tolerate the avowed anti-Americanism of its Marxist professors. Time and again, pushed by activists on both sides, it has reacted in extreme fashion and called for the critic's head. To survive the dilemma, Marxist criticism, like all other criticisms, must be criticism *for* American society, not against it. The Marxist truth must also be the truth *for* American society, not against it. In the end, a perfect America may be indistinguishable from a Marxist America.[2] Marxism may be said to have triumphed and achieved its objective when American society has been completely transformed in the Marxist image—just, truthful, and happy. It has been transformed without being destroyed. There is a significant difference between the two, and therein lies, I believe, the salavation for both academic freedom and Marxism in America. Both sides must concede the importance of the other for *their own* goal.

Marxist professors come with impeccable credentials as social critics. If all academic professors in American society turned truth-pursuing critics, the Marxist would be head and shoulders above them all. Reflecting on my personal experience, I have found the Marxists to be among the most widely read scholars. Their knowledge of intellectual history, political economy, and literature in general is far superior to that of average academic professors. In spite of their "Marxist" bias, or perhaps because of it, their breadth and scope in scholarship are often greater and more encompassing than those academics who claim "balance" and "objectivity" in their knowledge. As individual human beings, they are unfailingly men and women of decency and integrity. Rarely have I found among Marxist professors the kind of hustling, self-serving, servile attitudes for petty rewards or back-stabbing treachery that are common among academic professors. Their conviction for truth and justice and happiness is as fearless as it is deep. They are, in their work habits, dedicated, earnest, industrious. Indeed, they are among the finest of the American professoriate. Their only sin, for which they pay dearly, is that they believe in Marxism. As America's own dissidents, they are not welcome.

But if all these qualities of scholarship and character could be mobilized *for* America's own benefit, there would be no better academic critic than the Marxist professor. As his persuaded truth, not forced through socialization, his belief in Marxism is perhaps the purest truth there is. The task both for him and for American society is how to mobilize his excellence for America's benefit.

There is really no secret in solving the dilemma once the task is understood and agreed on. The Marxists must persuade American society that it is in *its* best interest to become a *better* society and that more of the status quo would not serve its best interest. It is as much a matter of style as it is that of substance. Marxism can be taught in ways that would benefit American society's most urgent task, namely, its own improvement toward perfection. It must be taught *without* invoking doctrinal Marxism. It must be the *ideas* from Marxism that help American society most beneficially. A self-improving and self-perfecting society is willing to learn from any source where the truth may be found. Whatever one's ideological color, it must be acknowledged that Karl Marx is now established beyond dispute (even with the collapse of Soviet communism) as one of history's greatest truth-sayers. Why would American society refuse to learn from his ideas if they would help its own improvement and perfection? It can be argued that America's granting of tenure and academic freedom is nothing but a smoke screen to pacify its own intelligentsia. Whatever its motive, the fact remains that the American professoriate is in possession of the rarest kind of intellectual freedom that the world has ever seen. There is no reason why Marxist professors cannot enjoy it like the rest.

Lest we forget, the purpose of tenure and academic freedom is the unfettered pursuit of the truth. In the end, when truth is pursued honestly, independently, and critically, it may all converge to be *one* kind of truth. When truth is pursued under the precondition of selflessness, every truth-seeker will converge upon similar conclusions about human happiness in community, society, and humanity. After all, the Marxist truth, if pursued selflessly, is also one of history's great ideas, perhaps more truthful than most. Why should American society find *that* truth unacceptable? Karl Marx's ideas of a happy, perfect society, taken as a whole, are not too different from those of Socrates, Jesus, Lincoln, Gandhi, or Martin Luther King, Jr.

Under the protection of tenure and academic freedom as a special privilege, what the Marxist professor may or may not do is the same as that for the more activist academic professor. His privilege (whether tenured or probationary) is for *academic* freedom, not for a movement. His freedom guarantees (if he is tenured) his *thought*, not action. He is not to be a revolutionary in the streets any more than an academic professor is. He is a professor pursuing the truth and teaching the truth he has found, which is protected, not actual speech or action that provokes immediate reaction. His audience is the larger society and posterity, as is the academic professor's. He may write and publish the truth that has a Marxist origin, but the truth must be there first *before* Marx. *As* a professor protected by academic freedom (tenured or not), his allegiance is to the truth first, and Marxism next. In the way he pursues truth, the way he presents it, and the way he persuades his society with it, and in other subtle ways, this difference must be taken seriously.

What the Marxist professor faces at a typical university is indeed formidable. He is asked to teach Marxism, or whatever American society can learn from it for its own benefit, without being a Marxist. The question then should be, How can Marxism benefit American society? Not, How to convert American society to Marxism? Marxism, personified in the professor, must be adapted to America's quest for improvement and perfection, not the other way around. Tenure and academic freedom, after all, are established to make American society a more truthful, more just, and happier place. If it takes Marxism to do it, then the Marxist professor will have to persuade America that it is in *its* own benefit to do so.

But the task is made slightly easier by the very nature of American society itself. As a liberal market society, America is much more adaptable to beneficial suggestions than are more doctrinally rigid social systems. It is not committed to any preconceived principle requiring absolute submission. America, after all, is a free-floating, self-interested nation, willing to compromise for its own benefit. The Soviets and Amish might die for a principle, but average Americans are not likely to die for "Americanism." Capitalism, touted as the pillar that upholds all that is America, is by no means carved in stone. People believe in it, or so they insist, only because it works or seems to work. They believe in the results, not in the doctrine. Those who believe in capitalism are the first to abandon it if it does not work, or if there is a better alternative. Even a Donald Trump or an Ivan Boesky will listen to a good deal, even a spiritually good deal. And human happiness, however it may be defined, is a potentially good deal that will get their attention. So is truth. So is justice. The only unyielding principle that governs American behavior is self-interest. And the main task for the Marxist or any academic professor is to show that self-interest is against truth, against justice, and against human happiness, and in the end against all that is dear to American life. That this is a difficult task, or almost impossible, to accomplish is irrelevant. The professor has no other duty than to persuade his society to the truth he has found. And in this act of persuasion he is soundly protected by academic freedom.

Conscience often takes a heavy toll on the believer. The protection that academic freedom accords in contemporary American society against such a toll is no mean variety. History is replete with instances where one often died for speaking the truth (e.g., Socrates and Jesus). Less traumatic, one was often subject to ostracism, poverty, ridicule, neglect, obscurity, and other such inconveniences simply because one believed in something. Whatever one believes in honestly, independently, and critically is one's truth, and the truth necessarily irritates authority and popular opinion. There are no such personal inconveniences as the price of truth at American universities, at least for the tenured professor. The protection accorded in tenure and academic freedom, however, is for university professors only and for the express pursuit of the truth only. It is not for freedom to carry on a movement or a mission. The Marxist professor may accept his present position in the American academy under these provisions. It is still considerably improved over the bygone era and is still freer than in other societies. Along with his other colleagues, he is no longer subject to great tortures and deprivations for his truth. He is merely asked to tell the truth in a way that would benefit the society that guarantees his own safety of thought. This may be a small price to pay for his freedom to speak the truth.

It is incumbent upon American society to do its part in this rethinking about Marxism. Its part consists of simply recognizing the idea that one's worst enemy is always the best source of truth about oneself. Whether we like it or not, what our worst enemy has to say about us is one truth we would rather avoid knowing. But that is one truth that would do us the *most good*. A man's character is perhaps best revealed by what his ex-wife says about him. Where the truth is pursued and accepted, one's worst enemy is one's best benefactor. Where falsehood is pursued and accepted, flattery and lying are most welcome. Hence, the greatest truth about American society has to come from its worst political enemies. Marxist criticism undoubtedly is thus the best form of self-revealing tonic that American society can find anywhere. Its own "friends" will say virtually nothing that is the painful truth about American society. And that will not help.

We in American society ardently applaud any sign of "Americanization" in our worst enemy, namely, the Soviet Union. We have wished that free enterprise would be taught in the Soviet university or practiced in the marketplace. We believe that the Soviet system will improve to the *extent* that such ideas influence their social consciousness and action. We applaud their dissidents precisely for that reason: they improve the Soviet system on *our* behalf. Why should this principle not work in *reverse*? What else would improve American capitalism than the influence of its worst enemy, namely, Marxism? Why could we not introduce Marxism into the American university curriculum and applaud our own dissidents, namely, the Marxist professors?

The conservative answer to these questions is obviously that we do not *believe* in Marxism. But the same conservative inertia has also given the professor tenure and academic freedom in the sole interest of the truth. Through tenure and academic freedom, American society has declared that truth comes before capitalism. To demand that the Marxist professor put truth before Marxism, the American university must demand that the same truth be put before *capitalism* as well.

After all the truth has been honestly, independently, and critically pursued, we may still end up poles apart between Marxism and capitalism. But that sort of pursuit has not yet taken place in the American academy in total earnest. The typical academic professor is neither a gentleman nor a scholar, much less a selfless seeker of the truth. He has been more the self-serving academic hustler than the truth-seeker. The typical Marxist professor has been unforgiving in his demand for the overthrow of American capitalism. He has delighted in the possibility that the protector of his own intellectual freedom is destined to fall. From these unyielding positions, neither side has considered the truth *for* American society before its own predetermined course of thought and action. Neither the self-serving academic professor nor the doctrinal Marxist has given the truth his whole commitment.

The best defense against one's critic is to make his criticism irrelevant by making it unnecessary. In Latin America, land reform has been one of the sore points that arouse the leftist guerillas to great passion. Their passion is so great that the dominant society must expend a great deal of its own energy and resource to fend off the guerilla attacks. Why would the government not simply institute a land reform that would make the criticism irrelevant by making it unnecessary? The truth about land reform arouses equally great passion from the landed class, which would rather go on with the fights at enormous expense. The real truth may be that the country and its posterity will be better off with the truth for land reform than the truth against it. Whatever the reason for the inability of land reform, the critic continues his attacks and the defender continues his costly defense. As long as this continues, the critic will find his criticism relevant and necessary.

Only self-interested falsehood would deny that Marx is perhaps America's best critic and one who could do it the most good. American society, while protecting academic freedom, may refuse to accept the Marxist truth. But the disinterested observer also notices that this will put America's claim to academic truth in great jeopardy and possibly reveal hypocrisy, which it would rather avoid. The Marxist critic says a good deal about America's injustice in wealth and poverty, domestic and foreign policy, and war and peace. This sort of criticism will be recognized as true and accepted as valid by American society *only if* it considers the truth beneficial to its own improvement and perfection. Recognizing and accepting these and other similar charges as valid would seem to require, on the surface, much courage and sacrifice. But the simple truth is that these charges are *good* for America's own self-interest. Only criticisms will improve a social system; only criticisms will prevent a power from its own inevitable self-corruption.

The academic professor himself also stands to benefit from Marxism. No serious professor in any academic field can do adequate thinking and teaching without having read Marx. No serious scholar's preparatory education can be complete without a solid knowledge of Marxist literature. No serious humanist can go about his daily business without being familiar with the Marxist tradition in Western thought. Anyone who seriously thinks about truth and justice and happiness in America or anywhere else is perhaps more deeply indebted to Marxist thought than he realizes or openly recognizes. Much more to the point, many of the concepts developed by Marx are crucial to understanding contemporary American society. In fact, often they are the only conceptual tools available. There is no conceptual equivalent, for example, of alienation in the non-Marxist literature, none as effective and accurate. No other concept illuminates the feelings of hopelessness, powerlessness, and meaninglessness in modern working life quite the way Marx's alienation does.

The importance of Marxist legacy in American social thought is evident in the works of virtually every major social critic—Veblen, Mills, Galbraith, Schumpeter, to name just a few—in the twentieth century. Without becoming "Marxist," they made intelligent use of Marxist thought to describe and analyze contemporary America. Some of the most insightful and dynamic analyses of American society have come from those who know Marx and have learned from him the essentials of social analysis. That Karl Marx has become the quintessential archvillain of American capitalism is the purely accidental work of history in the Soviet Union. Marxism with or without the Soviets (now without) would have remained part of the quintessential American scholarship regardless. It is his power of intellect and passion for humanity that are the basic inspirations of modern social criticism. It also makes up part of the grand tradition of Western humanistic quests—both secular and ecclesiastic—in which social criticism has taken the dominant role. In American tradition, Edward Bellamy's earlier utopian nationalism is as much part of Marxist legacy as the contemporary feminist and civil rights movement. In all, Americanized Marx has benefitted American society's own quest for truth, justice, and happiness. Marx pricks America's conscience whenever it gets groggy.

One of the persistent popular complaints about Marxism in writings or classrooms is the use of Marxist language. Many of the so-called Marxist concepts grate on the American mind and give that peculiarly "Marxist" color, which add to popular resentment against Marx. Terms like "dialectic" or "exploitation" are the bread-and-butter ingredients of Marxism, but they can be nicely translated into American terms that might avoid unnecessary inflammation in classrooms or in public forums. Manipulation by commercials on television, corruption in presidential campaigns, disproportionality in salaries of corporate presidents and athletes as opposed to secretaries and schoolteachers, and any number of such familiar cultural artifacts can be used to illustrate the point without resorting to those awful-sounding terms unique to Marxism. Where discretion is the better part of valor, there is no reason not to heed the simple wisdom.

After all has been said and done, no party may be satisfied with our suggestion for Americanizing Marx. Yet, there is little doubt that an Americanized Marx would serve everyone's purpose far better and in greater peace of mind than a Marx against America.

NOTES

1. The most recent case at this writing was reported in an article about an economics professor at Virginia Commonwealth University. See Debbra E. Blum "Professor Sues Va. Commonwealth U., Claims Politics Cost Her Tenure," *Chronicle of Higher Education*, 1 Feb. 1989.

2. Leon Samson, a socialist, made this observation to explain the difficulty of establishing a socialist movement in America. See Leon Samson, *Towards a United Front* (New York: Farrar and Reinhart, 1933).

Part IV

Betrayal of the Professor

Chapter 13

Professor as Professional

One of the most predominant intellectual assumptions of modern professors, and their most dominant psychological profile, is undoubtedly in "professionalization" and its attendant "professionalism." The academic professor, especially, sees professionalism as his appropriate mental outlook and professionalization as his relevant advancement in society. By and large he thinks and acts like a "professional" in a "professional" manner. His colleagues are professional associates and their gatherings constitute professional meetings. As a professional, he is intensely interested in the rules of personal conduct appropriate to his new status and the canons of academic production acceptable to his collective organization. This tendency toward professionalization, perhaps more than anything else in our time, profoundly affects his mindset and work habits, and as a result, the very meaning of truth itself. In a nutshell, what has been gained through tenure and academic freedom (individual truth) has been lost through professionalism.

There were times when commitment to an academic career constituted a "calling."[1] Along with the callings of the clergy, artists, and revolutionaries, the academic calling stood as a personal commitment to a set of values and ideals that far transcended worldly rewards. Along with the other callings, the academic career evolved around the notion of "truth," each calling defining its own truth. The clergy found it in their faith, artists in their art, and revolutionaries in their utopia. Alongside yet often above them, the academic truth often coincided with the other truths, and more often, it also defined the truth for the other callings.

With the coming of the modern industrialized world, all this has changed. The clergy, artists, and revolutionaries, along with professors, have become by and large *professional* ministers, artists, revolutionaries, and professors. It is the professional ethos that now occupies them as specific guide to general conduct; it is the professional reward that inspires their initial commitment; and it is the professional reliance on technical knowledge that identifies what is professionally acceptable and what is not. This last element of professionalism affects the academic professor more than any other. It is what drives his subconscious mind ever toward science, utility, and standard that he regards as professionally necessary. Above all, he is a professional man first, and an academic professor next.

The professionalizing tendency of academics culminated in the 1950s and 1960s when the floodgate to academic membership opened.[2] It allowed an influx of great numbers into academia, which resulted in a complete democratization of professors. It was no longer even a superficially elitist group, at least culturally if not economically. During this period of rapid growth for the American university the professoriate obtained a middle-class status. With this trend came the final push toward professionalization defined mainly by scientific, utilitarian, and standardized practices and canons. In it the original idealism for truth, however vague, was gradually replaced by "service" idealism in a more concrete, practical context of everyday life. The professionalized professor began to see himself not as a pursuer of some vaguely defined truth, but as a man of practical action, a solver of real problems, and a follower of scientific rationality.

Under the large historical umbrella of professionalization also came the tendency to unite the traditionally divided fields between functional sciences and academic departments. Technical expertise essential to professionalism brought the preponderance of rational and scientific models to their activity and thought. The chemist and the philosopher were now both professionals, although accorded slightly varying recognitions of their status, one thought to be more professional than the other. Nevertheless, the terms of professionalization applied to both and other such fields. Technicality and culture, science and politics, mathematics and experience converged under professionalism and were united in the minds of academic professionals. Virtually every field wanted to be a professional field, and by necessity virtually every field adopted the premise that the world—both material and moral—is one large, unified element subject to professional studies. Both chemists and philosophers were now fellow professionals, slightly different in methodologies yet essentially united under the premise of professionalism that both now shared.

In the last decade of this century, such is the largely predominant feature and profile of the academic man. With minor variations, the professor today defines himself first and last as a professional. The term "scholar" is nowadays seldom used and often in an irrelevant context of ceremony and rhetoric. No longer conceived of or perceived as a calling, the academic career is now defined almost exclusively in the "economic" model and "legalistic" model. The first sees academic life in a careerist sense, as a source of job, income, and economic security. In it, tenure is seen as a permanent job, and academic freedom as protection against unemployment. The second sees academic life in a contractual sense rather than in a symbolic context of personal commitment. The job is an objective fact of credentials, contractual specifics in job descriptions, and legally binding rules of dismissal only upon material evidence and adversary proceedings.

Perhaps the most profound effect of the change in the modern professor can be observed in the transformation of his "professorialism" (defined in *Webster's New Twentieth Century Dictionary, Unabridged*, Second Edition, as "the character, habits or manner of thinking of a professor") into professionalism. With it has evaporated the tenuous but necessary assumption in human thinking that nature and society, material possession and human happiness, science and politics, facts and truth, functional fields and academic fields are two separate spheres of action and thought. It has been on the assumption of such divisions that truth is searched and facts are researched, politics debated and rockets tested, love felt and cells counted. The character, habits, or manner of thinking of a professor are now those of a technical professional guided almost exclusively by the scientific model. By becoming professionalized, however, the academic professor has made himself a technician, not an honest, independent, critical mind in pursuit of his own truth. That this is so is necessarily in the *very nature of professionalism* itself that no artificial effort can avoid.

Professionalism is bound by rules, regulations, principles, and other established guidelines, some divine and some human. If it involves material objects, as in physical science, the guidelines are divinely predetermined by the physical workings of nature. The goal is to discover what the physical laws of nature *are*, not to create them or alter them. If it involves human objects, as in accounting, social work, or law, the guidelines are given in the respective regulatory rules of society. The professional does not make the guidelines; he merely follows them and goes wherever they may lead him. As a specialist skilled in the field, he cannot deviate from these pre-established rules of conduct, whether providential or social. He is by necessity beholden to them. He is, as a professional, no longer an autonomous thinker resolutely pursuing his own truth and free to create his own rules in the process. Professionalism is thus quite contrary to daring imagination, creative initiative, or unorthodox inquiries. The "creative lattitude" that is often cited as instrinsic to professionalism is essentially the creativity of a mission already defined. Every technical professional needs room to operate.

Naturally, as a professional one does not make decisions. The professional rules do. What is commonly referred to as professional decision-making is in fact a series of technical and standardized choices that the professional man cannot control. He may make the necessary distinction between two alternate courses of action, but the alternate courses of action are not his own making. They are produced by his profession. Whether a scientist or an academic, a *professional* does not create his own methodology of research or a journal in which to publish the results. He merely chooses one that best serves his task and purpose. Good professionals never make "personal" decisions; they either follow rules or wait for orders from above. The professionalized professor, no matter what his field, cannot make any independent decisions regarding society and individuals *outside* the rules already established. He cannot pursue the truth about them by his own rules of conduct. Decisions made by professionals might as well be made by computers if they were so capable, as some decisions *are* indeed made by computers.

It is not unlike the task for a man who must go home. The destination is already set by circumstances. He may experiment with a variety of ways to get there, some even novel or exciting or creative. He might even encounter a semi-mysterious revelation in his search for the best way. But get there he must. Whether to go home or not is not his decision. *How* to get there in the best technical sense is the question he must answer. "Scientific" enterprises, the now-universally accepted modes of technical decision-making, are nothing but a more complex series of finding ways to get home. The task has already been decided for him. He must accomplish it as cheaply—or as efficiently—as possible for those who have set the task for him.

This unavoidable fact in professionalism makes it equally unavoidable that the professor-as-professional's capacity is severely restricted to a subject that is clearly defined as a *technical* one. He much prefers that the definition come with its perimeters and ranges and available alternatives. Any effort at degrading or embellishing professionalism will be both unnecessary and inaccurate. Technical expertise is the beginning and ending of all professional activities. The technical imperative in professionalism need not be asserted, for it is so overwhelming that it can merely be assumed without assertion.

One of the primary driving forces for professionalism is its economic reward. A professor who thinks of himself as a professional does not think about scholarship as his intrinsic reward. He thinks about tenure, promotion, salary increase, and other signs of academic perks, and lets the rest take care of itself. He chooses his field of endeavor with both eyes on the economic implications. He invests time and money in return for economic security and even superiority, derived directly from the selling of his expertise and competence in the chosen field. That it happens to be a university, not the marketplace, is easily resolved by the overriding professional definition of his being. Lacking in talent for a more prestigious occupation, such as medicine or nuclear physics, one may consider a lesser field like philosophy or sociology. But considering the light intellectual requirement and routinized professional progression, such academic fields are no mean places for economic careerism. That their economic reward is meager (compared with some others) must be compensated for by the lightness and routineness of their task, not by the loftiness of their idealism. The professional imperative, although one may indignantly protest, makes the latter irrelevant as a factor and negligible in subconscious.

In this way, professionalism accords well with the supply and demand principle of a market society where talent is bid and sold. In this, the professor naturally thinks of himself as a commodity competing for the best price the market will bear. The more successful among them are perennially roving door-to-door salesmen, moving from one university to another in search of the highest price. The superstar professors are like all other superstars. They command fierce bidding for their service in what Professor Mary A. Burgan calls "The Superstar Syndrome."[3] Normally, a professionalized professor stays in one place only because he cannot get a higher price for his service elsewhere. A fierce protest from him would instantly be nullified by the simple fact that he has not served the interest of anyone since his matriculation except his own, with no sign of truth anywhere pursued. The fierceness of his protest is matched only by the emptiness of his record. His record, if examined with detached conscience, is purely that of a professional on the make, not that of a scholar in pursuit of the truth. Often, the professional protests too much about his devotion to service idealism to make his claim credible.

As professionalism draws the academic professor ever closer to the circle of more prestigious and established functional fields, for the obvious benefit of being associated with the prosperous brother, the functional professor makes a similar move in the *opposite* direction. He tends to define his functionality in the all-encompassing fields of human welfare. The scientist now wants to be the Scientist of Human Happiness. The golf instructor wants to enhance his pupil's self-actualization; the accountant wants to contribute to one's peace of mind; the mathematician wants to apply his knowledge to solving all social problems. The librarian wants to be the guardian of great ideas and books in society. No functional professor is now satisfied simply doing his technical thing. He wants to be the guru of all humanity and define its happiness for all mankind.

This trend is easily explained by the facts that (1) the academic professor no longer shows any interest in the inherently "political" questions of his society, and (2) professionalism is considered the know-it-all panacea of the contemporary world. The academic professor is too busy emulating the methods, models, and procedures of his brother functional professor to worry about his traditional task. Professionalism is so dominant a force in shaping the modern technical world that it is only natural that human happiness should also be defined by its technical experts and in their own terms. This view is so reasonably held that to assert it would be redundant. But implications from this trend do not bear happy conclusions, for in professionalism, truth and facts are once again harmonized into irrelevance and meaninglessness.

Technique belongs to functional fields, politics to no one in particular. There are technical experts in all material facts. A chemist is an expert in chemistry; a nuclear physicist in nuclear science; a real estate law professor in real estate laws, and so on. They hold, in their specific fields of expertise, knowledge that is not publicly available. But there is no such thing as a "politics" expert. From interpersonal relations (the smallest politics) to international relations (the largest politics), everyone is an expert so to speak. No sane person will consult a political scientist on the eve of a presidential election. No sane person will want a psychologist to pronounce the fitness of his or her prospective matrimonial partner. The mind is already made up one way or another. One may consult an astrologer or a medicine man for good oracles, but neither is a professional expert. For a broken bone, one will rely on an orthopedist. For a vote on nationalized health care, one will rely on oneself. It would be absurd to think that the bone expert is also an expert in the politics of who should get health care, who should pay, how much, and why.

The functional expert need not persuade his clients, students, or public in general about the fact of a broken bone. One look at the X-ray will settle that. But an academic professor must persuade, when he has come upon the truth, everyone who will hear him that it is for everyone's happiness that his truth be heard. The academic professor, however, claims no expertise. He merely shows his familiarity with the great ideas (or truths) and thinkers who have grappled with similar problems before and have come to certain conclusions. The conclusions are now reapplied, through his persuasion, to the political decisions of our own time. It is entirely possible, although not likely, that a functional professor has this familiarity with the truth of his own, independent of his own professional ethos and canons of conduct. Physicians sometimes write creatively. If they are successful, like Sir Arthur Conan Doyle in the nineteenth century and Robin Cook in our own days, however, they will quit their profession to become full-time writers. One kind of decision-making cannot take place within the framework of the other. One does not consistently vote Republican when he remains in the Democratic party.

Technical decisions are fairly straightforward. The difficulties, which are legion, are not the difficulties of the decisions themselves. They simply arise due to lack of adequate knowledge. But the experts will have to make do with what they have, which is considerable, and go ahead with their decisions and solutions to the task. The differences of opinion among experts are merely different technical interpretations, not opposing truths, and they are resolved within the ethos and canons of professionalism. The simplicity of technique, as opposed to the complexity of politics, has to do with the inherently "rational" approach that all professional tasks require. It is a decision of means and ends, economy, and logistical efficiency. Whatever is best for (1) the ends sought, (2) without spending unnecessary expenditure, and (3) with certainty, on the basis of rational calculation, will do the job. The uniformity of the material world makes it possible to choose the methods and procedures best suited for the problem at hand. Under normal circumstances, functional fields tend to be relatively free of biases regarding sex, race, and age. It is the technique, not the technician, that dominates. Where technique is held constant, whoever does the job best will get the job.

Politics, on the other hand, may simply be defined as a contending ground of different truths. No specific rules or guidelines apply. On one extreme, it is persuaded. On the other, it is forced. In between these extremes, a variety of ideas and opinions, sometimes authentic truths, contend with one another. Interpersonally as well as internationally, every political view has its defenders and apologists. Where such defense or apology is not necessary, politics does not exist. In dictatorial or totalitarian societies, politics is replaced by forced routines in thought and action. In free, open societies, politics is not only allowed, it is the full-time function of many members.

The nature of politics being uncertain and fluid, its conflict ranges from mild persuasion to organized propaganda, from legal disputes to international warfare. What emerges is that there is no correct political position other than the position of the winner, but only temporarily until the challenger replaces it. The uncertainty and fluidity of politics, and the unhappy results it causes, have been the primary motivation for developing what we now call academic fields of human thought. The solutions variously offered make up the total body of human knowledge and truths. The job of academic fields, everyone's job now more specified for the ostensibly best and brightest, is thus to make sense out of what is essentially a senseless situation. It will require nothing short of one's total dedication and commitment, for any hint of self-interest would instantly corrupt the view, the framework, and the conclusion of his truth. Political solutions, where the truth may lie, have nothing to do with logical reasoning, computerized calculations, or rational means-ends balance. If they did, we would be thoroughly dominated by mathematicians by now.

This fact of political uncertainty causes great inconveniences to dictators and scientists, the former in ruling and the latter in expert-advising. But it is also what makes our pursuit of truth possible and imperative. Where dictators and scientists triumph, there is no politics. Where there is no politics, no truth is searched or spoken. Dictators want to know how to control the population. Scientists want to know how to predict human behavior so that they can advise the dictators. Material scientists and functional experts want to control our world. The truth liberates us from it. It is an eternal battle between the two forces that is as old as time. Fortunately for us, the political idea of a brilliant mathematician has no more power of truthfulness than that of a shoe shiner. To think that the mathematician's political idea may be better than the shoe shiner's is to believe that the mathematician's marriage may be happier than the shoe shiner's. In the ethos and canons of contemporary professionalism, however, now fully supported by academic professors turned professionals, we tend to believe that it must be so. The mathematician thus becomes our official truth-teller.

It requires virtually no special effort to assume the above. Even a contentious, cantankerous skeptic will still accept science, at least in principle, as the modern oracle in all aspects of social life. To realize that it should not be so is difficult and takes a good deal of mental effort. Essentially the same difficulty is involved in pursuing one's own honest, independent, and critical truth. Technique is based on factual calculation, logical inference, a closed system of assumptions, predetermined rules and principles, and the inherent superiority of one alternative over another in a strictly rational sense. Politics is based on personal, moral, and emotional interpretations of social reality, in which all things are equally possible, defensible, and subject to change. The common assumption of professionalism is that the former and the latter are linked into a unified whole, and that knowledge about the former is applicable to the latter. Mathematicians would casually mention that all reality, both material and human, is made up of mathematical equations. Sociologists would feverishly study statistics and computer science to comprehend their society. The public would rather ask physicians about the dangers of nuclear war.

It would never occur to them that the great minds, being wiser, more just, and better than ours, have thought about our reality and that their great ideas are as close as the nearest local library. The technical imperative of professionalism is so overwhelming, so logically compelling, so all-encompassing that to think otherwise would be a suicidal heresy for the contemporary academic professor.

One of the consistent surprises for the functional professor, on the other hand, is to realize that his enterprise consists of tried and true techniques and his function in the process is that of a technician. In a world dominated by material science, it is easy for the functional professor to assume the role of an all-knowing oracle of truth. Indeed, it behooves him to no end to be told that in the scheme of things social and moral, his tiny scientific specialty amounts to no more than a grain of sand at a beach, if that. Only because he studies the human molecule does the functional professor tend to think he also studies the "human being." Because he can observe the molecule, he tends to assume that he also understands "human behavior." Habitually, he tends to equate technical symmetry with social perfection. If you add to this confusion the arrogance usually associated with political simple-mindedness and narrow technical training, you have the most explosive display of bloated self-image and the unthinking endorsement of the conservative social order among scientists. Never mind that they sometimes act "liberal" in certain issues.

With rare exceptions (so rare that one must do a double take when one finds them), scientists are much like academic professors in their general outlook: they are hustlers of research grants, and when they get one, they operate mainly as administrators of the technical procedures that they promised to follow in their grant proposal. Their "problems" are defined by grants, and their "solutions" by procedures. In this, they often mistake the rules of science for the rules of society, confuse the observation of things with the understanding of human behavior, and long for the simple solution of science applicable to the moral problems of society. Thus, the scientist joins the misguided academic professor in the search for irrelevance and irresponsibility—and professionalism.

The tenured academic professor is a free man, pursuing his own truth answerable only to his own conscience—until he becomes a professional. By accepting the ethos and canons of professionalism, by adopting its methodology and standard, he changes from a master of his own to a functionary, if not an outright slave. A philosopher as a free man requires a relatively small effort to be persuasive. A professional as a functionary, a handyman, an instrument of his professional enterprise—both natural and human—requires more than a perfunctory reflection to be convincing.

No scholar is free and independent unless he (or she) is free and independent from established orthodoxy. But professionalism *is* orthodoxy par excellence, which has a stranglehold on the thoughts and actions of its members. Anyone who is proud to be a professional presumes the supremacy of orthodoxy. With this acceptance of orthodoxy, however, one's public duty to be a free and independent scholar-critic is rejected. Professional allegiance to orthodoxy and scholarly honesty cannot coexist. This is especially—I should say almost exclusively—burdensome for academic professors.

The principle is fairly simple, in fact, too simple to assert strenuously. The professional, especially the scientific professional, is a functional agent of his profession. He may attempt to change some of the rules of professional conduct to his advantage in the periphery of his profession. But he could not possibly think of changing the very ethos and canons that make his profession possible. The scientist working on atomic bombs may try to make his and his fellow scientists' working conditions a little better, or even try to steer the basic purpose of atomic science toward a more humane use. But he could not possibly change the rules of atomic physics. An accountant may favor individual clients over corporate clients as a matter of personal principle. But he will not deem it his personal duty to try to change the very rules of money counting in America to favor individual clients. If he did, he would be in the political arena, not accounting. Likewise, the professional economist takes the ethos and canons of the market economy as settled. He will not question them any more than an aerospace engineer will question gravity. In the former, simple conservative inertia prevents him from questioning; in the latter, it is the law of nature. That a scientist or a technician sometimes balks, for some reason, at the very system that employs his talent should not obscure the fact that he almost always acquiesces to the needs of the larger society. And acquiesce he must to make his talent valuable to that very system. A chemist who refuses to work on some philosophical grounds would be fairly rare and, indeed, surprising to those who summon his knowledge in chemistry for particular use.

To be sure, the rational development that makes professionalism possible takes many practical messes on its way to maturity. But there is a clear method of rational development if one looks for a pattern. A scientific discovery or a technical invention may bear the discoverer's or the inventor's name for record-keeping purposes. But that it "belongs" to that particular person is strictly accidental. If it is not one person, it is another. Rational development does not belong to one technician, nor does it belong to one technical community. It belongs to the entire history of the scientific and rational development of mankind. The internal combustion engine, the microwave oven, the computer is no one's exclusive creation. (No wonder so many patents are reversed on appeal by competitors.) The complex process of deduction and induction is unceasing. No one, however great in achievement, is allowed to ignore or bypass this process. Nor is one to be blamed for having created a phenomenon, however unpleasant its consequence. No one blames Newton for gravity or Einstein for atomic power. No matter what consequences these discoveries may entail, it is nothing personal. The natural phenomena of gravity and atoms existed long before Newton and Einstein. The development of science in history, and its subsequent contribution to human pleasures and destructions, are based on the logic and inevitability of the given order. No man has ever exerted control over that order. No matter how exalted his role in it, he is but a functional tool of that order.

This notion is not likely to please the professional community, whether functional or academic. Only few professionals see their roles in the simplified nuts-and-bolts context of functionality. The rest, naturally, tend to see themselves as significant actors in the drama of scientific and rational development. As professionals, they tend to attribute human meaning to things and procedures that are strictly nonhuman. As professionals in an age that adores professionalism in all things, they tend to see themselves in a much more heroic light than simple logic would warrant. In their self-image of omniscience, they try to apply their professional scientific knowledge to explaining the mystic experiences of art and religion.

In his self-exaltation the professional simply forgets that he himself has no control over what he can and cannot do in his daily exercise of professional conduct. In his cool detachment, he does whatever is called upon him to perform according to his technical expertise. No professional knowledge is good or bad in itself by definition intrinsic to its development. There is no intrinsic moral quality in any scientific development that forms the basis of professionalism. The technical professional is a mere human tool in its historical unfolding. A geneticist cannot control the workings of genes and their structures, for they are not his to determine. Hence, no scientist is responsible for the consequences of his action. It is the *society's* political decision that is responsible for the consequences. The consequences of scientific discoveries, such as those made by Copernicus and Darwin, were not scientific consequences subsequent to the discovery. They were *political* ones that did not involve the discoverers at all. Before Copernicus, stars in the heavens still moved; before Darwin, organisms still evolved.

Some people would undoubtedly berate the view of professionalism and technical science presented so far as "too simplistic" and would argue that reality is much more "complex" than that. As always, however, those who describe reality as complex—too complex to say anything about it, in fact—are likely to be those who stand to benefit from that very "complexity." On the one hand, professors benefit as the putative *solvers* of complexity as their specialty by making it simple, and the more complex the task, the more valid their status claim. On the other, they also benefit as the *perpetrators* of complexity, as they have every reason to make things as complex as possible. There is genuine fear among professors of simplifying things, not unlike physicians who would be horrified of a disease-free world at the same time as they try to create one. Professors endeavor to understand things so that they become simple to understand—but not so simple as to threaten the very reason for their existence. Only those who see moral urgency in their tasks—and what is more urgent than the business of truth?—will be impatient with the notion that reality is too complex to comprehend or do anything about it. Most professors apparently see or feel no such urgency. Scientism and professionalism, the twin pillars of modern "complexity," comfortably serve their inertia. To them, reality is always "more complex than that." Complexity has the intellectual advantage of getting by with unclear and inactive thought. And professors are quite adept at exploring this advantage to its fullest extent.

Finally, the academic professor's fascination with technical professionalism reveals an interesting insight into patterns of knowledge production. Preoccupation with things technical and scientific, much impressed with logical and mathematical aspects of work, tends to be fairly typical of youthful exuberance. Virtually every academic person starts out determined to comprehend his reality logically and mathematically. But as he reaches maturity, if he makes the normal progress from youthful exuberance to thoughtful reflections of age, he tends to think less of his earlier fascination. Many thinking men and women have grown in their maturity into reflections on the human condition that are uncertain and undefined. They tend to think less surely of their earlier conviction that rational approaches will unlock all human secrets. The technical problem-solving model gradually loses its appeal in the mature mind. It now considers the "morals" and "politics" of man in his varying expressions and uncertainties to be the very crux of human understanding.

This intellectual growth, the replacement of a thing-model with a mind-model, is the progression from a Buzz Aldrin to a Socrates. The basic simplicity and symmetry in scientific rationality are replaced by more thoughtful agonies. The abundance of self-confidence and arrogance characteristic of youth now appears empty of significance. Fascination with facts gradually loses its appeal, to be replaced by pursuit of the truth. Examples of this transformation abound: Immanuel Kant from physical science to moral philosophy, Sigmund Freud from medicine to psychoanalysis, William James from medicine and physiology to philosophy, Bertrand Russell from logic and mathematics to social and moral philosophy, C. Wright Mills from empirical sociology to cultural criticism. There are whiz kids in computer science, mathematics, or business, but never in life philosophy. In terms of understanding society and life, one simply must mature. There is no short cut.

In spite of cultural adulation and economic reward attendant to professionalism, as noted, the professional remains essentially a technical functionary in society. By adopting the posture and identity of professionalism, the academic professor cannot help but abandon what little influence he may exert on his society as a scholar-critic. A professional academic is normally not part of the intellectual elite, which consists mainly of unattached writers, journalists, and political analysts. As a technical functionary without technique and without function, he is neither a fully accredited member of the professional world nor an honored member of the free intelligentsia. As an academic professor he has abandoned his earlier role. As a technical professional he is an outsider to the scientific community. Once aspiring to be a free, autonomous scholar, he is now enslaved in worldly ambition. He wants to be an economically respectable professional but he has no function to sell. Neither pursuing truth as a scholar nor performing any useful function as a technician, he drifts and schemes in his meaningless daily existence.

Yet he has some of the spirit of a scholar still left in him, which only increases his agony in moments of self-reflection. The contemporary academic man thus occupies a tenuous position between intellectual elite and technical functionary. But he is both unable and reluctant to be clearly in either position. To be a member of the intellectual elite, he lacks the necessary commitment to and passion for the truth. To be a professional technician, he lacks the marketable expertise that is imperative to professionalism. In the agony of ambiguity and hesitancy he tries to be both and succeeds in being neither. The intellectual world shuns him; the professional world ignores him. As a free intellectual in his rare self-image, he cannot muster the necessary scholarly substance and the imperative moral force inherent in it. As a technical professional in his economic role, he remains unhappy to be relegated to simple technical functionality, for he may still think highly of himself as a moralist.

By a strange twist of politics and technique in modern America, the academic in the meanwhile straddles the two worlds without defining either, yet attempting to benefit from the ambiguity. Protected by the inertia of tenure, however, this agony is made considerably more tolerable. He maintains his status as a fairly respectable university man. But his status is paper thin, and his respectability essentially maintained in deception. The life of falsehood for one sworn to truth is not easy.

This insecurity makes academic professionals, more so than functional professionals, extremely sensitive to criticism of their professional fields. As "professionals," they are habitually hostile toward any sign of nonorthodoxy. The fate of anyone branded as a "maverick" is not a good one. Sociologists used to treat C. Wright Mills, the most publicly celebrated sociologist in America, as a persona non grata. It is also widely acknowledged for economist John Kenneth Galbraith that among his professional colleagues he is not regarded as a "real" economist at all. (We can only wonder what kind of reception Socrates would get from present-day professional philosophers. Would he be considered a "real" philosopher?) Accordingly, works by those who transgress the accepted ethos and canons of professionalism are either silently ignored or, if this is not feasible, received with great hostility by professional academic reviewers. Professionalism and orthodoxy thus go hand in hand in mutually enforcing each other's defensive paranoia and narrow-minded-ness. There is nothing more impossible to correct than the errant mixture of arrogance, fear, and stupidity in human conduct. The academic professional epitomizes this impossibility more than anyone in American society.

NOTES

1. In the beginning of the AAUP's history, John Dewey referred to its task as "the integrity of our calling." Now, of course, no such reference occurs in contemporary AAUP documents. I have explored the contrast between profession and calling at greater length in my as yet unpublished book, *The Professional Class*.

2. See Commission on Academic Tenure in Higher Education, *Faculty Tenure*, (San Francisco: Jossey-Bass, 1973), 8–9.

3. Mary A. Burgan, "The Faculty and the Superstar Syndrome," in AAUP, May-June 1988, *Academe*, vol. 74, no. 3, 10-14. Also see Richard Schmitt, "Academic Freedom: The Future of a Confusion," in *The Concept of Academic Freedom*, ed. Edmund L. Pincoffs (Austin, TX: University of Texas Press, 1972), 111–30, for his comment on the "professional-mercenary" aspects of professors, which makes their claim to pursuit of the truth impossible to sustain.

Chapter 14

The Economic Model

Since the economic theme is among the most persistent, if not the most dominant, among academics it is well for us to consider the issue separately here. Nothing stirs the faculty to greater arousal than talk of money, although considering the scholarly image they project, they should be least susceptible to the lure of worldly reward. From their reaction a stranger might gather that their whole life focuses on a percentage point or two on their next salary scale. Obviously, there is little money on campus, and although comfortable, faculty compensation hardly ranks among the nation's more affluent. From year to year, most professors' salary does not change that much. When change occurs, if is fairly predictable. But this scantiness of reality is strangely over-matched by the eagerness with which professors greet money matters. (Their eagerness pivots largely on the biggest prize of them all, namely, tenure.) In fact, money is almost the only thing that academic professors confess to "feel strongly" about.

This heavy economic accent in academic dialogue—which accords well with the ethos and canons of professionalism—bodes ill for the professor and is incongruent with the objective reality of his life. It is on economic grounds that the academic professor's weakest flank is exposed. As an economic actor in an advanced market society, he plays a negligible role. Yet, it is precisely his "economic" approach to academic life, putting out the least for the predetermined reward, that stirs the public indignation, demanding greater productivity from professors. It is incongruent as a matter of reality in which the economic struggle yields such paltry results. John Kenneth Galbraith once remarked that wealth is the relentless enemy of understanding."[1] It might be said that poverty is also the relentless enemy of understanding.

In the absence of a more committed goal to define his energy and direction, the academic professor is singularly attracted by the economic factor. In this, if not in results or competence, he is no different from his counterpart in a corporation. Only the size of his reward, which is negligible, is different. Since he spends little or no time on thought that would demand his total devotion, he is naturally alert to the little differences that his relentless economic interest can discover between himself and his colleagues. A man freed from the basic necessities of life, thanks to tenure security, now wants to make his life a little less basic in however insignificant a way. One who thinks highly of money naturally thinks lowly of himself. One who thinks money is everything thinks little or nothing of his own life. Likewise, a professor whose pursuit of tenure is the economic ultimate naturally thinks little or nothing of his scholarly importance. Thus, tenure threatens to reduce his whole being to nothing. But he adjusts. He manages to transform nothing into something. To a man who has little else to do, even an insignificant event appears momentous.

Tenure confers two entirely different rights upon the professor. It assures him, being an economic actor, of job security for life, a simple sinecure that can be translated into an easy economic calculus. He has a lifetime job from which, under normal circumstances, he cannot be fired. This is strictly an economic definition and one that the professor is intensely aware of. He pursues this end of tenure unabashedly and will use any means to obtain it. The hierarchy of campus is defined by this aspect of tenure, and one's achievement is measured by its attainment. This is the *ordinary* economic end for which tenure is sought and viewed after it has been obtained.

As a scholar in the old-fashioned sense of one called to pursue an honorable end, the tenured professor is assured of *that* very freedom that is termed academic freedom. While tenure means both things at once, this latter emphasis makes it a *special* right. Special rights entail special obligations. The special right of academic freedom calls for the special obligation to perform, namely, pursuit of the truth. Although the economic factor in tenure is by no means insignificant, it simply has become invisible in this special emphasis. Tenure as job security has become meaningless in the face of the special right and obligation that tenure now confers upon the professor. To pursue the truth, the professor will obviously have to survive as an economic actor. But tenure, as much as economic survival itself, must *serve* a purpose. And that purpose is nothing less than total service of the truth.

In the present frame of mind, the professor calls upon an *extraordinary* privilege (tenure, academic freedom) for an *ordinary* (economic) end. When tenure is pursued and viewed as an economic end, as it is now, the professor forfeits his right to invoke the extraordinary grace of tenure and academic freedom. What he is asking in tenure is what *anyone* in American society with economic survival in view (which is just about everyone) is asking. Why should the professor be considered an exception to the case, by giving him tenure that no one else gets, when his end is just as unexceptional as anyone else's? Tenure is an academic imperative not available in any other way. But as an academic imperative, not a business one, it must demonstrate that it indeed exists for that academic imperative. The burden must now be placed heavily on the professor to demonstrate that very imperative. As an economic pursuer of tenure, he has no legs on which to stand. Moralists and crackpot critics seize the opportunity to launch their attack on the professoriate, which, on this ground, it richly deserves.[2] To the critics, an economically conscious professoriate is an abominable creature of self-interest.

Few things in an outright commercial society, an advanced form of market society where everyone pursues private gains as one's sole occupation, can claim the purpose of nobility. Among the ever-declining number of noble causes still stands the cause of truth embodied in academic scholarship. Even with its present taint, scholars command respect from society precisely because of the noble aim traditionally considered the essence of a scholar's life. The special recognition that scholars command, tenure privilege being one, has been established upon their lofty denial of crass commercialism and material gains. When an academic professor abandons this aura of nobility in purpose, he abandons a rather crucial pillar that sustains his claim to special status. With his blatant economic interest in plain view, the status collapses to the level of common banality. There is nothing special or noble about a professor who acts like a common economic animal. The smallness of his reward and the incompetence of his method shield him somewhat in this. But the attitude is eventually made public, and it becomes obvious to all that beneath his cap and gown the professor is a small-time hustler of the most banal kind. Once he is exposed, the cry for treating him just like any common economic animal on the make in the commercial world rises to a great height. In fact, there is nothing more pitifully vulnerable than an economically exposed professor. Without the traditional protection of scholarly nobility, he has nothing behind which to hide his naked but petty ambition.

Virtually everyone on campus, in the meantime, claims the right to tenure as a matter of principle. But principle claimed as principle, not on economic rationality, must be defensible in some principled ways. If a tradesman claims his right to peddle his wares on grounds of economic survival, few will be inclined to uphold that as a *principle*. More likely, the right will be granted on some ordinary, although quite necessary, grounds that the man is entitled to his own survival. The principle of free trade or other lofty ideals will be found irrelevant for the purpose in hand. But if a professor claims a right to economic survival as a principle to which he alone is entitled, people will naturally demand some positive proof to show that the claim is indeed a *principle*, not a trick to get an easy living out of it. Unlike the tradesman who is under no other obligation than what he is and needs, the professor must continuously demonstrate that his claim is indeed a claim of principle that is noble and defensible for the very privilege it accords. The moment he shows habits of behavior in common with the tradesman, his demand for the special claim will become untenable. Being well-educated in ways of using words, the professor may be able to hold off the assault for a while, but not indefinitely. With the passage of time, as more and more people realize the trick he has played on them, the assault will become more vocal and united. In not too distant a future the professor could be thrown out of his lofty but phony position of special claim.

Tenure seen as a blatantly economic sinecure attracts the kind of men and women to university life who are not good scholars. In a market society money corrupts everyone, and more money corrupts everyone more thoroughly. Medicine and law, two professional fields with strong economic rewards, tend to attract men and women who have little interest in curing the sick and defending the powerless as their primary goal. It is no mystery that, by and large, people who want to make money enter medicine and law. Academic life, which compensates for less money by providing an easier job, tends to attract the second-tier minds (after medicine and law) that have little or no interest in scholarship. They enter academia *to get* tenure. What small and routine "scholarship" they produce before tenure virtually stops after it. Their career evolves around tenure, not pursuit of the truth or whatever lesser form their scholarship might take. Tenure pursued as an almost exclusively economic factor allows no other intelligent interpretation. Being a college professor is certainly not the cushiest job in the world, to be sure. But considering the intellectual and moral demand it puts on the professor, which is woefully small, it is still one of the easiest ways for an average man to earn a living. Word spreads and graduate schools are seen as the breeding ground of such intellectual mediocrity and economic parasitism.

The temptation to equate tenure with economics is irresistible. Few resist and most succumb. Even respectable administrators and scholars speak of tenure reward as an "incentive" for higher productivity. The philosophy is, of course, imported directly from business. Professors must be motivated to work hard. To reward them economically, like all other industrial workers, is the best way to motivate them. But aside from its minor moral repugnancy, there is the inconvenient small difference between academic work and industrial work that makes this theory unworkable. For one thing, there is no way to measure the professor's output in precise quantitative terms. Elaborate peer evaluation on merit consideration, which often involves ranking works in order of "importance," is only a caricatured torture in academic rituals to measure it. For another, academic jobs are not as fluid as most industrial jobs. Academics do not easily move laterally from one place to another. In fact, one recent study puts it at close to zero percent.[3] When the measure of output is uncertain and fluid mobility nonexistent, no amount of whipping or exhortation will move the professor to a greater height of productivity. In reality, it does not. The academic professor, with rare pathologically ambitious exceptions, always does the minimum for the given level of economic reward.

But this attempt at industrial analogy is not entirely without some analytic value. Except for his inaptitude and the smallness of his ambition, the professor as an economic animal is really no different from his counterpart at IBM, Standard Oil, or any other normal corporation. His entirely salesmanlike approach to scholarly life, essentially as an economic endeavor, is wholly indistinguishable from that of his corporate counterpart. In spite of his self-image and claim to the contrary, the professor is a salesman in every way. Whatever he does is almost purely economically motivated to the end of maintaining his job. That he may show some particular interest in one thing or another in a scholarly field or research subject is a matter of random chance, since he has no personal commitment to anything in particular. One could do one's little "research" either at IBM or at the State Department. Concerning the basic strain of thought, the professor is as economically motivated as any corporate employee or government bureaucrat. What is commonly called scholarship is just a moderately well-packaged product of fairly average insignificance. Hence the importance of salesmanship in selling it. The way the success of the more successful salesman-scholars achieved is quite indistinguishable from that of any ordinary hustler.

Under present policy, job guarantee in tenure at American universities leads almost inevitably to sloth. In America's market society, the professor may not perform productively in its economic system. But he enjoys its perks. He has learned to do the very least for what is already given and permanently fixed. When job security is forever guaranteed, only extraordinary community pressure can prevent the worker from developing slothfulness on the job. Only in such tightly knit social groups as the Germans, Japanese, and the Amish may job security avoid bringing about eventual sloth in workmanship. In America's market society where minimum is performed when reward is predetermined, the economically conscious professor has every incentive to be indolent with his job. In the face of neither community pressure nor his own internal compulsion to work, the professor has every incentive to be lazy. The remarkable fact of having a job for good in a market society where no one gets that sort of privilege simply escapes the professor. Thinking like a common market man, but with an uncommon nonmarket privilege in his possession, the professor has no desire to make his life any more taxing than the next man. With tenure, he is as free as a child and as oblivious as a lunatic. He indeed has full academic freedom.

Under these circumstances, consider the hollowness of the following description of tenure and academic freedom: "The academy is free when the scholars who make it are free, as scholars. And the academy is free when its governing board is free to protect and to advance this freedom."[4] The academy has never been freer, the academic man never more secure, outside interference never more infrequent. Yet the professor has never been so timid. With tenure security, he might be expected to be more honest, more independent, and more critical in his pursuit of the truth, now that he has little to fear. His imagination would be more daring, his criticism bolder, his quest for human happiness more all-consuming. But what happens is exactly the opposite. With tenure, he becomes more enslaved than freed. With tenure as a hard-earned economic reward, not as a point of liberation, he is not about to do anything to jeopardize it. He becomes a scholarly nonentity; a routine uninspiring teacher; a predictably harmless figure on campus. By protecting it with timidity, rather than boldly using it as it is intended to be used, he jeopardizes it for his future. But in his shortsighted economic stupidity, he weakens the very pillar that sustains his tenuous economic hold in society. By making tenure essentially meaningless for scholarly pursuits, he eventually hands it back to its critics.

This economic perception of tenure is nowhere more graphically illustrated than by the moment the professor gets it. The day it is officially awarded is the day the professor has lived for. The whole world around him celebrates and congratulates him on that. He has reached the zenith of his existence. Why such celebration? If it is his scholarly accomplishment that is recognized and celebrated, why wasn't it so recognized and celebrated before? This celebration means only one thing: everyone, especially the professor, *knows* that he will *always have a job*. He will always have a job because he will never do *anything* that might jeopardize his job security. The moment that tenure liberates the professor, he becomes a slave. He silently swears to his eternal god that he will keep the job until he retires. To keep it, he will do absolutely nothing to jeopardize it. Instead of liberating him with academic freedom, tenure thus enslaves him with job security. He will now never do anything significant, original, critical, or unorthodox, to cause discomfort or irritate the powers that be. At the moment of his tenure, the free academic man submits himself to economic bondage.

The economic equation of tenure is unfortunate for the professor in another way. A tenured senior professor holds a monopoly on his job immune from market competition. No economic man in the marketplace considers his economic victory permanent, for the next round of battle is looming just ahead of him. It is the fact of life that, round after round, he must defend his position from his challengers. Two observations can be made against this view of economic life. One views the American economy as being fairly close to oligopoly, with virtually monopolistic consequences in effect. But this is largely for the corporation and institution, not the individual employee. Every employee must still fear the next occupant of his job. The second view allows for the fact that virtually every job in American society carries tacit tenure. No surgeon or lawyer or ordinary employee gets fired as long as the status quo holds and he does his job normally.[5] Yet, job security by grace or convention is rather different from job security guaranteed by legal contract to be broken only by adversary proceedings. This is what the professor with tenure has.

Only when the work to be performed is fairly routinized can we expect reward similarly fixed. For civil servants, soldiers, and schoolteachers, whose jobs are most predictable, reward can be fixed on a predictable scale. In other cases, as in the private market sector where the volume of work can depend on the performer, this fixed reward is deemed most unproductive and, thus, is mostly avoided. It would be almost catastrophic for a market society to reward its market workers with permanent tenure on a predictable reward scale. Nor would it help the tenured professor, who is expected to be creative and dynamic like a market worker, yet who is rewarded with fixed economic security for life.

In his enjoyment of economic freedom, the senior professor comfortably rejects the economic freedom of his challengers. The way the senior rejects the junior's right to challenge his position is nothing short of natural selection for survival in its most unforgiving extreme. The probationary period for the junior has been described by one as "nothing less than a brutalizing, dehumanizing, and discouraging experience."6 It is not far removed from Thomas Hobbes's famous description of life in nature as "solitary, poor, nasty, brutish, and short."7 It has nothing to do with academic freedom and much less with the truth, and it has everything to do with tenure as economic security pure and simple. Only the most uninitiated would connect this brutality with any notion of scholarly selectivity. For what emerges is not the best, but the most average—hence the worst. The newcomer never replaces a senior unless the senior dies or retires. The only requirement for the senior is to be there, and no senior has ever voluntarily vacated his position because of his own self-realized inadequacy. In this sense the new member is always *added* to the pool of seniors. When that happens, understandably, it is nothing short of the most august of occasions for the individual in academia. Small wonder that getting tenure is so celebrated!

This fact of tenure as economic security exposes an inherent contradiction in academic life that is ignored entirely for its ubiquitous presence. It is the contradiction between economic security and academic freedom. Those who seek academic freedom do not pursue economic security as their primary goal. To them, economic security consists of what is basically entailed in academic freedom. For those who pursue economic security primarily, academic freedom *is* economic security, for they are not interested in academic freedom as such. To them, academic freedom outside economic security has no intrinsic meaning. The contradiction consists of not getting academic freedom while *in need* of it; the other, getting academic freedom while *not* in need of it. The former is a waste of human resource and subsequent pains in the untenured; the latter a waste of public trust and resource in the tenured. Those who exercise academic freedom do not enjoy economic security (they normally get denied tenure). Those who enjoy economic security do not exercise academic freedom (they normally do nothing with it).

This eternally conflicting facet of academic life compels many thoughtful observers to passionate denouncements of present policy. To repeat my earlier theme, those who need tenure do not have it; those who have it do not need it. If one is competent, tenure is unnecessary. If not, tenure only means a reward for incompetence, which is not justifiable. If tenure is given to guarantee academic freedom, what does academic freedom defend? There is no easy way of solving the dilemma without admitting the awful bind into which the present policy has cornered the American professor.

Tenure as a system solidified in the 1960s when supply lagged behind demand in faculty. Now, supply far exceeds demand, yet the market cannot adjust. For in spite of all its market mentality and grabbiness, academic life is immune to market competition where it really counts. The younger, perhaps more dynamic, members are for a foreseeable future kept out of the monopoly game only the seniors can play. Individually the professor pursues the market economy model. As a group, the professoriate practices the cartel model. The struggle among the outsiders to join the insiders is enormous. It is a saga of small tragedies and inconsequential triumphs without which no campus lore is complete.

The academic professor is extremely anxious to maintain the benefit of a double life. On the one hand, he aspires to the idyllic life of a scholar, unconcerned about campus politics and economics and devoted to his scholarly duty. On the other, he wants to participate actively in the game of market society. Considering this dilemma impossible to resolve, few scholars go the first way. Many go the second. There are so few of the first type, in fact, that I have not seen them fit to discuss at any length. The dilemma of tenure's economic factor consists of the simple fact that scholarly pursuit of the truth is incompatible with its market reward.

But for the first group of scholars, this is entirely a false dilemma. The second type of academic professor, believing that his is a Hobson's choice (i.e., impossible either way), has decided to go with the market reward, thus forsaking his scholarly pursuit. For the first group, it is the best of both worlds, as I propose in the following consideration in which the dilemma can be reconciled. If the solution proves correct, we find that the scholar's "instrinsic value" in his scholarship is *identical* to the market reward his more economically conscious colleagues seek in place of scholarship. Once scholarship and market are reconciled, the anxious academic professor may rest with greater peace of mind.

The intrinsic value of all *voluntarily chosen* occupations —scholarly calling being one—always equals the pleasure derived by each occupant from his work. Artists, hobbiests, revolutionaries, amateur scholars, religious devotees, and the like would not think of their devotions as lacking in the way of concrete reward. Every minute, every day, every

moment they spend with their chosen field of "work" will be fulfilled to
the fullest extent. Otherwise, they would simply quit and find another
line of work. The fact that they have voluntarily chosen to be involved
explains its full intrinsic value. Institutional scholars—as opposed to
amateur scholars—have also chosen their fields voluntarily. In spite of
the misgivings we have about their motive or about their later economic
anxiety, most, if not all, academic professors can be assumed to have
chosen their fields voluntarily, not forced into it for sheer economic
survival. The very fact that their chosen fields are useless in the market
sense only lends our assumption its authoritative support. There is no
question about the intrinsic value—the pleasure of one's work itself—of
their chosen fields, as scholars would rather do their current work than
anything else.

All we have to do now is to reconcile intrinsic value with putative
market value, which I have claimed are always identical. This reconcil-
iation is easily accomplished if we consider a typical functional professor
who has chosen the job primarily for its market value. Say the accounting
instructor chose to be an accountant because of its market attraction,
although he might have felt more fulfilled pursuing something else. The
accountant, preparing himself for the job, expends an appropriate amount
of time, energy, and resource. While in preparation, he has an idea as
to how much his market value (not intrinsic value, which is close to zero)
is worth. He relies exclusively on established market patterns in setting
price for the service that he is about to render.

He knows the general range of his worth, specifically considering his
expenditure and function. One's market value is fairly easy to establish,
especially for one whose qualification calls for long-term plans and
investments. Such plans and investments cannot be made unless their
anticipated market value is fairly stable over time. The market value of
book-maker may fluctuate widely, but not that of doctors, lawyers, or
accountants. For the accountant in preparation, it is natural to consider
that all his time, energy, and resource expenditure "deserves" the current
market value of an accountant. If, say, the going rate for an accountant
in his first year after graduate school is $50,000 a year, he would naturally
consider that amount exactly "right" for his expenditure to qualify for
the job. He feels it right because it is neither above nor below his
expectations in relation to his expenditure. Therefore, his total expenditure and market value can now be regarded as identical. This identity is
what keeps our market system functioning and stable.

Now, our academic professor has made a similar expenditure of time,
energy, and resource to qualify for *his* scholarly role. He might not

exactly think of it as a function or a job, perhaps more as a role. Whatever, there is a set of rules that calls for specific qualifications for scholarly roles. Just like the accountant, the scholar has put in his hours in preparation for the eventual role. How much does he expect to get out of his own expenditure of time, energy, and resource? Just like the accountant, the scholar expects to get what he "deserves" that is just "right" for him. This is nothing less than his total intrinsic value. Unlike his accounting counterpart, the scholar gets all his in intrinsic value, not in market value. But the rewards in both are identical. Hence we arrive at the simple deduction that scholarly intrinsic value and market value are always identical. This is true, of course, as long as the scholar has voluntarily chosen his field for its intrinsic value, not for its market value (which is close to zero). The scholar is satisfied with his just reward, as is the accountant with his.

There remains one small detail, of course, to be worked out. It is the scholar's livelihood. While the accountant's is taken care of by the market, the scholar's is taken care of by an artificially institutionalized means known as tenure. However, while enjoying the best of both worlds, intrinsic value being worth the same as market value, the scholar confuses the two and often becomes unhappy. There is no doubt that on the average an academic professor's salary lags behind that of the more prestigious and useful functional professional on the same campus. This causes considerable bad feelings among colleagues simply because the academic professor wants to be satisfied with *both* intrinsic value *and* market value in the identical *amount*. This cannot be done. Although his salary is smaller than the accountant's, he gets what the accountant can never enjoy, namely, his work's intrinsic value, which is always identical with the accountant's market value. Otherwise, the scholar would not have chosen his field voluntarily.

If the scholar's original aim was high market value, then he should have chosen another field and invested his time, energy, and resource appropriately for that task. As long as he makes a comfortable living with his scholarship, as he obviously does with tenure, he should be content with the full intrinsic value of his work, which his market counterpart apparently cannot. It is entirely possible that one can really enjoy counting someone's money, which may amount to the scholar's intrinsic value. But I would discount such claims as exceptions bordering on pathology. The fact remains that accounting, like medicine and law, is basically a trade that one learns for a living. Children of the extremely rich rarely choose to be practicing doctors, lawyers, or accountants. Many from ordinary middle-class families, on the other hand, choose to be starving artists rather than wealthy accountants. We should never underestimate the intrinsic value of scholarship. Neither should the scholar himself, for his own peace of mind, for he gets what he rightly deserves at all times. He is much better off than he sometimes feels. But when one thinks economically, rarely is one satisfied.

To further highlight the nature of pure intrinsic value, what the scholar derives from his scholarship is no different from what a person of intense religious experience may derive from his faith. The scholar's vow to seek the honest, independent, and critical truth has the familiar ring of a spiritual commitment more commonly observed in the ecclesiastic literature. What other secular vow could commit one to such total selflessness for pursuit of the truth? Academic ceremonies and processions often resemble religious ones, professors being the High Priests of the Order of Truth. This secular truth would demand nothing less than an absolute commitment to itself and itself only. It demands in absolute terms of tenure and academic freedom that Thou Shall Not Have Other Interests That Might Corrupt Thee.

It is difficult indeed to reconcile the fall of the secular high priest with the imperatives of an economically driven and rapidly professionalizing occupation. The demand of purity remains as the vestige of an age whose spirit is fast fading. In its place, technicians and professionals and economically conscious scholars are puzzling over the role that once defined their purity. Unable to play the role yet reluctant to discard it, they find it easier to play it halfway. Committed wholly neither to the discomfort of truth nor to the comfort of deceit, they survive in a life that is half true and half false. In this corrupting state of conservative inertia, naturally, neither half of the professor ends up being fully happy or fulfilled.

NOTES

1. John Kenneth Galbraith, *The Affluent Society* (New York: The New American Library, 1963), 13.

2. See, for example, Charles J. Sykes, *ProfScam* (Washington, D.C.: Regnery Gateway, 1988).

3. Christine M. Licata, *Post-Tenure Faculty Evaluation* (Washington, D.C.: Association for the Study of Higher Education, 1986), 3.

4. Robert MacIver, *Academic Freedom in Our Time* (New York: Columbia University Press, 1955), 4.

5. For example, see John Livingston, "Tenure Everyone?" in *The Tenure Debate*, ed. Bardwell Smith (San Francisco: Jossey-Bass, 1973), 54–73, for the second observation. For the first, John Kenneth Galbraith, *The New Industrial State* (New York: The New American Library, 1967) is a superb source.

6. Rolf Sartorius, "Tenure and Academic Freedom," in *The Concept of Academic Freedom*, ed. Edmund L. Pincoffs (Austin, TX: University of Texas Press, 1972), 140.

7. Thomas Hobbes *Leviathan* (New York: Collier Books, 1971) p. 100.

Chapter 15

Gresham's Law

With the massive size of each academic field in the university, it is perhaps impossible to avoid mediocrity and conformity. Under present policy for tenure, what a scholar must do for his minimum attainment and maintenance is not much: he needs only to conform to the orthodoxy of views, publish a few articles of trivia, and sport a pleasing personality in regard to his posture toward the seniority. After tenure, this record of mediocrity and conformity must continue in order to ensure one's regular advancement through the academic ranks. In every rank and in every year of one's academic career, the best policy is to do the least and be least troublesome.

Every university wants an "excellent," "first rate" faculty. But what this faculty should look like is determined by faculty members themselves. Faculty members are first hired by faculty members. Then they are granted tenure or denied it by faculty members. They advance in the ranks or stay behind on the decisions made by faculty members. The faculty itself has become the de facto administrators of things pertaining to faculty members. The "peers" as a collectivity have become a most fearsome and feared instrument of thought control never imagined even under the old Grand Inquisition. The fear they can strike, the power they can exercise, and the control they can exert have made the peers perhaps the most terrifying of all controlling mechanisms in modern times.

When there is so much at stake for the faculty, this concentration of absolute power in the hands of the peers casts an ominous shadow across everything academic. In this, as in anything else, Gresham's Law tends to prevail. Many bad ones keep out few good ones. The tight control the peers exert over their own kind is mercilessly unforgiving toward heretics. As always, they will close ranks toward the center. It is almost always the conservative inertia that prevails, and it is almost always academic freedom that is threatened at the end. It is the power of numbers at work, the democratic formula for mediocrity and conformity, that the modern American faculty now personifies.

The sheer number of academic faculty makes standardized procedure for peer evaluation impossible to avoid. Clark Kerr once called the university "elitist," "the elite of merit."[1] But the way merit is assessed makes it anything but elitist. Quite the contrary, the modern university is highly *democratic*, not elitist. The size of the university would not make it anything but democratic. Democracy necessitates standardization. Standardization inevitably gravitates toward the middle, the average, the mediocre. In scholarship as well as in popular taste, in politics as well as in economics, things numerous are things mediocre. The modern university, of necessity, cannot be anything but the citadel of mediocrity.

Most democratic cultures deserve to survive or even prosper with this burden of mediocrity only if it does not replace merit. In fact, mediocrity is the precondition for merit by excellence. Democratic mediocrity is tolerated on the grounds that while the many mediocre are rewarded, the excellent few are also among the rewarded. As an intrinsic function, these democratic cultures must make sure that the excellent few are not sacrificed for the many mediocre. In America's democratic academic culture, Gresham's law holds iron-strong. In it, mediocrity *is* the standard of excellence. By the most elaborate procedures imaginable, which are also necessary ingredients of mediocrity, it keeps merit out of its ranks. The mediocrity of the many can be forgiven only if it cushions the merit of a few who need such protection. But the university hierarchy not only fails to protect the excellent few, it has made the mediocre *the excellent*.

Under present policy it is much more of a burden to stand out for some reason than not to stand out at all. To be sure, incompetents also get denied tenure or are weeded out in the process. But almost invariably, the excellent stand out much more clearly and annoyingly than the incompetent. There is a huge gap between mediocre many and excellent few. There is but a small—one might say negligible—gap between mediocre and incompetent. Pure incompetence has a greater chance of survival by sheer number and conservative inertia under the present system of peer inquisition than the meritorious few. Just consider who occupies all the visible positions of "excellence." Professorial eminence, the ability to be recognized among the academic multitude, is almost always associated with mediocre achievements repeated enough times to be ingrained in public memory: a position in national organizations, chairmanship of this committee or that, publication of a string of articles only peers can understand, a distinction called expertise in one's field, and so on. None a product of honest, independent, and critical pursuit of the truth. Certainly not the kind of merit that a Socrates, a Marx, a Veblen, or a Mills would enjoy. We know what happened to Socrates; Marx could not get a university job; Veblen never had a permanent university job; Mills barely got tenure at Columbia University. In academic practices that follow the market model, one must assume the worst as the necessary outcome. In the marketplace, the worst commonly sell the best; in academia, the most forgettable also tend to attain eminence.

Naturally elaborate procedures are necessary if substance is in question. A department of English would hire a Shakespeare on sight. But it would demand from the many unknown an elaborate demonstration of their worth. Elaborate procedures for peer evaluation of merits and demerits are established to safeguard the process, not the substance, of evaluation. It is the safeguarding of mediocrity, not excellence. Certainly no excellence, not even a Shakespeare's, could survive such grinding procedures of modern academic evaluation. In the process, everything becomes standardized, and standardization inevitably brings about trivialization. The procedure reduces all things to objective criteria. It asks and records how many papers presented, how many journal articles published, how many books written. Also asked would be the meetings where the papers were presented, the journals where the articles were published, the places where the books were quoted. All these, in turn, would be ranked to assess the proper merit of each. But the idea of the evaluators actually *reading* the papers, articles, or books and independently evaluating them, unless as an afterthought to a foregone conclusion, would not normally occur to them. It is not standard and is taken as only marginally significant to the process. Nowhere does the process say how to assess quality. So the process necessitates the next step: quality is presumed to exist in quantity.

This standardized procedure puts everyone under similar obligations for productivity. Each department has its own notion of how many articles, how many books, or how many other signs of productivity may be deemed appropriate for tenure, promotion, and other perks of academic life. It is a "publish or perish" grindstone in its magnificently scheduled run. The schedule is announced at the beginning of one's appointment, and a certain degree of productivity (e.g. two articles, one book) would be expected within the probationary time period. One must sometimes decide whether to go for a quick turnaround article or to aim for a longer turnaround book. The commissar has pronounced the quota and the production line must grind it out. Whether or not there is any important idea one wishes to pursue, or whether or not there is any point in doing anything at all, the quota is merciless. The scholar is now a factory worker in the academic system. He must grind it out or he himself is out. Predictably, desperation drives him to group projects, textbook writing, quick survey results, or other standard solutions.

Equally predictably, routines emerge in the academic world to command its attention as the new standard of excellence. There emerge "established" journals, the most prestigiously held and competitively selective ones in each field. They are the outlets for official orthodoxy and party lines; they are the house organs that are touted as the badge of excellence. The most mediocre, most acceptable, most numerously held views are now elevated to the level of excellence by the sheer force of conformity. The so-called established journals accept for publication only the most *established* ideas and nothing else. Worse yet, the established ideas are tightly held by a faction or a clique, a special group among the mediocre. These established journals encourage, or virtually dictate, what kind of ideas should be pursued in the field. The prevailing ideas and format are closely enforced and deviation scrutinized. Anyone who may have a new challenge or a critical idea dares not even approach the established journal. In academic fields where honest, independent, and critical insights are the very lifeblood, the established journals demand uniformity of thought and style. "The truth" has already been decided in each field, the idea implies, and no deviation will be allowed. One must follow established subjects and established methods and come to established conclusions. Academics are generous toward incompetents but will not forgive heretics, critics, or deviants from orthodoxy. Their "truth" has the advantage of being established as orthodoxy requiring only a routine submission, not assertion, to pass as "the truth." But these defenders of orthodoxy are also the most ferociously critical of any mention of "truth" in any other context.

Once in a while even the mediocre community of scholars, in a self-affirming ritual, needs to isolate someone from the rest as the target of their collective scorn. They pick out the extremely old or burned-out or stubborn refusniks and brand them as "dead wood." The branding of dead wood is almost always done on the basis of routine production or lack of it. The dead wood, for one reason or another, just would not produce his quota like everyone else. Since he is likely to be a tenured senior, the criticism is mild and normally expressed in his absence. (Criticism among professors is almost always mild, for everyone has a skeleton in his own closet.) But what makes him the subject of such professional chastisement? His refusal to participate in the trivial, insignificant, standardized knowledge production that passes for academic productivity and scholarship? If he were in the Soviet Union he would certainly be a proud dissident and a darling of American academics. Why, he is our own dissident, proudly refusing to participate in what he considers essentially a mindless exercise in futility. He rightfully feels that not one truth is pursued or pronounced in this exercise. He would rather not do it and just enjoy his teaching duties until he retires. While there is no doubt about the genuine dead wood—the impossibly lazy and dormant—in the academic community, at least his scholarly spirit and integrity may not be as dead as they might be in the younger, more productive practitioners of mediocrity and sycophancy. At least he is an honest loafer and suffers no self-delusions of scholarly grandeur.

Standardization routinized according to mediocre expectations makes academic life fairly even-keeled and predictable. Everyone knows his exact quota and works on fulfilling it. What everyone is expected to accomplish in his scholarship is never extraordinary. It is precisely within the range of what a mediocre mind can accomplish within a fairly generous period of time. Besides, the methodology and theory that are established as professional orthodoxy make things much easier to follow. All one has to do is be a good soldier and march to the orders. The procedure has been spoken and all is set. But why is the real academic life, then, so nasty, brutish, and short?

Standardized scholarship does not solve all the problems of academic life. There is the small matter of selectivity that makes all things in academia competitive. Juniors must compete for tenure, and seniors for advancement, sabbaticals, raises, extra perks, whatever, although on a far less strenuous scale. Especially for the junior, fulfilling the established quota only satisfies the minimum requirement. He must still *please* his seniors. In fact, he must please his seniors better than does his competitor. Above all, he must have a *pleasing personality*. Standardized, routinized, and trivialized scholarship, by virtue of the ease with which it can be accomplished, thus leaves only one variable as unstandardizable, unroutinizable, and untrivializable, namely, his personality. In this strange way, personality after all becomes the most significant factor in a junior's fight for survival. The personality factor is so important that it will, if pleasing, overcome any deficiency in scholarship, or if displeasing, override any excellence in scholarship. Since having a pleasing personality in relation to its environment is largely a matter of luck, this factor alone accounts for the unceasing tension that is part of academic life. Given standardized mediocrity, one lives or dies on personality.

The personality factor is particularly significant in academic fields, as opposed to functional ones, for the simple reason that academic orthodoxy is not nearly as airtight as functional orthodoxy. Personality in functional fields is less of a factor than competence. In academic fields, competence can be redefined and regauged according to which yardstick is applied. This uncertainty makes everyone nervous and elevates the factor of personality to a still higher plane of importance. A pleasing personality in chemistry may simply be considered an individual's behavioral attribute. But a pleasing personality in philosophy or sociology implies his *thought-conformity*, a demonstration that he implicitly understands the rules of inquiry, the methodology, the subject, and the conclusion therein. A pleasing fellow in an academic field is also a pleasingly pliable junior who comprehends the prevailing yardstick of conformity that is expected of him. A "flawed methodology" can always be overcome by a flawless personality. But a flawed personality will not overcome a flawless methodology under inspection by his seniors. The blessed academics are those with a pleasing personality, not flawless quest for the truth. For the most part, therefore, getting tenure is largely a matter of luck, not merit. Hence the air of fear, paranoia, and feverish hoping and guessing at tenure time.

It is precisely at the point of personality that junior members become separated between tenurable and untenurable. Juniors with a pleasing personality (not the same as a pleasant personality, however) will become seniors by getting tenure and will go on to what is described as a successful academic career. Juniors without a pleasing personality will be denied tenure and will likely face a series of critical tests for their resolve in survival. Unfortunately for the university, it is the wrong juniors who are selected for tenure and successful academic careers. For those who succeed by wits, submissiveness, and sycophancy (all the requisites of academic tenure) tend to make the worst tyrants once they become powerful enough themselves. The test of one's true personality comes when there is little external requirement for pleasantness, generosity, or fairness. In no other event does the senior display his true personality more than when he is about to lord over a haplessly submissive junior. It is the moment of paramount truth about oneself, both granter and grantee of tenure, for different reasons. What normally emerges during tenure deliberation is, then, perhaps the worst aspect of academic falsehood and personal corruption.

Based on the description given above, we find two common types of senior faculty now dominating the academic scene in America: the "schemers" and "incompetents."

The schemers, a numerical minority, are the ringleaders, keenly alert to the shifts of power in the department, in the school, in the university, and often in the national arena as well. They know who is in and who is out, who is on the way up and who is on the way down. They are instinctively equipped with the knowledge for attachment; they know the right person to ally themselves with and to distance themselves from. Their vita is devoid of substance yet covers all the right committees, research projects, and personalities. They show little or no interest in any scholarly activity yet manage to fulfill the minimal requirement for advancement into higher ranks, normally in administration. They are the academic politicians, ingratiating and domineering when necessary. They represent much of what is wrong with the American academy. Whenever decision making falls into their hands they have their shining moment of glory. No opportunity passes them by unused or unnoticed if it serves their ever-scheming minds for personal advantage.

The incompetents make up the numerical majority on any campus. They are basically good soldiers and cannon-fodder for the scheming leaders. They constitute what Andrew Hacker once called the men and women of "middling intelligence" who, in a more discriminating era, would have held far less exalted status.[2] Their sin, unlike the schemers', is one of omission. They do the least to get by, often becoming candidates for the campus title of dead wood. The incompetents contribute to the present ills of academia by doing nothing to make it right. But doing anything about it is simply beyond their reach. Their conceptual power in grasping reality is as weak or nonexistent as their intellectual power in penetrating it. Minimum numbers of articles will be written, papers presented, classes taught. Even conscientious or meticulous on the superficial level of routines and insignificance, they often show signs of honesty and willingness to be persuaded. Unlike the schemers, they do not thrive on corruption, and personally they may exhibit exemplary integrity. But in the end, sins of omission are indistinguishable from sins of commission. And knowingly or otherwise, they ultimately partake in the hypocrisy and corruption on campus.

Then, to complete the picture, we might mention the "rejects," who by their distinguishing characteristics of honesty of thought, independence of mind, and critical pursuit of truth, are normally denied tenure and weeded out early on. They are never very numerous and play an insignificant role in the current composition of university life in America. The ghost of their presence is felt only by their absence.

Tenure was explicitly granted to protect the professor from authority. Just now, authority has receded in importance. In its place has emerged a senior faculty that is now the junior professor's primary source of fear. With his relentless pressure for mediocrity and conformity, the senior takes away the junior's academic freedom. In no uncertain terms, the senior member has become the greatest enemy of academic freedom in America. But the way this is done is insidious and, on the surface, highly rational. Like the marketplace theology of supply and demand, peer control over professors seems simple and rational. Yet its implications, as we have seen, are as terrifying as they are insidious. No one can fight the model of supply and demand with the arsenal of simple-mindedness. Nothing commands greater accolades of democratic fairness and justice than the concept of "peer review." Who can argue against such an open, natural, and elaborately safeguarding system of evaluation all carried out by one's own peers? It is too simple to argue or criticize. The senior has a gridlock on the system and his control is as complete as it is deemed democratic. From this position he commands the worst form of academic tyranny and thought control, and he practices the most repugnant form of political sycophancy and intellectual inertia. That peers are doing it to their own peers renders all things in their name unquestionably justifiable and right.

Unfortunately for new ideas, the peers are ubiquitous. They make up the marjority in every academic field. Numbers are on their side, as are the textbooks, the committee memberships, the editorial boards, the tenured seniority, and so on. They are now the academic equivalent of Big Brother. Their views are held as orthodoxy, almost with the certainty of science and law. They confuse orthodox party lines with "scientific facts," majority agreement with accuracy, and the comfort of conformity with being in the right. They may pay lip service to "creativity" and "originality," but their definition is so diluted as to be meaningless in practical application. In academic fields where honest, independent, and critical insights are the very lifeblood, the peers punish deviation. All articles that pass peer judgment are more or less an exercise in conformity. The peers, with rare exceptions of courage and foresight, will not accept deviation from standardized rules and expectations. Whenever unanimity of thought among the peers prevails in an academic field, therefore, stagnant and slothful thinking is presumed to prevail. Increasingly, academics have become comfortable in living with Big Brother and performing his errands for him.

When academic freedom is conceived of as a right, the right to do as one pleases usually becomes the right *not* to do as one pleases. A right to do *anything* in academia, as always, inevitably degenerates into a right to do *nothing*. It is a progression from which few have been immune. Conservative inertia, to do as little as possible, is overwhelming both individually and institutionally. Freedom to do as one pleases is almost always freedom to do nothing, if consequences are the same. The professor's right to pursue the truth thus almost always becomes his right to pursue falsehood by sycophancy or pursue nothing by sloth. Standardization of scholarship protects professors from the accusation of each other. Peer evaluation shuts off the possible internal criticism from their own ranks. Thus squandering precious principles of tenure and academic freedom, the seniors have devised an airtight system of self-corruption and false scholarship. They bring into their own ranks only those who share their corruption and falsehood. The mediocre junior with pleasing personality is normally the one.

Stationed halfway between the insulated senior and the public stands the university administrator. The administrator himself has normally risen from the faculty ranks and implicitly understands the inner workings of that body. He is also the institution's link to the outside world. He speaks to the public, the legislature, and also the student body. Perhaps most significant, he is positioned hierarchically to countermand faculty decisions and actions. It is not easy for the administrator to override a faculty recommendation and face the consequence. There is nothing more ferocious than a protest from the faculty whose self-interest has been thwarted by the administration. Most sane administrators try to avoid this.

But the key administrator—dean, academic vice president, president— is the only force of any significance that can bear upon the present situation of tenure and academic freedom. He can (1) exert enormous pressure on the faculty to pursue honest, independent, and critical scholarship as is its duty; (2) using his office, protect the dynamic junior not likely to be approved by seniors for tenure and remind the faculty of the original purpose of tenure and academic freedom; and (3) if necessary, threaten to take the matter to the legislature or the public to correct the present trend of complacent "do-nothingism" among the faculty.

This is indeed a slender hope, or a "best case" scenario, given the mutually enforcing conviviality that most administrators and faculty share. But a courageous administrator may be far more effective, though far rarer than a courageous professor, because the former can do much more than the latter. The "worst case" scenario has the administrators emerging from the most scheming and power-grabbing ranks of anti-scholars in the faculty. These administrators lead and encourage the conservative inertia of the academic community. Even as the campus may be growing in size and financially prosperous, corruption and hypocrisy may still be mixed with mediocre scholarship and with lionized untruth as the standard fare for faculty reward. Worse yet, they may connive with the scheming professors to rid themselves of the more dynamic, committed, and innovative scholars. In the least, they may resort to do-nothing conservative inertia and consequently fail to rescue the junior members in need of their countervailing intervention.

As always, the best and worst possibilities among administrators are still the same as those among professors. The absolute majority of college presidents have consistently come from academic, rather than functional, fields. Hence they share the intimate traits, best and worst, of the academic professor. The best possibilities, as in all things in life, require courage both public and private. The worst possibilities promise inertia, the status quo, and short-term satisfaction. Given the choice, the worst of human nature, as in self-interest and corrupting power, tends eventually to get the upper hand. Courage, so little of which is required in our age of protected scholarship and truth, has never been so scarce.

NOTES

1. Clark Kerr, *The Uses of the University* (Cambridge: Harvard University Press, 1963), 121.

2. See "Democracy and the Scholarly Calling," in Andrew Hacker, *The End of the American Era* (New York: Atheneum, 1973).

Chapter 16

Teaching and Professing: An Epilogue

In following the conventions of public communication I am going to use this last chapter for my parting thought on what would make scholarship more truthful. It is perhaps no more than wishful thinking, considering the odds. Professors are normally the most formidable defenders of established habits. The academic mind is nothing if not at least stubborn. I hope, and let us all hope, that it is also vulnerable to reflection and reason, for these qualities are the very lifeblood as well as salvation of scholarship.

Whatever the effect, my job would have been done well if I have alerted my academic colleagues, and the general public, to two obvious possibilities. We can all ascend to the height of truth and human happiness, or we can descend to the hell of damnation and ignominy. History may wait for its own turn to bestow on us its merciless verdict. But our more immediate society will certainly not.

It is easy to agree that many ordinary professors in all capacities and on various levels (now close to one million, both academic and functional, in America) do their job and go home at the end of the day, essentially satisfied with their work. Peace of mind associated with this workmanlike routine performance may have its own moral defense. After all, many professors think of their occupation as a "job" and their activity as "work." But scholarship is not like working a nine-to-five day at a corporate office or a shift at a factory. It is almost wholly defined by independence of mind, honesty in criticism, and freedom to seek an alternative system of thought and action. Tenure is no ordinary contract, as searching for the truth is no ordinary task. No routine performance, however sincerely and studiously performed, however acceptable in other occupations, will do for a scholar and professor. The existence of tenure and academic freedom quickly disposes of any agreement with this workaday definition of the professor's job.

Any system that requires an existence of more than one generation (a state, a corporation) also requires a large army of apologists to defend it. All the schools of business and departments of economics, for example, are the academic arms of America's economic system, and all the business teachers and economists its academic apologists. Near unanimity also prevails in philosophy, sociology, psychology, political science, history, and other fields in support of the status quo. The Great Conservative Inertia makes anything else difficult, if not impossible. Most professors at most universities spend most of their time and energy mostly apologizing for and defending the system. It is not necessary to be conscious of one's apologistic role to perform it effectively. In fact, by not being conscious of one's role—by making it a "routine"—one's performance becomes more effective. An academic professor who is not self-conscious of his role in the service of his routine occupation unknowingly performs this convenient role. His service to the system is vital to its existence. But his service is for the system's *existence*, not improvement or perfection in the course of a more truthful or just existence.

Every system exists to exist, it has been said. By doing his daily routine, a professor only serves a system that serves itself, and nothing else. But the scholar's role is to criticize the system, not to serve its justification. In his routine service as a teacher, he teaches the existing orthodoxy for the system; as a scholar, he upholds the prevailing theory of the system; as an economic agent, he unconsciously accepts the party-line model of a market society. Few other instances of corruption in society are as intolerable as those committed by scholars. For society expects, and makes provisions for, them to be different, to be honest, critical, and independent. Thus, a professor's "routine" day is an evil day, and his "routine" activity is nothing but another evil deed.

It is the peculiar nature of scholarship in pursuit of the truth to require a singularity of personal and public life on the part of the academic professor. More crucially than for the functional professor, the scholar tends to be held to the integrity of private character and public virtue. One who teaches moral philosophy in public is expected to be a man of belief in private. In short, tradition holds that a man must practice what he preaches. And preach the academic professor does in his daily routine as a scholar in the classroom and as a writer to the larger society. A highly bigoted man can still be a good chemist or accountant or Spanish instructor or librarian or golf teacher. But the same man cannot possibly be a good teacher in an academic field that encompasses society and life. His academic commitment demands his *whole* self, private belief and public confession, to be consistent. It is much more difficult to become a "competent" philosopher than a competent chemist. The former demands that one be a competent *human being* as well. An incompetent human being cannot possibly be a competent philosopher.

It has become one of the undisputable facts of campus life to divide faculty work into "teaching," "service," and "scholarship." This classification of the professor's performance is then elaborated into more detailed gradations within each area. Teaching, service, and scholarship have become the cornerstones of all faculty evaluation. For the academic professor, this is at best an irrelevant and at worst a false classification. Internally and externally, he is a scholar devoted to pursuit of the truth. In the course of his work he may teach his students, he may lecture on the subject to the community, and he may publish his scholarly thought. What he teaches, what he lectures, and what he publishes as a scholar are all the same—or ought to be the same. He cannot, upon demand, transform himself into an "objective" teacher in the classroom, a pleasing soothsayer for the community, or a good soldier for his professional orthodoxy. He is the same person in all categories; his belief in the truth is the same in speaking to strangers as it is for his own colleagues. It is demanded of him that he be a whole, consistent person of integrity. He is a *scholar* at all times in pursuit of the truth. Tenure and academic freedom could demand nothing less than that from him. As a man of special privilege in society, he could offer nothing less than that in return. He must *teach* and *profess* the same truth.

The best, most ideal scholar-teacher is always one who has *synthesized* the great ideas (or the "historical truth") as his intellectual preparation and *internalized* them as his personal virtues. The first comes from his familiarity with all the known ideas, many of them "great," about society and life. This prepares him for his intellectual task. The second comes from his personal growth as a human being, most intimately experienced and observed in himself and in his social environment. When he sees an instance of injustice, he habitually links it with the great ideas of injustice that have been articulated before. In this, his immediate personal experience is constantly given its proper historical objectivity and intellectual scope. Both as a scholar and as a human being, he is guided by the broad scope of great ideas that magnify and give meaning to his daily experience and awareness. The two are in constant communication within him, inseparably and dynamically enforcing each other's enrichment.

This process allows the historical ideas to become part of the scholar's living reality, relevant and instructive. The first without the second makes the great ideas fossilized and stagnant, irrelevant to contemporary reality. The second without the first makes the subjective experience superficially all-important, all-absorbing, and all-encompassing. A morally incompetent teacher will not represent Socrates' teachings competently although he may confess to be fond of his philosophy. A mechanically inclined teacher will not practice the "Socratic method" of teaching adequately although he may think of himself as its devout practitioner. As always, a half-truthful teacher is worse than an all-lying one, for his may easily be taken as the whole truth.

The scholar-teacher must be true to himself for his falsehood cannot be concealed. A Marxist teacher must teach what he honestly believes to be the truth, and for the benefit of those he teaches, not his or his hero's. As a scholar he is beholden to the truth; as a teacher he is beholden to his society. These often conflicting forces are fortunately reconciled in tenure security and academic freedom in America. Thus, one need not be sacrificed for the other. It is what he *believes* to be true to all community, society, and humanity, not what *benefits* himself the most. In utter absence of self-interest, the teacher need not fear the consequences of not being "objective" or "broad" enough in his classroom. The truth honestly, independently, and critically derived and broadened by experience will make his teaching objective and broad if such terms are still necessary to describe it. The so-called objectivity and broadness are already over-accomplished in the public schools, later intensified in the general cultural and economic ethos. The university does not exist for the continuation of this sort of untruthful education or forced truth in socialization. Scholarship is what keeps the truth from what Walter Metzger calls society's need for "immediate solidarity and self-preservation."[1]

For the scholar-teacher it is *what* to teach that occupies his prime concern, not *how* to teach. A halting, awkward teacher who speaks the truth is infinitely preferable to a smooth-talking salesman-teacher who speaks with a forked tongue. Technique of teaching is important if the substance of teaching is either irrelevant or settled. The first involves academic teaching that is half-true or untrue because the teacher is a self-serving moral incompetent and standardized routinizer in mediocrity. To him, as to a salesman, how to present one's package is the only important issue; what the package contains is irrelevant. The second involves functional fields whose rules of functionality—as in chemistry or accounting—allow no deviation and still are functional. No chemist or accounting teacher worries about what to teach, for it is simply settled and is beyond his pondering or control. The question that remains is how to teach effectively, now that what to teach has been settled.

Unlike the functional teacher, the scholar-teacher necessarily practices, elitism as opposed to democracy. The chemist or accountant must teach what is universally known to be true, at least in his own country, which represents *everyman's* chemistry or accounting. It is democracy in practice par excellence. The scholar-teacher, however, cannot do that. What he chooses for his students must be the very *best* there is in human thought. *Everyman's* thought will not do. A literature teacher selects what is historically regarded as the very best in literature; a philosopher the very best of philosophy; the sociologist the very best in social thought; and so on. The good teacher may connect the very best thought to the student's everyday life experience but will not substitute the former with the latter. Only the insecure or incompetent teacher caters to the student's immediate personal experience without going anywhere further or forward with it. Good teaching—and more important, truthfulness—essentially consists of *elevating* the mundane, routine, insignificant experience to something significant, ennobling, and even heroic; in short, something historically important and lasting.

To profess is to have something that ought to be said. Being a "professor" consists of the ability and willingness to deal with *ideas*. A Ph.D. is a permanent, static title. The title of professor is not. It must be attained and retained on the basis of continuous renewal. Once he ceases to deal with ideas, he has nothing to profess. When he has nothing to profess, he is no longer a professor. There are many professors on campus; few still profess.

What one professes is what one expresses in either speech or writing. The style of the professor's expression reflects the substance of his thought. If his style is "academically" turgid, obscurantist, and frigid, it does not bode well for the soundness or substantiveness of his thought. The narrower his audience, however, the more academic his style tends to become. Those who write for the smallest audience, the professional colleagues in one's narrowly defined specialty, tend to have the worst style of writing. Considering the academic substance of society and life, this sort of academic style only evokes caricatured ridicule from the public, and deservedly so.

The subject of all academic fields is society and life, about which a great many people outside academia have something to say. They say it with lucidity and simplicity of style unmatched in the academic circle. The former, while perhaps lacking in formal meaning and perspective, makes itself relevant. The latter, while perhaps formally and analytically sound, makes its formal analysis empty of the feel of real life. In this sense, formal education, especially the kind one gets in graduate school, is often the worst enemy of simple comprehension. For in society and life, all distinctions between educated and uneducated disappear. There is no such thing as an educated or uneducated society; nor learned life or ignorant life. There are only happy or unhappy societies and lives. Whether wholly or in segment, the professor's thought encompasses these societies and lives, and there is no reason why he cannot express his ideas more intelligently for a wider audience. After all, it is everyone's society and life he is talking about.

Unfortunately, much of what passes for academic thought is irrelevant as ideas and muddled as communication intended for the consumption of one's equally irrelevant and muddled colleagues. If one were to think seriously about the audience outside his narrow specialty, the substance of his thinking and style of writing would be radically affected. The narrow circle of approval that he seeks gives him the comfort of irrelevance and muddledness in his writing. Unlike functional research, life in society is always a *whole* and *continuous* experience. There is no such thing as a voter who is also not a parent, consumer, or neighbor. Nor is a man much different at night as a human being from what he is during the day. Studying one particular segment in great detail, while convenient for the study, will yield little or no value for the purpose of comprehension and action. It is much preferable—no, imperative—that an academic scholar comprehend a little bit of everything, rather than everything of a little bit.

An ideally suited scholar learns *from*, not just *about*, the subject of his study. A good anthropologist learns from the natives he studies; a mediocre one merely learns about them. Only in academic fields are scholars expected to learn something about themselves in the course of their routine study. With each study, their whole self-knowledge matures as well. The best scholar, paraphrasing Socrates, is one whose self-knowledge is always pushed to its limit. By the same token, there is no one more idiotic on campus than a pompous know-it-all who is totally oblivious to his shortcomings. No one will dare tell a professor what an idiot he is.

The principle of academic freedom guarantees the professor's freedom to *express* his ideas. In his classrooms he is guaranteed to teach in peace. But is it *not* guaranteed that his writings should also be freely expressed?

Contrary to the moment's reaction to this observation, the professor's ideas have no guarantee that they would find an audience. The channel of expression today is controlled by two forces, each as tightly as an iron grip. One is the colleague-controlled channel of academic journals. The control over this channel is so complete and autocratic that the outsiders with unorthodox ideas have no access.[2] The other is commercial publishing. But this channel is controlled by the iron law of market conditions. It will allow only what will sell. Most scholars would find this market constraint an almost insurmountable obstacle. For important ideas are not marketable. What *is* marketable is normally unrelated to scholarship. Textbooks are marketable but what is written in them are either orthodox party lines or popular nonsense, or often both. The textbooks are more a product of word-processing than scholarship; their multi-authorship, an increasingly popular device, heads off any potential controversy.[3] This is all part of commercialism natural to the market. Neither source is open or appropriate for the scholar to express his ideas, especially unorthodox or unpopular ones. Where is his freedom to express them?

Corollary to the above, the indisputable "publish or perish" of academic life should cease. Not everyone has something to say at regular intervals. Not everyone has something worth saying upon demand. This is one of the more irrational, if not ridiculous, assumptions of scholarship routinely applied to professors: that *all* professors are alike in their ability, willingness, and involvement in dealing with ideas. Not everyone should write. Not everything should be written about. We must drastically *reduce* what is to be written and published by professors.

Likewise, all distinctions between published and unpublished works should cease. What matters is that the professor has thought of these ideas, not whether they are published or not. The former is a matter of substance; the latter, of packaging. Einstein's formulas or Schubert's symphonies would be just as good whether engraved on a gold plate or scribbled on a grocery bag. As long as the work is in evidence and available to public inspection, the fact of publication in a specific format is irrelevant and immaterial. Only insubstantial material, as a rule, insists on good packaging for effect.

To make the foregoing suggestions possible to practice, I would recommend that the university community make *all* writings of professors available in some definite form. Physically, this could be something between photocopies and printed copies, which many universities and departments already do for limited monographs and papers. An appropriate number of copies should be made available in solid binding to all members of the academic, if not functional, community. Every scholar, now free from both the professionally controlled journals and the market controlled outlets would be at peace with himself knowing that his ideas *will* have a ready-made audience. The quality of his ideas will no longer be judged by whether they are printed or not and in what specific journal, or by a small circle of specialists who share his own defects. Only the entire academic community, the broadest limits for his scholarly audience, and even the general audience beyond it, may judge the quality of one's ideas. In the judging of scholarship, nothing ever substitutes for reputation accumulated widely and over time.

As a condition for this arrangement guaranteeing part of the professor's academic freedom, he must also promise to write for *all* academic colleagues regardless of disciplinary boundaries. This would reverse the currently reckless tendency among scholars to specialize into the most minisculely infinite division of human thought and into almost certain oblivion. (As specialization protects ignorance, it also promotes irrelevance.) Most academics would be frightened out of their wits if they thought other scholars outside their own disciplinary specialty would read their writings. It might therefore enhance the quality of their thinking and writing and also reduce the volume of research papers and silly scholarly articles no one can possibly find useful. This forces one to be a broadly thinking scholar rather than a narrow specialist whose "scholarship" serves no one's interest but his and his specialty's. Academic freedom is not established to serve a scholar's or his specialty's narrow interest, but to serve the interest of the whole society. Ideally, every word written by a scholar should mean something. It should make the reader (the student, the public) react—with awareness, anger, action—as a result of reading it. As specialists write for other specialists, rarely is anyone moved by each other's words.

Thus, under this new circumstance, a sociologist would write for philosophers, English literature instructors, political economists, political scientists, historians, whatever. Scholars would once again be communicating with one another, the absence of which everyone swears is deplorable at present. After all, they are all part of what is fondly described as the "community of scholars." This practice would bring sanity back to what is obviously an insane situation: the notorious practice of professors writing for their own kind.

History has repeatedly shown us that all good works by scholars are read by virtually every thoughtful person in every generation, regardless of specialty or—not infrequently—of education. Good scholars by their instinctive tug of mind always consider all of community, society, humanity, and posterity whenever they think and write. Nothing less would be considered adequate, especially for a scholar whose livelihood and freedom of thought are absolutely guaranteed by his society. Reminding himself of the Oath of Tenure, his own imaginary version, will do his scholarly soul a lot of good, too.

NOTES

1. Walter Metzger in Richard Hofstadter and Walter P. Metzger, *The Development of Academic Freedom in the United States* (New York: Columbia University Press, 1965), 506.

2. See Steve McNamee, Cecil Willis and Ann Rotchford, "Gender Differences in Patterns of Publication in Leading Sociology Journals, 1960–1985," *The American Sociologist*, Summer 1990; see also Cecil Willis and Stephen J. McNamee," Social Networks and Science and Patterns of Publication in Leading Sociology Journals, 1960 to 1985," *Knowledge*, Vol. 11, no. 4, 1990, pp. 363–381. In their research on faculty productivity, Steve McNamee, Cecil Willis, and Ann Rotchford have found that of all the articles published in the "top four journals" in sociology between 1960 and 1985, close to one-quarter of all authors were affiliated with the ten most prestigious institutions in America, although these departments comprise only 0.5 percent of all departments of sociology in the country.

3. Herbert Gans, President of the American Sociological Association in 1988, was dismayed to learn that the "vast majority" of sociology textbooks were written by nonsociologists. See his presidential speech, "Sociology in America: The Discipline and the Public," *American Sociological Review*, 54 (February 1–16), 7.

Bibliography

Academe. Washington, D.C.: American Association of University Professors, various issues.

Bloom, Allan. *The Closing of the American Mind*. New York: Simon & Schuster, 1987.

Byse, Clark, and Louis Joughin. *Tenure in American Higher Education*. Ithaca, NY: Cornell University Press, 1959.

The Code. Chapel Hill, North Carolina: Board of Governors, University of North Carolina, 1988.

Commission on Academic Tenure in Higher Education. *Faculty Tenure*. San Francisco: Jossey-Bass, 1973.

Demerath, Nicholas J., et al., *Power, Presidents and Professors*. New York: Basic Books, 1967.

Galbraith, John Kenneth. *The Affluent Society*. New York: New American Library, 1958.

_____. *The New Industrial State*. New York: New American Library, 1967.

Gans, Herbert "Sociology in America: The Discipline and the Public," *American Sociological Review*. Volume 54 (February: 1–16).

Hacker, Andrew. *The End of the American Era*. New York: Atheneum, 1969.

Hofstadter, Richard. and Walter P. Metzger, *The Development of Academic Freedom in the United States*. New York: Columbia University Press, 1965.

Hook, Sidney, ed., *In Defense of Academic Freedom*. New York: Pegasus, 1971.

Huer, Jon. *Art, Beauty and Pornography*. Buffalo, NY: Prometheus, 1987.

_____. *The Fallacies of Social Science*. New York: Peter Lang, 1990.

Jencks, Christopher, and David Riesman, *The Academic Revolution*. Garden City, New York: Doubleday, 1968.

Kerr, Clark. *The Uses of the University*. Cambridge, MA: Harvard University Press, 1963.

Lasch, Christopher. *The Culture of Narcissism*. New York: Norton, 1979.

Licata, Christine M. *Post-Tenure Faculty Evaluation*. New York: Association for the Study of Higher Education, 1986.

MacIver, Robert. *Academic Freedom in Our Time*. New York: Columbia University Press, 1955.

McNamee, Stephen J., Cecil Willis and Ann M. Rotchford. "Gender Defferences in Patterns of Publication in Leading Sociology Journals, 1960–1985." Forthcoming in *The American Sociologist*, 1990.

McNamee, Stephen J., and Cecil Willis. "Taylorism in the Periphery: The Decentralization of Research Productivity in Sociology." Presented at the 1986 Southern Sociological Meetings. April 9–12, New Orleans, LA.

Memory, J. D., et al., "Physics As a Team Sport," *American Journal of Physics* 53 (3), March 1985.

Metzger, Walter P, ed. *Dimensions of Academic Freedom*. Urbana, Illinois: University of Illinois Press, 1969.

Mills, C. Wright. *White Collar*. New York: Oxford University Press, 1959.

_____. *Power, Politics, and People*, Irving Louis Horowitz, ed. New York: Oxford University Press, 1964.

Morgenthau, Hans. *The Purpose of American Politics*. New York: Vintage, 1960.

Olson, Robert G. *Meaning and Argument: Elements of Logic*. New York: Harcourt, Brace & World, 1969.

Pincoffs, Edmund L., ed. *The Concept of Academic Freedom*. Austin, TX: University of Texas Press, 1972.

Riesman, David. *The Lonely Crowd*. New Haven, CT: Yale University Press, 1950.

Robinson, Joan. *Economic Philosophy*. Chicago: Aldine, 1962.

Sennett, Richard. *The Fall of the Public Man*. New York: Vintage, 1974.

Smith, Bardwell, ed., *The Tenure Debate*. San Francisco: Jossey-Bass, 1973.

Sykes, Charles J. *ProfScam*. Washington, DC.: Regnery Gateway, 1988.

de Tocqueville, Alexis. *The Old Regime and the French Revolution*. Garden City, NY: Doubleday, 1955.

Volmer, Howard and Donald Mills, eds. *Professionalization*. Englewood Cliffs, NJ: Prentice-Hall, 1966.

Whyte, William H. *The Organization Man*. Garden City, New York: Doubleday, 1957.

Arthur S. Wilke, ed., *The Hidden Professoriate*. Westport, CT: Greenwood Press, 1979.

Willis, Cecil, and Stephen McNamee. "Social Networks of Science and Patterns of Publication in Leading Sociology Journals, 1960 to 1985," Knowledge, Vol. 11, no. 4. June 1990, pp. 363–381.

Index

American Association of University
Professors (AAUP), 7–10, 31
Association of American Colleges
(AAC), 8, 9, 11
Abortion, 128–29
Academic fields: and functional fields,
59, 70, 80; and professionalism,
155–69; and research, 82–85; as
apologists, 196; as calling, 155;
contribution by, 99–100; defined,
17; intrinsic value of, 180–82; inward looking in, 35–36; outlets in,
200–201; real value of, 20–21; specialization in, 37, 40, 62, 75, 201–
2; tenure and, 17–18; uselessness
of, 19–20, 27
Academic freedom: abuse of, 105;
among academic professors, 32–33,
86; and Constitution, 125; intrinsic
value in, 179–82; and Marxists,
143–44, 145; and oath to state,
140; in "perfect society," 104–5; as
inapplicable to market fields, 17–
20; in political activity, 125–26;
purpose of, 11, 172; in social criticism, 105; tenure and, 85–86; truth
and, 53–54
Academic professor: and academic
freedom, 31–32; and administration, 8–9; approach to scholarship
among, 128–29, 133, 135; and All-
American issues, 131–32; compared to industrial worker, 188;
conservative inertia among, 186,
194, 196; controversy, 131; "dead
wood," 188–89; diversity among,
74–76; "do-nothingism," of, 193,
195–96; economic interest among,
171–77; elitism among, 125, 168–
69, 186; expertise of, 129; freedom
of speech, 136–37; "Gresham's
Law," 185; history and ideas for,
92–93; imitation of science by, 60–
61, 81; in trouble, *xiv–xv*; introduced, *xiv*; and job security,
78–79; liberalism among, 127, 130,
163; and McCarthy Era, 10, 140;
narrow-mindedness among, 168;
and neutrality, 98–99; and partisan
issues, 127–32; 135–36; 139–40;
and political activity, 125–37; and
professionalism, 157, 158–60, 164–
66; peer evaluation, 185–86, 187,
192–94; personal development,
165–67; personality factor, 189–90;
productivity of, 31, 48, 175–76;
professionalization of, 155–57;
prominence attained, 186–87; "pub-

Social criticism: "constructive," 111–
12; and credibility, 139; in Japan,
104; by Marxists, 145; and power,
116, 123; as precondition for tenure, 106–7, 108–9, 111, 196; as
self-criticism, 109
Socialism, 46, 57, 84, 92
Social science: in classics, 37; social
scientist, *xiv*, 16; as "unemployment field," 17
Sociology: and academic freedom,
100; average sociologist, 94; best
of, 199; disappearance of, 13, 42;
democratized scholarship in, 39–
40; dynamic, 108; as game, 40;
"good" sociology, 38; grantsmanship, 39; narrow vision of, 36–39;
orthodoxy and, 23, 36, 40; packaging in, 41; scientific research and,
38–39, 85; sociologist, 13, 18, 29,
35–37, 79, 97; study of, 35, 40,
41, 48; theory in, 17, 41
Socrates, 6, 26, 43, 48, 55, 62, 69,
95, 147, 148, 167, 168, 187, 200
South Africa, 106, 122
Soviet dissidents, 110, 189
Soviet Union, 57, 78, 103, 147, 149,
151
Specialization, 37, 40, 62, 75, 202
Standardization, 39–40, 98, 186–88,
189, 193
Standard Oil, 175
"State of Nature," 126, 134
"Super citizens," 104, 137–38
"Superstar Syndrome," 159
Surplus production, 138
Supply and demand, 27, 192
Supreme Order (of society), 43

Tautology, 46, 89
Textbook, 97, 129, 201
Theology, *xiv*
de Tocqueville, Alexis, 105
Trump, Donald, 148
Truth: and academic freedom, 53–55;
average truth, 94; as belief, 57–58,
84, 198; commitment to, 182, 198;
and consequences, 44, 56–57; con-
trasted with facts, 56–59; as criticism, 105; and economic factor,
172–73, 176; everyman's truth,
199; and facts, introduced, 22–23;
and funding, 86; "Great Truths
(Ideas)," 68, 94, 197; as independent of research, 85; and justice,
70–71, 107, 140; legal truth, 29;
and Marxism, 146–47; materializa-
tion of, 90–93; and objectivity, 64–
65; and "ought to," 107; and
orthodoxy, 56, 96–97, 98, 99, 107,
131, 188, 192; and partisan issues,
128, 135–36; as personal knowledge, 64, 200; and persuasion, 58,
60, 106, 139, 161; and productivity, 30–31; and professionalism,
164; pursuit as ordinary task, 68,
74; and research, 82–83; and self-
interest, 69–72; as self-knowledge,
64–65, 200; and specialization, 62–
63; and social facts, 60–61; and
standardization, 39–40, 98, 186–
89, 193; state and pursuit of, 77;
suppressed in tenure, 32–33; and
tautology, 89; and teaching, 64–65,
197–99; and tenure, 23, 25–26, 53–
54; and untruth, 53–54, 58, 67–70,
132–33, 140

University of California, Los Angeles,
143
University of Wisconsin (Board of Regents), 106
U.S. Supreme Court, 29, 43

Value, 46–47
Van Alstyne, Williams, 125
Veblen, Thorstein, 27, 78, 81, 96,
110, 133, 151

Wall Street, 28
White Collar (Mills), 38
Whyte, William, 70
Willis, Cecil, 39
Women's studies, 139–40

ABOUT THE AUTHOR

JON HUER is Associate Professor in the Department of Sociology at the University of North Carolina at Wilmington, and is the author of a dozen or so books critical of American society and its many institutions. Among them, the following titles are of special interest to the readers of *Tenure for Socrates*: *The Dead End* (1977), *The Great Art Hoax* (1990), *The Fallacies of Social Science* (1990), *Art, Beauty, and Pornography* (1987), and his yet-unpublished volumes, *Darwin's Progress* and *The Professional Class*. He received his Ph.D. from the University of California, Los Angeles, in 1974.